Leviticus and Numbers

Westminster Bible Companion

Series Editors

Patrick D. Miller
David L. Bartlett

Leviticus and Numbers

RICHARD N. BOYCE

Westminster John Knox Press
LOUISVILLE • LONDON

Book design by Publishers' WorkGroup
Cover design by Drew Stevens

First edition
Published by Westminster John Knox Press
Louisville, Kentucky

This book is printed on acid-free paper that meets the American National Standards Institute Z39.48 standard. ♾

PRINTED IN THE UNITED STATES OF AMERICA

08 09 10 11 12 13 14 15 16 17 — 10 9 8 7 6 5 4 3 2 1

Library of Congress Cataloging-in-Publication Data

Boyce, Richard Nelson.
    Leviticus and Numbers / Richard N. Boyce. — 1st ed.
        p. cm. — (Westminster Bible companion)
    Includes bibliographical references.
    ISBN 978-0-664-25525-1 (alk. paper)
    1. Bible. O.T. Leviticus—Commentaries.   2. Bible. O.T. Numbers—
Commentaries.   I. Title.
    BS1255.53.B69   2008
    222'.13077—dc22   2007032145

Contents

PART 2: IN THE WILDERNESS, THE JOURNEY OF GOD'S PEOPLE (NUMBERS 10:11–21:9)

Series Foreword

This series of study guides to the Bible is offered to the church and more specifically to the laity. In daily devotions, in church school classes, and in listening to the preached word, individual Christians turn to the Bible for a sustaining word, a challenging word, and a sense of direction. The word that Scripture brings may be highly personal as one deals with the demands and surprises, the joys and sorrows, of daily life. It also may have broader dimensions as people wrestle with moral and theological issues that involve us all. In every congregation and denomination, controversies arise that send ministry and laity alike back to the Word of God to find direction for dealing with difficult matters that confront us.

A significant number of lay women and men in the church also find themselves called to the service of teaching. Most of the time they will be teaching the Bible. In many churches, the primary sustained attention to the Bible and the discovery of its riches for our lives have come from the ongoing teaching of the Bible by persons who have not engaged in formal theological education. They have been willing, and often eager, to study the Bible in order to help others drink from its living water.

This volume is part of a series of books, the Westminster Bible Companion, intended to help the laity of the church read the Bible more clearly and intelligently. Whether such reading is for personal direction or for the teaching of others, the reader cannot avoid the difficulties of trying to understand these words from long ago. The Scriptures are clear and clearly available to everyone as they call us to faith in the God who is revealed in Jesus Christ and as they offer to every human being the word of salvation. No companion volumes are necessary in order to hear such words truly. Yet every reader of Scripture who pauses to ponder and think further about any text has questions that are not immediately answerable simply by reading the text of Scripture. Such questions may be about historical and geographical details or about words that are obscure or so loaded with meaning that one cannot tell at a glance what is at stake. They may be about the fundamental meaning of a passage or about what connection a particular text might have to our contemporary world. Or a teacher preparing for a church school class may simply want to know: What should I say about this biblical passage when I have to teach it next Sunday? It is our hope that these volumes, written by teachers and pastors with long experience studying and teaching Bible in the church, will help members of the church who want and need to study the Bible with their questions.

The New Revised Standard Version of the Bible is the basis for the interpretive comments that each author provides. The NRSV text is presented at the beginning of the discussion so that the reader may have at hand in a single volume both the Scripture passage and the exposition of its meaning. In some instances, where inclusion of the entire passage is not necessary for understanding either the text or the interpreter's discussion, the presentation of the NRSV text may be abbreviated. Usually, the whole of the biblical text is given.

We hope this series will serve the community of faith, opening the Word of God to all the people, so that they may be sustained and guided by it.

Introduction

Wandering and wondering are part of the same process, and he is most mistaken, most in error, whenever he quits exploring.

William Least Heat Moon,
Blue Highways: A Journey into America

The quickest path from Egypt to Palestine is right along the coast, a trip of a couple of hundred miles, up through the territory now including the Gaza strip. If a traveler's only objective is to get from A to B, that's the route to go—whether you're on foot, on camel, or on plane.

But what if a traveler has purposes other than transit? What if some preparation is needed before you reach your destination? What if there are lessons to be learned "on the road" that will help you survive and thrive once "in the land"? What if there are skills to be practiced, tests to be faced, punishments to be endured, and gifts to be received before you are ready to "cross the river to the other side"?

Well then, a traveler might detour south toward the mountains of the Sinai peninsula; a reader might slow down in flipping from Exodus to Deuteronomy; a disciple might come to learn that the journey is as important as the destination, since the destination has a relationship at its heart.

Obviously, you are the type of person who's open to taking a detour. Though you may have bought this book out of compulsion ("I have to have the whole set!"), you would not be reading this introduction if your goals were simply a lectionary sermon or lesson (two in Leviticus, five in Numbers) or a proof text for some topical debate (too often the only motivation for traversing such "barren" stretches of Scripture).

But please be forewarned. The way will not be easy. While some portions of the Bible not only come alive but apply themselves almost by the telling (the stories of Jacob in the Old Testament; the parable of the Prodigal Son in the New), this is not the case when one's passage concerns a revised census (Num. 26), a divinely inspired plague (Num. 11), or an exquisitely detailed list of bodily discharges (Lev. 15). Handed such material for a Sunday school lesson or a weekday Bible study, the teacher may well feel worse than Moses in the wilderness when confronted with a spring masquerading as a flinty rock (Num. 20). Strike, and strike, and strike again, and you will find no water!

However, with a little patience (as the Israelites slowly learned) and with a constant sense of the wider story (stretching from the creation in Genesis to the conquest in Joshua and then far, far beyond), you may come to wish that this journey would not end (as did the author on his better days). Like the newlyweds who yearn to get out of their cramped first apartment, then spend the rest of their marriage remembering "those days"; like the congregation that dreams of being a big one, then looks back on its early days as its best; so the Jewish synagogue and the Christian church later looked back on Leviticus and Numbers as much more than a transition. These were indeed "the worst of times" ("But they had a wanton craving in the wilderness, and put God to the test in the desert"; Ps. 106:14), but also, in their way, "the best of times" ("I remember the devotion of your youth, your love as a bride, how you followed me in the wilderness, in a land not sown"; Jer. 2:2).

Before seeing why this was so at each stage of Israel's wilderness journey, however, we need to recite a little history: not only the history of this detour through the desert, but also the history of its interpretation down through the centuries. As we shall see, God's people have walked this path at least *three* times before—once literally, twice as a journey of reinterpretation.

A JOURNEY FROM ONE LAND TO THE NEXT

God's people's first trip through the wilderness was a divinely guided journey from one land, Egypt, to another land, Palestine, sometime around 1300 BCE. It was a trip of at least 600 miles (three times the straight shot!); it lasted approximately forty years (most of which can be attributed to the "delay" of Num. 14); it was carried out by the mode of transportation common to most biblical travelers: on foot. Though present-day scholars argue about the exact date, route, and number of tribes who participated in this march, few question its basic outline (at least with regard to a core group of tribes whose narrative eventually became fundamental for all). Once the Hebrews were slaves in Egypt; later they were settled as a people in Palestine. The wilderness journey was the trip that took them from A to B, thanks be to God!

Leviticus–Numbers must first be read, then, as the thanksgiving offered by this nation of travelers once they arrived in God's Promised Land. In its simplest form, this interpretation is made clear by the chronological list of desert stops in this "march" from "the land of Egypt" to "the plains of Moab" (see the travelogue in Num. 33, perhaps one of the oldest pieces of material in this entire block of material). More broadly, this basic interpretation provides the outline for the rest of the material's arrangement (note headings of the parts in the Table of Contents: "At Sinai"; "In the Wilderness"; "At Camp in Moab"), giving even the instructional material a "forward-moving" tilt (e.g., "Instructions *at Sinai*"; Instructions *in the Wilderness*"; "Instructions *for the Conquest*"). Most basically, this way of reading the story locates these two books between the deliverance from slavery in Exodus and the conquest of the land in Joshua, a location that holds steady whenever these people gather to remember this first journey once more (note the progression in Ps. 106: "Our ancestors, when they were in Egypt," v. 7; "But they had a wanton craving in the wilderness," v. 14; "They did not destroy the peoples, as the LORD commanded them, but they mingled with the nations and learned to do as they did," vv. 34–35).

The first collective interpretation of this "detour" is thus a thanksgiving for the journey itself, a journey that has prepared this people for their life as a nation now arrived ("When you have eaten your fill and have built fine houses and live in them, . . . then do not exalt yourself, forgetting the LORD your God, . . . who led you through the great and terrible wilderness"; Deut. 8:12–15). How did we get from Egypt to Palestine? By God's hand! How did we know how to live once we got there? Through the Lord's instruction! How can we continue to trust that as God has been with us in the past, God will travel with us into the future? By remembering the story and keeping it alive as we continue our march as God's people!

To read the Bible, then, by skipping from Exodus to Deuteronomy would be like learning the story of Jesus by skipping from Bethlehem to the empty tomb, or reciting the Apostles' Creed by jumping from "I believe in God the Father" to "I believe in the Holy Ghost" (see James Mays's introduction to *Leviticus–Numbers*, 8). We lose the heart of the story. We forget the means of our salvation. We lose the tangible ground for our hope.

A JOURNEY FROM ONE TEMPLE TO THE NEXT

There are clues in the material itself, however, that this reading of Leviticus–Numbers—a journey from one land to another—was not the only one kept alive by God's people through the years. In 587 BCE the Hebrew people lost this land to which they had journeyed, they were led back out through the wilderness to Babylon, and they began to dream of taking this "detour" once again. Evidence of this second journey through this material, while not as obvious as the first, is abundant and widely dispersed and helps explain much of our frustration when we attempt to read this material as mere travelogue.

First, while geographical markers may provide a broad outline for this material, they have to be rather diligently "uncovered" and finally prove fairly inconsistent, both *within* the material and *without* (cf. the more detailed chronology of Ps. 106 and the itinerary cited in Num. 33). The story begins to sound much less like a march and more like a wandering with little forward momentum—close to the experience of God's people as exiles in the sixth century BCE and beyond.

Second, the preparation these wanderers are undergoing seems to deal much less with the settlement of the land (Who will be king? Who is in charge of the army? Who will settle where?), and much more with the operation of the Temple (Who will be priest? Who is in charge of the sacrifices? Who offers what?). A different kind of journey seems to be going on here, one that moves from a first attempt at worship in Palestine before the exile to a second chance after the exile. Yes, a second detour of God's people has begun.

Third, and most important, rather than a God whose main characteristic is that of Deliverer, Savior, Travel-Guide, this material, especially in its instructions, celebrates the God who is holy. The command to be holy as God is holy becomes the main marching order for this second march. God has come to dwell with us. The Lord is his name! How can we both survive and give thanks for this visitation? Be ye holy as God is holy! How will we settle the land once we arrive? Keep yourselves separate and maintain your worship in Temple and home!

If the primary texts for the first journey were Leviticus–Numbers' *narrative* sections, the primary texts for this journey must be the *instructional* sections. The forward momentum slows down. The elaborate sacrifices and rituals become difficult to imagine for any people on the march (with mostly manna and quails to offer!). The reader begins to wonder if this journey has anything to do with transit, or rather the transformation of a people's worship between one Temple and the next.

A JOURNEY FROM ONE WORLD TO THE NEXT

There are at least two major problems with the approaches so far described: journey from one land to another, *and* journey from one temple to another.

First, in their current form, these books end without the people ever reaching their destination. While this issue is usually addressed with reference to the break between Deuteronomy and Joshua (why do the five books of Moses, the Pentateuch, end with God's people still on the far side of the Jordan?), this same problem arises with the end of Numbers ("These are the commandments and the ordinances that the LORD commanded through Moses to the Israelites in the plains of Moab by the Jordan at Jericho"; 36:13). Here the forward momentum seems to stall completely, with the next verses of the story circling back upon themselves, "These are the words that Moses spoke to all Israel beyond the Jordan—in the wilderness" (Deut. 1:1). You would think that a narrative whose primary intent is to preserve the miracle of a divinely inspired journey would at least get the sojourners to their destination *now*, rather than nearly forty chapters later in Joshua 3! Is this really a narrative about a journey from one land to another after all?

Second, if Leviticus–Numbers, in its present form, is essentially an instructional guidebook for establishing a new temple to succeed the old, it is highly curious that all the instructions are framed as guidelines for establishing a *portable* shrine for a *portable* people rather than a *permanent* temple set in *one place* forever. The intricacies of the sacrifices, the elaborate order of the priesthood, and the agrarian content of many of the gifts offered point toward a form of worship more appropriate for a settled people in a settled temple; yet the focal point of all Israel's service and devotion is an ark with poles for carrying, within a tent of meeting able to be pitched. You would think that a set of instructions meant for the restoration of temple worship following the exile would include, at least, the dimensions for the aforementioned temple and, at most, the laying of its cornerstone! Is this really a set of instructions concerning a journey from one temple to another?

Two historical events *outside* the text must now be brought into play, one within the life of God's people Israel (to whom the words of these books were first directed) and the other within the life of God's people, the church (for whom these words are still accepted as revelatory):

The destruction of the Jerusalem Temple. In 70 CE, the Romans destroyed the Temple in Jerusalem, a demolition that is still in effect to this day. We can only begin to imagine how this event must have affected the first-century Jew. One thing, however, is certain. If the key to maintaining one's relationship with the Holy God lay primarily in the restoration of priestly practice, with the destruction of the Temple this route was cut off. One might expect that the materials proposing this route would then be discarded. But they were not. Rather, the wilderness detour began to take on a whole new vitality.

What if neither the settlement of the land nor the restoration of the Temple would take place in this world (modern Zionism notwithstanding)? What if the rituals of sacrifice and the stories of defeat and conquest had to be read from a whole new perspective? What if the wilderness experience began to be seen not as a *stage* of one's journey, but the *whole* journey itself—at least into the foreseeable future, when the Jews as a people are destined to be a nation of wanderers?

Then the whole forward momentum of the story eases up. Both the instructions given and the narratives recounted become revelatory words for life between-the-times. Is the manna yet falling? Who are the cattle, goats, and birds of sacrifice? What do the categories of clean/unclean, victory/defeat, Egypt/Palestine mean in a world where God's Temple has been destroyed? Yes, what if the travelers have purposes other than transit? What if some preparation is needed before we reach our destination? What if there are lessons to be learned, skills to be practiced, tests to be faced, punishments to be endured, and gifts to be received before we are ready to "cross the river to the other side"?

Life, death, and resurrection of Jesus Christ. If the destruction of the Temple was a revolutionary development in the history of Israel's faith, the life, death, and resurrection of Jesus Christ was the event that caused a whole new branch to be grafted onto the original vine. Through Jesus, the church becomes the new Israel, a community of believers who, from the beginning, saw themselves as living life between-the-times—between the time of Christ's first coming in Nazareth of Galilee, and his coming again at the end of time. God's people thus begin the search for some interim ethic and some kingdom stories in order to shine as Christ's disciples until the kingdom fully comes.

If Christ is the ultimate sacrifice, once-for-all, where are the priestly actions of sacrifice carried out among God's people today? If the new Moses calls the dietary laws into question, yet vows not to eliminate one jot or tittle, how do Christians decide what to eat and not eat today? If the Lord's Messiah comes to this world and lives the life of a wanderer, mingling with unclean people, refusing to take up the sword in either offense or defense, is not *this* the life to which his disciples are called, and if so, what use are Leviticus and Numbers? Now the pace really slows and the journey threatens to lose direction altogether.

And yet, if the God revealed in the Christ is the same God who reveals the divine character through the laws and narratives of Leviticus–Numbers, somewhere there must be a common thread and link between, under, and through these two testaments (like the "crimson yarn" that connects many of the priestly sacrifices; cf. Lev. 14:4 and Num. 19:6).

The irony and the central challenge of this study companion is that the thread and link may be clearer here (in these materials where the hunger for land and temple has been diverted to an entirely different plane) than in other more mundane and widely read portions of the Scriptures (where more worldly versions of God's kingdom are yet in progress). The dream of something new, first voiced by the foreigner Balaam ("I see him, but not now; I behold him, but not near—a star shall come out of Jacob, and a scepter shall rise out of Israel," Num. 24:17), detours off through the writings of the letter to the Hebrews ("If they had been thinking of the land that they had left behind, they would have had opportunity to return. But as it is, they desire a better country, that is, a heavenly one"; 11:15–16), only to draw us back and focus our attention on this detour in the wilderness once again ("All of these died in faith without having received the promises, but from a distance they saw and greeted them. They confessed that they were strangers and foreigners on the earth, for people who speak in this way make it clear that they are seeking a homeland"; 11:13–14).

What does this wilderness journey have to teach Christ's church afresh at the beginning of a new millennium? How has its call to holiness been transformed by the advent of God's Holy One? Is it possible that this detour may prove to be the designated route for the earthly life of God's people here and now, today?

Then, maybe, a traveler might detour south toward the mountains of the Sinai peninsula; a reader might slow down in flipping from Exodus to Deuteronomy; a disciple might come to learn that the journey is as important as the destination, since the destination has a relationship at its heart.

* * * * *

William Least Heat Moon set out one day to meet this country called America. He wanted to know something of its character, its purpose, and its mystery. Such a journey, he decided, is best accomplished not on the interstates of this land, but rather on the "blue highways," the "least of these" designations on most maps. It is in the most barren stretches, the least traveled portions of our national geography, that our country's character is most apt to be revealed.

So we, at the beginning of a new millennium, set out in this study to meet the Lord God. We too want to know something of God's character, God's purpose, and God's mystery. True, many before have succeeded in this task by sticking to the interstates, such as the stories of Exodus or the instructions of the Ten Commandments. But here we will stick mostly to the "blue highways" of the Scriptures, such as the stories of the Midianites' defeat or the rules for cleaning houses plagued with leprosy. Perhaps it is in the most barren stretches, the least-traveled portions of our spiritual geography, that our God's character (and thus the requisite character of God's chosen people) is most apt to be revealed.

Note. It must be understood at the beginning that what may indeed be a "blue highway" for the church has always been closer to "interstate" in the synagogue. Leviticus–Numbers comprise two-fifths of the Pentateuch, the five books that serve as the core books in the Hebrew canon. Of the 613 laws that the rabbis have traditionally designated as fundamental guidelines for the Jewish life, 247 (or roughly 40%) come from the book of Leviticus alone. So revered has this one book been in the life of later Jewish commentary that it was once given the designation of *Sipra*, "The Book." Surely for a church that claims that "all scripture is inspired by God and is useful for teaching, for reproof, for correction, and for training in righteousness" (2 Tim. 3:16) such an extreme disparity in treatment is strange indeed!

Part 1: At Sinai, Preparation for the Journey

Leviticus 1:1–27:34;
Numbers 1:1–10:10

A. General Instructions "on Mount Sinai"
Leviticus 1:1–27:34

No sooner do you screw up the courage to tackle Leviticus, than you hit chapter 1. With no warning, you find yourself sucked into a detailed and bloody procedure for the sacrifice of cattle, sheep, and birds: "He shall remove its crop with its contents and throw it at the east side of the altar, in the place for ashes" (1:16). This then is followed by *six* more chapters of sacrificial techniques and technicalities, where the details multiply and overwhelm: "The whole broad tail, which shall be removed close to the backbone, the fat that covers the entrails, and all the fat that is around the entrails; the two kidneys with the fat that is on them at the loins, and the appendage of the liver, which you shall remove with the kidneys" (3:9b–10). And you thought you were embarking on a Bible study! This sounds more like a course in anatomy, or witchcraft, or worse! What in the world have we gotten ourselves into?

First, let us get our bearings.

Remember (though it will seldom feel like it in Leviticus!), God's people are getting ready to travel. After heading south out of Egypt, God's glory drew near to them on Mount Sinai: "Now Mount Sinai was wrapped in smoke, because the LORD had descended upon it in fire; the smoke went up like the smoke of a kiln, while the whole mountain shook violently" (Exod. 19:18). After much negotiation, Moses convinces the Lord to go with them on their journey: "He said, 'If now I have found favor in your sight, O Lord, I pray, let the Lord go with us. Although this is a stiff-necked people, pardon our iniquity and our sin, and take us for your inheritance'" (34:9). Chapter after chapter of building ensues, and God's traveling temple, the tabernacle, is completed. Then, just five verses before our beginning, God's glory has descended: "Then the cloud covered the tent of meeting, and the glory of the LORD filled the tabernacle" (40:34).

This is the point. God's people here, in Leviticus 1, are confronted with a dilemma. Like the prophet Isaiah, ushered into the presence of the Lord God Almighty, they cry out: "Woe are we! We are lost, for we are a people of unclean lips, and we live among nations of unclean lips; yet our eyes have seen the King, the LORD of hosts" (cf. Isa. 6:5). Such a close encounter posed problems when the Lord was *on the mountain*: "When all the people witnessed the thunder and lightning, the sound of the trumpet, and the mountain smoking, they were afraid and trembled and stood at a distance" (Exod. 20:18). What in the world does one do when the Lord has climbed *into the backseat*? "For the cloud of the LORD was on the tabernacle by day, and fire was in the cloud by night, before the eyes of all the house of Israel at each stage of their journey" (40:38).

As we shall see, the rest of Leviticus–Numbers (indeed the rest of the Scriptures!) can be seen as an answer to this dilemma. Put bluntly—as priests tiptoe in and out of the Holy of Holies; as the Israelites scrutinize what they eat, drink, and wear; as God's people try to make distinctions between their day-to-day lives and those of the nations round about them—the Bible describes a world where God is *too much* rather than *too little* present. Believe it or not, there is a reason why much of Leviticus reads like instructions for entering a nuclear reactor or a scene of alien invasion. That we today are more acutely aware of God's absence than presence and tend to locate God's glory more in selected holy sites rather than with us on the road goes a long way toward explaining our confusion with the book of Leviticus in particular, and the Bible in general. It certainly goes a long way toward explaining our deep-seated difficulties with the notion of sacrifice, which, with no prior announcement, suddenly appears in Leviticus 1. Our problem, we think (amazingly, for Christians!), is how to get God close. The Bible's problem, more often, is what to do when God draws *very* close, maybe even to "tabernacle" with us, on the way: "The Word became flesh and lived among us, and we have seen his glory, the glory as of a father's only son, full of grace and truth" (John 1:14). Leviticus's "Manual of Sacrifice" (a possible title for the first seven chapters of Leviticus), one of the most profound answers to this dilemma in all of Scripture, begins right here.

At this introductory stage, a few key points.

God cannot be bought. Let us be clear. Sacrifice is *not*, repeat, is *not* a means of securing the Lord's presence and glory. As the narrative framework makes clear, the Lord is *already with* God's people (Exod. 40:34). Through Moses' intercession, the Lord has promised to travel with this people on the way (40:38). Though the meaning of sacrifice is multifaceted and mysterious (especially for nonherding and nonagrarian people like us today!), this much must be said: sacrifice, even in Leviticus, has more to do with repositioning *us* than with repositioning *God*.

Something must be done. However, whenever the Lord chooses to draw near, some solution is necessary. Sometimes it may be as simple as taking off one's shoes, as Moses did when confronted by God's glory in a burning bush (Exod. 3:5). Other times it may require attention not only to one's shoes, but one's clothes as well, as with the people before their encounter with God on the mountain (19:10). But most of the time, especially when God's presence becomes more persistent, the sacrifice is more costly indeed, due to the utter, awesome extravagance of our God: "Live in love, as Christ loved us and gave himself up for us, a fragrant offering and sacrifice to God" (Eph. 5:2).

In defense of those who slaughter. Going in, from the beginning, let us rule out any cold-hearted, creature-hating assessment of the Israelites on our part. Any farmer who has tended the grain from seed to ear cannot place it lightly on the altar. Any herdspeople who have nurtured cattle from calves to cows and sheep from lambs to ewes cannot slaughter them at the tabernacle without cost. Remember, the Israelites did not laugh at the story of a poor man who brought up one little ewe lamb as one of his children—eating his meager fare, drinking from his cup, and lying in his bosom, so that "it was like a daughter to him" (2 Sam. 12:3). Later, this same people recognized that a good shepherd not only calls his sheep by name (John 10:3), but searches for one which is lost (Luke 15:4), and even, when necessary, lays down his life for the flock (John 10:11). Such a people possess a profound respect for the value of life: human, animal, vegetable. Sacrifice for *them* (maybe more than for *us!*) is no *easy* solution.

Maybe the best way for "nonliturgical slaughterers" to prepare for a reading of the Manual of Sacrifice is this: Put yourself in the shoes of the father in the parable of the Prodigal Son (Luke 15:11–32). Your child who was lost has been found. Your child who was dead is now alive. Something must be done! Bring out the best robe! Put a ring on his finger, and sandals on his feet! "And get the fatted calf and kill it" (v. 23)—not because you are heart*less*, but heart-*full*. Something must be done! Now, make the face of the one returning reflective of the very presence of God. Allow the arms of the one receiving to be the arms of God's people. Now, and only now, are you in the right frame of mind (and heart) to read the Manual of Sacrifice.

So then, back to Leviticus 1.

1. Instructions on Sacrifice
Leviticus 1:1–7:38

FOR ALL THE PEOPLE
Leviticus 1:1–6:7; 7:22–36

We begin in chapter 1 with sacrificial instructions *for all the people*. This is important, for while this third book of the Bible is probably wrongly named Leviticus (most of the instructions for the Levites come in Numbers, not here) and has more accurately been named "Priestly Guidelines" (*torat-kohanim*) in rabbinical tradition, maybe the best title for this book is simply *wayyiqrā'* ("And he [the LORD] called"), the first Hebrew word in Leviticus. God speaks to Moses in verse 1, then commands him to speak to "the people of Israel" in verse 2, *not* to just the Levites or the priests. Though Leviticus contains a couple of brief narrative sections and is bracketed on both ends by some of the most powerful narratives in the Bible, it is primarily a set of instructions for the priests, for the people, and for the sojourners in Israel's midst. In the "Manual of Sacrifice" we will approach these procedures from two different angles: first, instructions *relevant for all the people*; then, instructions relevant *for the priests only*. Different angles will provide us different insights. We begin with *all the people*.

Three Voluntary Offerings
Leviticus 1:1–3:17

Burnt Offerings
Leviticus 1:1–17

1:1 **The LORD summoned Moses and spoke to him from the tent of meeting, saying:** [2] **Speak to the people of Israel and say to them: When any of you bring an offering of livestock to the LORD, you shall bring your offering from the herd or from the flock.** [3] **If the offering is a burnt offering from the herd, you shall offer a male without blemish; you shall bring it to the entrance of the** tent of meeting, for acceptance in your behalf before the LORD. [4] You shall lay your hand on the head of the burnt offering, and it shall be acceptable in your behalf as atonement for you. [5] The bull shall be slaughtered before the LORD; and Aaron's sons the priests shall offer the blood, dashing the blood against all sides of the altar that is at the entrance of the tent of meeting. [6] The burnt offering shall be flayed and cut up into its parts. [7] The sons of the priest Aaron shall put fire on the altar and arrange wood on the fire. [8] Aaron's sons the priests shall arrange the parts, with the head and the suet, on the wood that is on the fire on the altar; [9] but its entrails and its legs shall be washed with water. Then the priest shall turn the whole into smoke on the altar as a burnt offering, an offering by fire of pleasing odor to the LORD.

The first sacrifice we encounter is the Burnt Offering (from the Hebrew word ʿōlāh, meaning "whole," from which is derived our word "holocaust," a word freighted with many meanings indeed). Like the Grain and Well-being Offerings that follow (see Table 1), the Burnt Offering is not provoked by any intentional or unintentional wrongdoing on the person's part, nor is it mandated by any date on the ceremonial calendar. Like the "offering" portion of the old phrase "tithes and offerings"; like the "love offering," which is supposed to be free of constraint or requirement; indeed, like all true praise, the Burnt Offering arises quite

Table 1.   Offerings in the Manual of Sacrifice, Leviticus 1–7

Voluntary Offerings	Purpose	Content	Beneficiaries
Burnt	Unspecified	Whole cow, sheep/goat, bird	Only God
Grain	Unspecified	Flour, cakes, barley	God and priests
Well-Being	Unspecified	Parts of cow or sheep/goat	God, priests, worshiper and friends
Atoning Offerings			
Purification	Purification of wrongdoer	Parts of sheep/goats, bird, grain; rest: burned (animal), to the priest (grain)	God, priests
Reparation	Reparations to wronged, Purification of wrongdoer	Reparations, and ram or equivalent	God, wronged, priests
For Priests Alone			
Ordination	Daily act of praise	Flour	God

simply out of the desire of a grateful person to offer something pleasing to one's God ("an offering by fire of pleasing odor to the LORD"; Lev. 1:9). Some comments.

1. Note the *extravagant nature* of these gifts. Though there is a descending order of costliness to these sacrifices—from cattle, to sheep and goats, to birds (a concrete example of the accommodating graciousness of the Lord)—none of these may be cast-offs or burdens marked for the glue factory ("a male without blemish"; 1:3). For a family of nomadic herders, this sacrifice came from the center of their security, their prized cattle and flocks. Surely we must ask what would be a similar sacrifice for us: retirement accounts, nest eggs, church endowment funds?

2. Note that this was *no "hands-off" affair.* The worshiper laid a hand on the animal and slaughtered the animal (cf. 3:2), the priests serving only to transport the parts to the holy places. You couldn't just drop your money in the plate. You had to caress, then cut.

3. The details of the slaughter reveal the Israelites to be *a people who knew their animals* ("its crop with its contents," 1:16) in contrast to most of us ("Is this a breast or a thigh?"). This was a costly encounter between creatures who knew one another well, not a casual slaughter between strangers (holocausts more the order of our day!).

4. This offering, more than any other offering (probably why it is first in the list), accrued *no benefit to priest or parishioner.* Everything was "turned into smoke" for the Lord; no parts were recyclable. As such, it stands as a symbol of truly selfless sacrifice—like the brilliant solo in the nonmusical congregation or the well-wrought blessing at a family reunion.

5. Even this sacrifice, which lists no wrongdoing on the part of the worshiper, has not only praise, but also *atonement* between God and God's people at its core: "You shall lay your hand on the head of the burnt offering, and it shall be acceptable in your behalf as atonement for you" (1:4). The writers of Leviticus will never let us forget that all of the law is concerned with relationships. Perhaps voluntary, sacrificial, and selfless praise is the best gift we can offer God to restore our relationship to God. Perhaps voluntary, sacrificial, and selfless praise is the best gift God can offer us to restore us to the people we are supposed to be. Though we often think that we are put on this earth to be productive, to be successful, or even to be helpful, our root purpose lies elsewhere. "What is the chief end of man?" asked the old,

noninclusive Westminster Shorter Catechism. Answer: "To glorify and enjoy God forever." Or, to address worship more specifically:

> God expects a church to meet for divine worship without ulterior motives. Thus, worship is not convened so that church budgets can be pledged, volunteers for ministry enlisted, programs promoted, attendance goals met, or personal problems solved. Authentic worship takes place only in order to honor God. People gather to worship God in order to give everything to God. (C. Welton Gaddy, *The Gift of Worship*, as quoted in Marva Dawn's *Reaching Out without Dumbing Down*, 82)

Note. One of the fun questions this offering has provoked for me goes like this. An elder walks into the pastor's study and announces, "Preacher, I want you to come out to the church parking lot with me. This morning I'm overwhelmed by God's goodness, and I'm under compulsion to do something extravagant. See this stack of $100s? Let's go outside and burn 'em!" What would you do?

Be clear. If you simply say, "No, no. Let's take that money and give it to Church World Service," you may unintentionally demonstrate that you are more enamored by the power of money than the power of worship! A prize cow was as close to a stack of bills as the Israelites got. It could fill the stomachs and provide security for many people. But if this cow was selected by its owner for a Burnt Offering, all this life-giving potential "went up in smoke."

It all reminds me of a similar reaction to a similar extravagant offering in John 12:1–7: "Mary took a pound of costly perfume made of pure nard, anointed Jesus' feet, and wiped them with her hair. The house was filled with the fragrance of the perfume." Just remember that the person who protests this offering is named Judas. Perhaps our aversion to Leviticus 1 is more than just skin-deep.

Grain Offerings
Leviticus 2:1–16

2:1 **When anyone presents a grain offering to the Lord, the offering shall be of choice flour; the worshiper shall pour oil on it, and put frankincense on it, ² and bring it to Aaron's sons the priests. After taking from it a handful of the choice flour and oil, with all its frankincense, the priest shall turn this token portion into smoke on the altar, an offering by fire of pleasing odor to the Lord. ³ And what is left of the grain offering shall be for Aaron and his sons, a most holy part of the offerings by fire to the Lord.**

A less precious, yet still costly alternative to animal sacrifice was the offering of grain, presented as flour, cakes, or grain. Like the Burnt Offering, this offering is not motivated by any specific wrongdoing. As with the Burnt Offering, there is a range of acceptable alternatives, though this time they vary more in preparational skills and equipment than in cost: if you can't handle or don't own an oven (v. 4), try a griddle or a pan (vv. 5 and 7)! Like the Burnt Offering, this sacrifice requires the best one can offer: "choice flour," "new grain from fresh ears."

What can we learn from the specifics?

First, Grain Offerings, like most of the offerings listed, were not unique to Israel. Particularly when it comes to agricultural offerings, Israel lived most of its life surrounded by practitioners of the same. The differences, therefore, lie in the details, such as the use of "unleavened" bread only (v. 11, reminding the Israelites of their exodus from Egypt, bread for a people "in a hurry"); the admixture of frankincense (v. 2, underlining the costly nature of this gift, and pointing forward to the gifts of the magi in Matt. 2); and the requirement of salt (v. 13, which takes on added punch when we are charged to be the salt that flavors, preserves, and makes acceptable the offering up of the earth and ourselves in the fires of God's service; cf. Matt. 5:13). Again and again, Israel and the church take what others have and make it their own. Sacramentally, with water at baptism and bread and wine at communion, we call it setting things apart "from an ordinary unto an extraordinary usage."

Second, in contrast to the Burnt Offering, the priests receive some benefit from what is offered: "What is left of the grain offering shall be for Aaron and his sons, a most holy part of the offerings by fire to the LORD" (v. 3). Although this may be seen as a sign of the Lord's largesse, it also begins a system for supporting the work of the priests that will prove both blessing (underwriting the work of the apostles; cf. 1 Cor. 9:13–14) and bane (cf. the simplicity of this scene with the complexity of what Christ overturned in the Temple, Matt. 21:12–13).

Lastly, one cannot read about Grain Offerings without thinking of a quote in Deuteronomy (8:3), later used by Jesus during his temptation (Matt. 4:4). At its heart, the Grain Offering is an acted-out testimony that we do not live by bread alone. We live, first of all, by the bread of God's word—made tangible during this journey by the daily manna in the wilderness (see Exod. 16), and later once-for-all in Jesus Christ (John 6). We live, second of all, by saying thanks for that word by offering up some portion of our own grains. How appropriate it is for us speakers of English that the money of our weekly offerings is also known as "bread." Perhaps if we saw this offering as a way of saying thanks for God's response to our daily prayer ("Give us, Lord, our daily bread"), then any emphasis on the tithe would no longer be necessary.

Offerings of Well-Being
Leviticus 3:1–17

3:1 **If the offering is a sacrifice of well-being, if you offer an animal of the herd, whether male or female, you shall offer one without blemish before the Lord. ² You shall lay your hand on the head of the offering and slaughter it at the entrance of the tent of meeting; and Aaron's sons the priests shall dash the blood against all sides of the altar. ³ You shall offer from the sacrifice of well-being, as an offering by fire to the Lord, the fat that covers the entrails and all the fat that is around the entrails; ⁴ the two kidneys with the fat that is on them at the loins, and the appendage of the liver, which he shall remove with the kidneys. ⁵ Then Aaron's sons shall turn these into smoke on the altar, with the burnt offering that is on the wood on the fire, as an offering by fire of pleasing odor to the Lord.**

The third of the Voluntary Offerings, the Well-Being Offering, looks little different from the Burnt Offering at first glance. It too involves cattle or sheep or goats (though it excludes birds and includes females as well as males). It too is motivated not by any specific wrongdoing, but simply by the desire to promote and strengthen the relationship between God and God's people, especially through prayer and thanksgiving. It too requires the best: animals without blemish and their choicest parts. Especially desirable is the fat, a priceless source of energy and vitality for a desert culture (making room for an interesting liturgical chant for our oversated age: "All fat is the Lord's!" v. 16).

A quick perusal of various Well-Being Offerings in practice (Jacob and Laban, Gen. 31:54; Moses and Jethro, Exod. 18:12; and Saul and Samuel, 1 Sam. 9) reveals that, after this sacrifice, a unique event occurs. A meal takes place, with the priest getting a select portion, and the other gathered worshipers sharing the rest. Thus, while this offering (like the Burnt and Grain Offerings) is initiated by an individual worshiper, it redounds to the benefit of not only God and the priests, but also those the worshiper gathers with him or her.

Several observations must be made.

First, how appropriate it is that the root Hebrew word for this sacrifice is also the source for the noun *shalom*: "whole," "peace," "restored." Though this sacrifice may not be motivated by any obvious tear or rip in the relationship between the worshiper and God, or in the relationship between the worshiper and one's family and neighbors, its celebration can help bring wholeness, peace, and well-being to both areas of life. It thus serves as a reflection of the communal celebration Israel experienced in her covenant meal at Sinai (Exod. 24:11) as well as a foretaste of other banquets to come (Ps. 23:5; Isa. 25:6; Matt. 22:1–10; Luke 14:15–24; 15:23).

Second, note that the host of this celebration is not the worshiper, but the Lord. Why? Because the worshiper offers as a sacrifice *the whole animal to the Lord*. What comes back is thus no longer the worshiper's, but the Lord's. Therefore, while the food offered here is not the choicest (that is, what is offered up), and while this food though "holy" does *not* somehow participate in the divine essence ("this is my body and my blood"), nevertheless this meal of Well-Being cannot help but remind us of another meal of Well-Being that takes place not at the Lord's house or tabernacle, but in an upper room (Mark 14:12–26).

Last, even though this sacrifice involves reparation for no obvious sin, it cannot be accidental that it follows after, or is placed on top of, the Burnt Offering, which functioned for atonement as well as thanksgiving (see above). As there is always an element of reconciliation and restoration present in New Testament offerings ("So when you are offering your gift at the altar, if you remember that your brother or sister has something against you . . ."; Matt. 5:23), so there must always be some element of reconciliation and restoration in the Well-Being Offering meal. Surely this is one reason Paul was so infuriated at the abuses of the Corinthian supper (1 Cor. 11:17–34). Surely it is at the heart of the power of both the sacred and the secular meals of the church today (note the library of reading on the topic of meals as spiritual practice; e.g., in Larry Rasmussen's chapter on "Shaping Communities," in Bass, *Practicing Our Faith*, he states: "Decisions on who gets to sit at the table, in what places, and in accord with what table manners are reflective of the order of a community—in the church, but also in the wider social order"; 130).

Once there was a reading by a noted Christian author at a denominational college in North Carolina (some identities are best left obscure!). Following the presentation, there was a question-and-answer period during which one particularly intent student asked the speaker about his attendance at church. "I don't go much anymore," the speaker said. "Most preachers seem bored with what they are going to say before they say it." Most of the audience laughed appreciatively. But the student persisted, "But have you tried anything *other* than worship?" "Like what?" the presenter asked. "A church night supper!?" The crowd roared. "Well," the student responded, silencing the crowd and the speaker, "that would be a start. Yes, that would be a start." And maybe, in some fundamental way, it all started here, in Leviticus 3.

Two Atoning Offerings
Leviticus 4:1-6:7

Purification and Reparation Offerings
Leviticus 4:1–6:7

4:1 The LORD spoke to Moses, saying, ² Speak to the people of Israel, saying: When anyone sins unintentionally in any of the LORD's commandments about things not to be done, and does any one of them: ³ If it is the anointed priest who sins, thus bringing guilt on the people, he shall offer for the sin that he has committed a bull of the herd without blemish as a sin offering to the LORD. ⁴ He shall bring the bull to the entrance of the tent of meeting before the LORD and lay his hand on the head of the bull; the bull shall be slaughtered before the LORD. ⁵ The anointed priest shall take some of the blood of the bull and bring it into the tent of meeting. ⁶ The priest shall dip his finger in the blood and sprinkle some of the blood seven times before the LORD in front of the curtain of the sanctuary. ⁷ The priest shall put some of the blood on the horns of the altar of fragrant incense that is in the tent of meeting before the LORD; and the rest of the blood of the bull he shall pour out at the base of the altar of burnt offering, which is at the entrance of the tent of meeting. ⁸ He shall remove all the fat from the bull of sin offering: the fat that covers the entrails and all the fat that is around the entrails; ⁹ the two kidneys with the fat that is on them at the loins; and the appendage of the liver, which he shall remove with the kidneys, ¹⁰ just as these are removed from the ox of the sacrifice of well-being. The priest shall turn them into smoke upon the altar of burnt offering. ¹¹ But the skin of the bull and all its flesh, as well as its head, its legs, its entrails, and its dung—¹² all the rest of the bull—he shall carry out to a clean place outside the camp, to the ash heap, and shall burn it on a wood fire; at the ash heap it shall be burned.

5:1 When any of you sin in that you have heard a public adjuration to testify and—though able to testify as one who has seen or learned of the matter—do not speak up, you are subject to punishment. ² Or when any of you touch any unclean thing—whether the carcass of an unclean beast or the carcass of unclean livestock or the carcass of an unclean swarming thing—and are unaware of it, you have become unclean, and are guilty. ³ Or when you touch human uncleanness—any uncleanness by which one can become unclean—and are unaware of it, when you come to know it, you shall be guilty. ⁴ Or when any of you utter aloud a rash oath for a bad or a good purpose, whatever people utter in an oath, and are unaware of it, when you come to know it, you shall in any of these be guilty. [5] When you realize your guilt in any of these, you shall confess the sin that you have committed. [6] And you shall bring to the Lord, as your penalty for the sin that you have committed, a female from the flock, a sheep or a goat, as a sin offering; and the priest shall make atonement on your behalf for your sin.

5:14 The Lord spoke to Moses, saying: [15] When any of you commit a trespass and sin unintentionally in any of the holy things of the Lord, you shall bring, as your guilt offering to the Lord, a ram without blemish from the flock, convertible into silver by the sanctuary shekel; it is a guilt offering. [16] And you shall make restitution for the holy thing in which you were remiss, and shall add one-fifth to it and give it to the priest. The priest shall make atonement on your behalf with the ram of the guilt offering, and you shall be forgiven. [17] If any of you sin without knowing it, doing any of the things that by the Lord's commandments ought not to be done, you have incurred guilt, and are subject to punishment.

6:1 The Lord spoke to Moses, saying: [2] When any of you sin and commit a trespass against the Lord by deceiving a neighbor in a matter of a deposit or a pledge, or by robbery, or if you have defrauded a neighbor, [3] or have found something lost and lied about it—if you swear falsely regarding any of the various things that one may do and sin thereby—[4] when you have sinned and realize your guilt, and would restore what you took by robbery or by fraud or the deposit that was committed to you, or the lost thing that you found, [5] or anything else about which you have sworn falsely, you shall repay the principal amount and shall add one-fifth to it. You shall pay it to its owner when you realize your guilt. [6] And you shall bring to the priest, as your guilt offering to the Lord, a ram without blemish from the flock, or its equivalent, for a guilt offering. [7] The priest shall make atonement on your behalf before the Lord, and you shall be forgiven for any of the things that one may do and incur guilt thereby.

With these sacrifices, we move from the more or less "voluntary" offerings to those meant to "atone," to "purify," to "repair a breach" in the relationship between the worshiper and God. Something has been done which must be "paid" for. Some act has wounded the relationship, and it must now be "restored." The "atoning" function of sacrifice that heretofore hovered at the fringe (as if in deference to the immediacy of God's glory's arrival), now moves to the heart of the ritual: "Thus the priest shall make atonement on your behalf, and you shall be forgiven" (Lev. 4:31; cf. 4:26, 35; 5:6, 10, 13, 16, 18; 6:7). The key distinction between these two types of atoning offerings (which often merge and overlap in practice) is the addition of "reparation" in the second type, restoring the relationship with both God *and* neighbor.

What must we say about these two?

First, the "unintentional" nature of all these sins has been much discussed (4:2; 5:15, 17). While the proximity of the Lord in this camp may well make the commission of any intentional sin hard to imagine, any translation of this term at face value creates problems. How can a priest be ignorant of the law (4:3–12)? How can sins like robbery, fraud, or false testimony be understood as "unintentional" (6:2–7)? The best that might be said here is that all these sacrifices are meant for purification and reparation regarding sins "wandered into" versus sins "high-handedly" performed (see Num. 15:30–31). These sins meet with sterner measures, as do the sins against the Holy Spirit later in Scripture.

Second, it is essential to note the writer's assumption that all people are prone to such sins: priest, ruler, congregation, commoner. While we may be offended by the implication that the identical sin by one person requires a higher price if performed by another (a cow if you are a king, a dove if you are a peasant), not only is there much wisdom in this (cf. the Epistles' strong warnings against sin by the leaders of the church), but it never negates the fact that all sinners must pay. Here there is an immediate link to the laws of Deuteronomy, which include laws under which even the king must live (Deut. 17).

Third, it should be no surprise to the reader of the Bible how cultic and noncultic, sacred and secular sins overlap—from mishandling of "holy things" (Lev. 5:15) to deceiving one's neighbor (6:2). This melding of "church" and "everyday" business becomes even clearer in the Holiness Code to follow (esp. Lev. 19).

Fourth, the requirements for Reparation Offerings demonstrate that one's business is only half over when one's human victim has been made good with interest (apparently set at twice the tithe, or 20%). One also has to make reparation to God ("And you shall bring to the priest, as your guilt offering to the LORD . . ."; 6:6). Here is revealed the profound truth that all sin is somehow sin against God. Thus the psalmist cries: "Against you, you alone, have I sinned, and done what is evil in your sight" (Ps. 51:4).

Last, if a solution must be found to the problem of a Holy God tabernacling amid an unholy people in general, how much more is the problem exacerbated in cases of obvious breach? In all these cases, much more than taking off one's shoes or washing one's clothes is required. This is no cheap grace, but a costly forgiveness indeed.

Surely a good companion reading to this section of Leviticus is Anne Tyler's novel concerning reparation and reconciliation, *Saint Maybe*. Ian has inadvertently caused the death of his brother by accusing his sister-in-law of infidelity. Later he finds himself in "The Church of the Second Chance" and feels himself forgiven by God. "Don't you think I'm forgiven?" Ian asks Reverend Emmett:

> "Goodness, no," Reverend Emmett said briskly. Ian's mouth fell open. He wondered if he'd misunderstood. He said, "I'm not forgiven?"
> "Oh, no."
> "But . . . I thought that was kind of the point," Ian said. "I thought God forgives everything."
> "He does," Reverend Emmett said. "But you can't just say, 'I'm sorry, God.' Why, anyone could do that much! You have to offer reparation—concrete, practical reparation, according to the rules of our church." (133)

And, we might add, at least to some extent, according to the rules of Leviticus 4–6. "'Let us not love in word, neither in tongue,'" Reverend Emmett said, "'but in deed and in truth.' First John three, eighteen" (134).

Additional Instructions
Leviticus 7:22–38

7:22 The LORD spoke to Moses, saying: 23 Speak to the people of Israel, saying: You shall eat no fat of ox or sheep or goat. 24 The fat of an animal that died or was torn by wild animals may be put to any use, but you must not eat it. 25 If any one of you eats the fat from an animal of which an offering by fire may be made to the LORD, you who eat it shall be cut off from your kin. 26 You must not eat any blood whatever, either of bird or of animal, in any of your settlements. 27 Any one of you who eats any blood shall be cut off from your kin. 28 The LORD spoke to Moses, saying: 29 Speak to the people of Israel, saying: Any one of you who would offer to the LORD your sacrifice of well-being must yourself bring to the LORD your offering from your sacrifice of well-being. 30 Your own hands shall bring the LORD's offering by fire; you shall bring the fat with the breast, so that the breast may be raised as an elevation offering before the LORD. 31 The priest shall turn the fat into smoke on the altar, but the breast shall belong to Aaron and his sons. 32 And the right thigh from your sacrifices of well-being you shall give to the priest as an offering; 33 the one among the sons of Aaron who offers the blood and fat of the offering of well-being shall have the right thigh for a portion. 34 For I have taken the breast of the elevation offering, and the thigh that is offered, from the people of Israel, from their sacrifices of well-being, and have given them to Aaron the priest and to his sons, as a perpetual due from the people of Israel. 35 This is the portion allotted to Aaron and to his sons from the offerings made by fire to the LORD, once they have been brought forward to serve the LORD as priests; 36 these the LORD commanded to be given them, when he anointed them, as a perpetual due from the people of Israel throughout their generations. [37] This is the ritual of the burnt offering, the grain offering, the sin offering, the guilt offering, the offering of ordination, and the sacrifice of well-being, [38] which the LORD commanded Moses on Mount Sinai, when he commanded the people of Israel to bring their offerings to the LORD, in the wilderness of Sinai.

Prohibition of Fat and Blood
Leviticus 7:22–27

Before leaving the first run-through of the Manual of Sacrifice, the people are reminded of God's claim on two portions of any animal sacrifice: the fat and the blood. The fat is a precious portion of the animal from *the human point of view* (high in energy, good to the taste, warming for the body) and thus represents God's people's willingness to lay aside the choicest portions for God. The blood is a precious portion of the animal from *the divine point of view*, representing life itself, and able to appeal to God for intervention when life has been wrongly taken (see the story of Abel's blood crying out to God following his surreptitious murder by Cain; Gen. 4).

What "fat" portions of God's created order do we reserve for God alone? The best of our music, our language, our intellect? Do we set aside the choicest portions of our days, our communities, our lives for God, or leave God only the gristle? When we share with others, do we hold back the fatted calf and offer them our mite-bitten chickens instead? "You shall eat no fat," reads Leviticus. Leave the best for God.

As for blood, where do we now believe that life resides? In the human egg and sperm? In strands of DNA and RNA? In the marvelous imaginations of little children? How do we show forth our honor for these life-loaded ingredients of God's good creation as we offer back this creation to God in praise? If we disdain the extra expense, care, and training required of the kosher butcher (whose special expertise is the proper handling of blood), where are we willing to invest such expense, care, and training? Are there not areas of our lives that should be as hands-off for us as blood was for the Israelites? Some things are too precious to become matters for human consumption. If improperly used, *this* blood too may cry out.

Portions for Priests
Leviticus 7:28–36

As the regulations for the Manual of Sacrifice wind down and the trauma of God's descent into the camp lessens, another issue begins to come to the fore: what is the relation between the worshiper and the priest? More specifically, should there not be greater clarity about what the bringer of the sacrifice does and what the priest does? what the Lord receives and what the priest receives? This concern, directed to the priests in the section to follow, is here directed to the people.

Several things should be noted.

First, the people yet have a role to play. "With your own hands" shall the offering be brought to the Lord and, by implication, the appropriate sections presented to the priests. The congregation is no passive audience or coerced captive in this divine drama. They must have a hand in the liturgy and make their offerings to God and the priest personally. It would be beneficial to compare this "interactive" worship with our worship today.

Second, clearly the issue of priestly benefits was a pressing topic at later stages in Israel's history. As we shall see, the tribe of Aaron received no portion in the division of the lands of Canaan. Thus they were ever dependent on the offerings of God's people for their livelihood. Even within these texts themselves, one can detect an ongoing debate concerning the proper balance between seeing that the priests' basic needs are met, and the priests getting rich off the people's devotion. "Let's see, the priests in general get the breast; the officiating priest, the thigh. The church staff in general get a cut from the regular offering; the officiant in charge gets the wedding honorarium."

If the love of money is the root of all evil, one should not be surprised by the level of emotion surrounding topics of clergy pay, the use of paid workers versus volunteers in the life of the church, and the whole topic of the more worldly benefits that sometimes accrue to those who immerse themselves in the activities of the church. "So-and-so's an elder; why not make her a partner?" Part of the "humanness" of the Levitical writings rests in the amount of space dedicated to this more mundane topic of "who gets what" after the main offering is done. It will come up again and again (as it does today!). This is a Lord who knows God's people. Would that we were as concerned with what goes up *to God* as what comes down *to us*, or our brothers and sisters in the faith.

Finally, this section ends with a review of the five offerings now covered: Burnt, Grain, Purification, Reparation, Well-Being. But into the mix is introduced a sixth: the Ordination Offering. Now that the offerings have been described, it is time to get the ball rolling. But first, we need some priests. After a few concluding instructions to them, the first offerings of ordination will take place.

FOR THE PRIESTS ONLY, FIVE OFFERINGS
Leviticus 6:8–7:21, 37–38

6:8 The Lord spoke to Moses, saying: [9] Command Aaron and his sons, saying: This is the ritual of the burnt offering. The burnt offering itself shall remain on the hearth upon the altar all night until the morning, while the fire on the altar shall be kept burning. [10] The priest shall put on his linen vestments after putting on his linen undergarments next to his body; and he shall take up the ashes to which the fire has reduced the burnt offering on the altar, and place them beside the altar. [11] Then he shall take off his vestments and put on other garments, and carry the ashes out to a clean place outside the camp. [12] The fire on the altar shall be kept burning; it shall not go out. Every morning the priest shall add wood to it, lay out the burnt offering on it, and turn into smoke the fat pieces of the offerings of well-being. [13] A perpetual fire shall be kept burning on the altar; it shall not go out.

If Leviticus 1–6 was hard slogging, Leviticus 6–7 seems even worse. Having walked our way through the sacrifices from the people's point of view, we now must traverse the same terrain for the priests. Why should anyone besides a Levitical priest care about such regulations? This kind of material, with its seemingly endless details of priestly practice, may appeal to the anthropologist or archaeologist, but how so the teacher or preacher?

In practice. First, these are sacrifices meant to be *put into practice.* As long as we talk about plans in the abstract, we don't need to mess with the details. We don't have to worry about who stands where, or who carries what. But if you are determined to put something into practice, you *have* to deal with the details. No sooner are these sacrifices commanded by God, than the details for their implementation are given to the priests. This is not just blue-sky dreaming. This is a "manual of operation." If we no longer choose to follow the details of *these* sacrifices to the letter, there should be some corresponding rules for *our* manual of sacrifice.

Essential. Second, this is *essential business.* Two entire chapters of the Bible are dedicated to this insider's view of the sacrifices. That's as much as for the creation of the world, as much as for the birth of the Messiah! This is not just important; even more, it is essential business. When we are dealing with the things of God, we are dealing with what is most precious for us as human beings. No area of our lives is more important or worthy of such meticulous concern. It would be interesting to speculate about that to which we'd devote similar space today: advice on personal health, tips on home mortgages, strategies for church stewardship? Here, the business is the Lord's worship. No detail is too small and no amount of effort too great to be included.

Details. Third, character is most visible *in the details.* Often we can learn most about a person by observing the smaller details of her life: how does she maintain her car, how up-to-date is her checkbook? Here we find the Lord instructing God's priests on the *details* of priestly sacrifice. Perhaps here, in these "domestic" instructions, the character of God becomes most visible. Some examples:

1. *A perpetual fire.* The fire on the altar shall never go out, it shall be kept burning (Lev. 6:12). Viewed one way, this seems the willfulness of a demanding God. Viewed another way, however, it is a picture of praise. The holy fire that first comes down to consume the sacrifices about to be offered up (Lev. 10) must never be allowed to sputter out—not through the wanderings in the wilderness, not during the days when they are scattered. Why? Because this fire flames as a symbol of a never-sleeping God ("He who keeps Israel will neither slumber nor sleep"; Ps. 121:4). God's receptivity is a light shining in the darkness. The darkness shall not overcome it.

2. *It is most holy.* The details of Leviticus 6–7 even include instructions for the cleanup of altar utensils: "An earthen vessel in which it [flesh] was boiled shall be broken; but if it is boiled in a bronze vessel, that shall be scoured and rinsed in water" (6:28). As vital as hygiene is for a surgeon, more vital still is proper care by the priests. Why? Because as important as health and lack of infection are for modern people, the presence of the holy and the lack of uncleanness is of even greater importance. The Lord wants to offer God's holy presence to God's people. Those things used for that purpose must be maintained for that purpose. If a careful cleaning cannot purify them from the taint of the purification offering they have carried, then they must be destroyed. What is more important? Keeping a pot (or an arm or leg for that matter; cf. Matt. 5:29–30), or protecting the gracious boundary between God and God's people? Look to the details.

3. *Daily offerings.* Though the sacrifices so far described follow no apparent schedule, as we move to details, the necessity of some daily observance arises: "one-tenth of an ephah of choice flour as a regular offering, half of it in the morning and half in the evening" (Lev. 6:20). Why? As God's mercies fall daily, so the people's praises should rise daily. This is a God who is with us in the camp.

4. *No leftovers.* Like the gathering of the manna and the quails, so the food of sacrifices is not allowed to accumulate: "It shall be eaten on the day that you offer your sacrifice, and what is left of it shall be

eaten the next day; but what is left of the flesh of sacrifice shall be burned up on the third day" (Lev. 7:16–17). There is the strong sense that every day should bring its own sacrifices, and thus its own returns. There is no room here for Sunday-only faith, or a once-in-a-lifetime profession. This is a God who longs for fresh commerce with God's people day in and day out.

5. *Clean/unclean.* Though this concern will later consume chapters of Leviticus, it is here introduced in the details: "When any one of you touches any unclean thing—human uncleanness or an unclean animal or any unclean creature—and then eats flesh from the LORD's sacrifice of well-being, you shall be cut off from your kin" (7:21). As important as life and life with one's kin may be, there is something more important: our communal fellowship with God. Again and again, in the details and in the broader strokes, it quickly becomes apparent that no treasure should be counted so dear as to cost the sacrifice of this relationship. One of the central tasks of the priests is to "cut off" in order that life might continue. There will be much more on this in the chapters to follow.

CONCLUDING OBSERVATIONS ON THE MANUAL OF SACRIFICE

Having traversed the range of sacrifices available, as well as the details required of the priests, some summary comments and comparisons are now in order.

First, it should now be clear that the presence of a Holy God amid an unholy people presents a problem. Without this God in their midst, the people would surely perish; yet with this God so gloriously nearby, they may well perish sooner! The entire sacrificial system, in all its magnificent and gory detail, is tangible testimony to this fact. If we, as Christians, decide that this solution is untenable, surely we must search for another.

Second, though the problem arises whether any obvious sin has been committed or not, the problem only intensifies when the sins become specific. Here the key word is *when*, not *if*. As the entire biblical narrative in general and the Leviticus–Numbers narrative in particular make clear, give God's people long enough, and they will foul up. Not only unintentionally, but also intentionally; not just in trivial matters, but also in matters at the heart of the relationship. Again, some solution must be found.

So, third, a solution in two parts:

1. Without a doubt, one of the greatest benefits of studying the Manual of Sacrifice is quite simple. Having realized the costly nature of the sacrifices God's proximity provokes in Leviticus (prize cattle gutted, doves' heads wrung off), we become even more amazed by the costly nature of the Sacrifice that God's proximity produces in Christ ("He humbled himself and became obedient to the point of death— even death on a cross"; Phil. 2:8). In Christ, we believe, God offers up everything with no benefit to Godself: the Burnt Offering. In Christ, we believe, God breaks open God's own body as bread for the world: the Grain Offering. In Christ, we believe, God shares with us God's very substance at a feast that makes well all of creation: the Well-Being Offering. In Christ, we believe, God purifies our brokenness: the Purification Offering. In Christ, we believe, God makes reparation for all our wrongs: the Reparation Offering. Surely this is a once-for-all offering, as declared by the author of the letter to the Hebrews (10:10).

2. Yet, even in Hebrews, Christ's sacrifice for all does not obviate the need for extravagant sacrifices in response: "Through him, then, let us continually offer a sacrifice of praise to God, that is, the fruit of lips that confess his name. Do not neglect to do good and to share what you have, for such sacrifices are pleasing to God" (13:15–16). If, through Christ's reconciling sacrifice, we have actually been brought even *closer* into God's presence than the encamped Israelites, then the Manual of Sacrifice of the Christian should put to shame the Manual of Sacrifice of Leviticus. Surely this is what drove Paul to add our *own* bodies to the bodies of cattle, sheep, and goats previously offered: "I appeal to you therefore, brothers and sisters, by the mercies of God, to present your bodies as a living sacrifice, holy and acceptable to God, which is your spiritual worship" (Rom. 12:1). Both the contemplation of the Sacrifice and the extravagance of the response are captured perfectly in the words of an Isaac Watts hymn familiar to us all:

> When I survey the wondrous cross
> On which the Prince of glory died,
> My richest gain I count but loss,
> And pour contempt on all my pride.
>
> Were the whole realm of nature mine,
> That were a present far too small;
> Love so amazing, so divine,
> Demands my soul, my life, my all.

2. Inauguration of Israel's Worship
Leviticus 8:1–10:20

One might expect the inauguration of Israel's worship to await the dedication of Israel's permanent temple in the Promised Land. Why begin worship *in the wilderness*? Animals for sacrifice, though present at the beginning ("A mixed crowd also went up with them, and livestock in great numbers, both flocks and herds"; Exod. 12:38), seem to have gone missing on the way ("If only we had meat to eat!" Num. 11:4). Surely, in the wilderness, there must have been more pressing needs than suiting up a bunch of priests (wouldn't *we* be more eager to inaugurate scouting and foraging parties?). Why not just lay down the rules for worship, then put them in practice when we get there, to the land, to a building—where everyone has a pew to sit on, a parking space to park in, and a cemetery to be buried in? What's all the rush?

The simple answer is *worship cannot wait.* Just as the descent of God's glory immediately inspired the need for sacrifice, so the Manual of Sacrifice immediately provokes the desire to put it in practice. As the presence of the Holy God requires the implementation of radical and costly response, so this radical and costly response can only be handled by a group of people who are set apart. This is a matter of life and death ("You shall remain at the entrance of the tent of meeting day and night for seven days, . . . so that you do not die"; Lev. 8:35). The need for worship runs as deep as the need for food and drink (maybe it was *because* the Israelites needed so many animals *for worship* that they had no meat *to eat!*). Remember, the problem is not too little, but too much God. There is no vacation from our vocation. It is *always* time for worship. The time to act is *now*.

Note. The interaction between instruction and narrative is one of the characteristics of the Bible in general and Leviticus–Numbers in particular. The Scriptures make it clear that these words are not "items for consideration," but "manuals for operation." God's people are not meant to be just *hearers*, but also *doers* of the word. Just as the Lord speaks and

31

worlds are created at the beginning of Scripture, so (when things are going right!) the Lord instructs and the Lord's people implement. The lack of lag time between speaking and doing is first and foremost a demonstration of God's power (in contrast to idols' lack of power). But the immediacy of the response in Leviticus 8 is also a measure of the creature's responsiveness. Here at the beginning of Leviticus (as is true for the whole second half of Exodus), we live in one of those rare times where the Lord commands and the people obey (cf. Gen. 12:4 and Mark 1:18, 20). Be forewarned: this will soon change. Yet the very rarity and fragility of such occasions make them all the more precious in God's sight—and our own!

THE ORDINATION OF THE PRIESTS
Leviticus 8:1–36

8:1 The Lord spoke to Moses, saying: [2] Take Aaron and his sons with him, the vestments, the anointing oil, the bull of sin offering, the two rams, and the basket of unleavened bread; [3] and assemble the whole congregation at the entrance of the tent of meeting. [4] And Moses did as the Lord commanded him. When the congregation was assembled at the entrance of the tent of meeting, [5] Moses said to the congregation, "This is what the Lord has commanded to be done." [6] Then Moses brought Aaron and his sons forward, and washed them with water. [7] He put the tunic on him, fastened the sash around him, clothed him with the robe, and put the ephod on him. He then put the decorated band of the ephod around him, tying the ephod to him with it. [8] He placed the breastpiece on him, and in the breastpiece he put the Urim and the Thummim. [9] And he set the turban on his head, and on the turban, in front, he set the golden ornament, the holy crown, as the Lord commanded Moses. [10] Then Moses took the anointing oil and anointed the tabernacle and all that was in it, and consecrated them. [11] He sprinkled some of it on the altar seven times, and anointed the altar and all its utensils, and the basin and its base, to consecrate them. [12] He poured some of the anointing oil on Aaron's head and anointed him, to consecrate him. [13] And Moses brought forward Aaron's sons, and clothed them with tunics, and fastened sashes around them, and tied headdresses on them, as the Lord commanded Moses.

8:31 And Moses said to Aaron and his sons, "Boil the flesh at the entrance of the tent of meeting, and eat it there with the bread that is in the basket of ordination offerings, as I was commanded, 'Aaron and his sons shall eat it'; [32] and what remains of the flesh and the bread you shall burn with fire. [33] You shall not go outside the entrance of the tent of meeting for seven days, until the day when your period of ordination is completed. For it will take seven days to ordain you; [34] as has been done today, the Lord has commanded to be done to make atonement for you. [35] **You shall remain at the entrance of the tent of meeting day and night for seven days, keeping the Lord's charge so that you do not die; for so I am commanded."** [36] **Aaron and his sons did all the things that the Lord commanded through Moses.**

As animals have been set apart for sacrifice, so now a group of God's people must be set apart to offer the sacrifices. From the word "go," this narrative can or should move on at least *two* levels. First, what does it have to say to those who would handle things set apart for God *on behalf of others* (those who handle God's word, who lift up the people's prayers)? And, second, what does it have to say to *all God's people*, who exercise the function of priest following the ministry of Christ?

Several points are here in order. Setting apart requires proper clothing, extravagant anointing, costly sacrifice, formative communion, and preparatory time.

Proper clothing. Ever since Adam and Eve's discovery of shame in the garden, proper attire in the presence of God has been a concern of God's people. Though certain types of clothing might be best suited for encounters with the world (cf. Eph. 6), how should one dress oneself before entering the sanctuary of God? Clearly, it would be wrong to neglect the broader scriptural principle of pushing the question of clothing below the surface of mere attire ("As God's chosen ones, holy and beloved, clothe yourselves with compassion, kindness, humility, meekness, and patience"; Col. 3:12). Surely it must be recognized that fancy clothes risk excluding some from worship due to their inability to pay (I've encountered a congregation in Scotland where the men refused to wear ties due to the poverty of their surrounding neighborhood). Nevertheless, there does seem to be some purpose in the community developing symbolic clothing (even if extravagantly "simple"!) to remind everyone to whom we are drawing close. The person who would draw close to the Lord of the Universe appropriately puts on some reflectively royal clothes. This would be a good place to discuss not only ministerial robes and collars, but also the whole issue of "church clothes." Have we lost something by jettisoning such Saturday-night activities as the polishing of shoes, the starching of shirts, and the pressing of Sunday dresses?

Extravagant anointing. Only a culture that hungers for anointing can understand the symbolism of Psalm 133: "It is like the precious oil on the head, running down upon the beard, on the beard of Aaron, running down over the collar of his robes." Anointing was Israel's most tangible symbol for "setting apart"—of prophet, priest, and king. It thus becomes the dream of every faithful Israelite (Psalm 23:5), a precursor for the waters of baptism. What is of particular interest here is that not only the people, but also the tabernacle is anointed. Once again, extravagant measures for an extravagant God.

Costly sacrifice. Now, for the first time, the Manual of Sacrifice is put into operation, only with this twist: technically, all these sacrifices are sacrifices to make the sacrifice possible. They cover not only the full range of available sacrifices, but also involve those being prepared in some peculiarly intimate ways ("Moses took some of its blood and put it on the lobe of Aaron's right ear and on the thumb of his right hand and on the big toe of his right foot"; Lev. 8:23). This calls to mind the total dedication required of anyone who would serve the Lord ("You shall love the LORD your God with all your heart, and with all your soul, and with all your might"; Deut. 6:5). Not one part of the person and not one part of this place can remain untouched ceremonially in order to be set apart for service.

Formative communion. Though Moses acts single-handedly in the performance of this ordination, he ordains not just one person, but also a group (Aaron and his sons). At the sacrificial meal (Lev. 8:31–32), they are drawn closer together, not only to God, but also to one another. The joint commissioning role of this holy meal surely points toward another appropriate level of meaning for Christian Communion/Eucharist.

Preparatory time. Though the Lord can do things quickly, sometimes God chooses to do things slowly, perhaps not so much for God's sake as our own. It took seven days to create the world. Likewise, it takes seven days to ordain a priest. Both are creation stories: creating a universe out of nothing; out of a wandering slave, creating a creature fit to serve. We rush such procedures (whether we're talking ordination or confirmation) at our own peril. Blessed, claim the Scriptures, are "those who *wait* for the LORD" (Isa. 40:31).

In a time of extreme casualness in worship and service, Leviticus 8 might serve as a model for proper preparation for the Lord's service. Preparation for this service began back in Exodus 28 (where the Lord provided instructions for the vestments for the priesthood). This ritual shall now be repeated whenever new persons are needed in the sanctuary's service. Far more space in the Bible has been devoted to this seven-day procedure than is devoted to the seven-day creation of the world or the one-day exodus from Egypt. Again, we might ponder how we set individuals (seminary education, officer training, ordination ceremonies) and all God's people apart (preparation for Holy Communion) for worship. Is this really an area where cost and corner-cutting is desired?

THE BEGINNING OF TABERNACLE SERVICE
Leviticus 9:1–7, 22–24

9 **On the eighth day Moses summoned Aaron and his sons and the elders of Israel.** [2] **He said to Aaron, "Take a bull calf for a sin offering and a ram for a burnt offering, without blemish, and offer them before the LORD.** [3] **And say to the people of Israel, 'Take a male goat for a sin offering; a calf and a lamb, yearlings without blemish, for a burnt offering;** [4] **and an ox and a ram for an offering of well-being to sacrifice before the LORD; and a grain offering mixed with oil. For today the LORD will appear to you.'"** [5] **They brought what Moses commanded to the front of the tent of meeting; and the whole congregation drew near and stood before the LORD.** [6] **And Moses said, "This is the thing that the LORD commanded you to do, so that the glory of the LORD may appear to you."** [7] **Then Moses said to Aaron, "Draw near to the altar and sacrifice your sin offering and your burnt offering, and make atonement for yourself and for the people; and sacrifice the offering of the people, and make atonement for them; as the LORD has commanded."**

9:22 **Aaron lifted his hands toward the people and blessed them; and he came down after sacrificing the sin offering, the burnt offering, and the offering of well-being.** [23] **Moses and Aaron entered the tent of meeting, and then came out and blessed the people; and the glory of the LORD appeared to all the people.** [24] **Fire came out from the LORD and consumed the burnt offering and the fat on the altar; and when all the people saw it, they shouted and fell on their faces.**

"Everything is now ready. Let all the people come." Days and days of preparation, verse after verse of instruction, and it all comes down to this. Upon the completion of the tent of meeting, the Lord's glory had come to dwell in the midst of God's people. But this glory was yet at a distance and not directly visible to them. Now begins the service that will bring this glory close, not only this day, but in perpetuity.

First a representative series of offerings is performed. Then an Aaronic blessing is pronounced, with Moses' assistance. Then God's glory appears to all the people, consuming the offering and causing the people to shout and fall down.

This is undoubtedly one of the high points in all of Scripture! Unlike the theophany on Mount Sinai (which occurs at a distance) and the transfiguration (which is visible only to a few), this appearance is seen and celebrated by *all* the people and is linked to a service and locale accessible to God's people on a *regular* basis. We must therefore be very careful what we do and don't say about it.

First of all, we must stress again that this service alone does not secure the Lord's presence; if read in isolation, though, the language comes perilously close to that: "This is the thing that the LORD commanded you to do, so that the glory of the LORD may appear to you" (Lev. 9:6). The Lord is *already* with this people as a cloud, pillar, and abiding presence. What proper worship enables is all the people's *accessibility* to this glory. It provokes a visible sign of an invisible grace, a regular manifestation of a constant reality. When we shun this gift, it threatens not so much *God's* position as *our own.*

Second, deeper even than the desire that God do something for us, is our hunger for God to reveal Godself to us. Over and over in the Scriptures, those who draw closest to God hunger to know God more intimately, to have the light of God's countenance shine upon them, to see God face-to-face. An experience that is usually reserved for only the most intimate of God's partners and, even for them, must be handled in the most delicate fashion (lest they die!) is here made open to all, at the conclusion of a ceremony repeatable in all its details. Worship thus becomes the "regular" means of experiencing the grace of a quite "irregular" God. Though God remains a holy, mysterious, and free Lord, this is not a God who is far off, but near: as near as this week's sacrifices of praise and priestly benedictions.

Third, perhaps the most remarkable thing about this chapter is that another one follows! In a quite basic way, the deepest purpose for God's people has now been met: "Master, now you are dismissing your servant in peace, . . . for my eyes have seen your salvation, which you have prepared in the presence of all peoples, a light for revelation to the Gentiles and for glory to your people Israel" (Luke 2:29–32). But, if one doesn't die (literally) in the midst of prayer or worship or service, one must eventually stand up from where one has fallen and move on. Most congregations do. Israel certainly did—with some good results, and some bad.

TABERNACLE SERVICE GOES AWRY
Leviticus 10:1–20

> 10:1 **Now Aaron's sons, Nadab and Abihu, each took his censer, put fire in it, and laid incense on it; and they offered unholy fire before the LORD, such as he had not commanded them. ² And fire came out from the presence of the LORD and consumed them, and they died before the LORD. ³ Then Moses said to Aaron, "This is what the LORD meant when he said, 'Through those who are near me I will show myself holy, and before all the people I will be glorified.'"**

And Aaron was silent. ⁴ Moses summoned Mishael and Elzaphan, sons of Uzziel the uncle of Aaron, and said to them, "Come forward, and carry your kinsmen away from the front of the sanctuary to a place outside the camp." ⁵ They came forward and carried them by their tunics out of the camp, as Moses had ordered. ⁶ And Moses said to Aaron and to his sons Eleazar and Ithamar, "Do not dishevel your hair, and do not tear your vestments, or you will die and wrath will strike all the congregation; but your kindred, the whole house of Israel, may mourn the burning that the Lord has sent. ⁷ You shall not go outside the entrance of the tent of meeting, or you will die; for the anointing oil of the Lord is on you." And they did as Moses had ordered.

10:16 Then Moses made inquiry about the goat of the sin offering, and— it had already been burned! He was angry with Eleazar and Ithamar, Aaron's remaining sons, and said, ¹⁷ "Why did you not eat the sin offering in the sacred area? For it is most holy, and God has given it to you that you may remove the guilt of the congregation, to make atonement on their behalf before the Lord. ¹⁸ Its blood was not brought into the inner part of the sanctuary. You should certainly have eaten it in the sanctuary, as I commanded." ¹⁹ And Aaron spoke to Moses, "See, today they offered their sin offering and their burnt offering before the Lord; and yet such things as these have befallen me! If I had eaten the sin offering today, would it have been agreeable to the Lord?" ²⁰ And when Moses heard that, he agreed.

There is a pattern in the Bible that continues to the end. If things get terribly bad, wait, and the story will eventually take a better turn. Conversely, as is the case here, if things get terribly good—God commanding, the people obeying—wait, things will eventually take a turn for the worse.

Following the glories of Israel's first day of formal worship, things quickly fall apart: due to overzealous worship, overlooked details, and disagreements among the leadership. The "good news" is obvious: when *we* mess up, even regarding the handling of holy things, we are not alone. If it happened on the first day of worship, it can and will happen again. Nevertheless, the call is a call for vigilance, here more than in any other area of our lives.

Overzealous worship (the story of Nadab and Abihu). Though the usual sin of God's people is undoubtedly too little worship, it now becomes obvious that there is such a thing as too much worship. Specifically, the story of Nadab and Abihu warns us against worship procedures not explicitly commanded by the Lord. Whether such "innovations" are meant to procure special favor for the participants or whether they simply represent the human desire to follow God's fire with more of our own, humanly inspired worship (a few extra flourishes at the baptismal font, a few personal emendations to the Lord's Prayer) is dangerous and can lead to devastating results. Though this might seem to mark the Lord as callous or ungrateful, it better represents the zeal with which God protects the gift of worship already given. Aaron and his sons are forbidden to mourn following this incident (10:6), lest their devotion to Nadab and Abihu appear to outweigh their dedication to the Lord's worship. Further, an additional requirement of sobriety is added, so that they might be ever careful in their work in the sanctuary and their teaching in the community (vv. 8–9).

Overlooked details. Here a clarifying detail pops up that adds to the requirements of the Manual of Sacrifice offered earlier, specifically designating *the place* for eating the Grain versus the Well-Being Offering (vv. 12–15). Only as God's people begin the practice of worship does it become clear that they had not fully captured the procedure at the end of the first lesson. It is a measure of Moses' and the Lord's grace that time and again in these materials (often immediately following a narrative where some misunderstanding of procedure has occurred) some clarifying word or procedure is provided. Growth in faith and practice is never over. We continue to learn as we go along.

Disagreements among the leadership. It is not clear exactly why Aaron and Moses disagree over the eating of the goat of the Purification Offering. Apparently, Moses is following the letter of the law requiring the priest to consume the offering in the court of the tent of meeting (6:26). Aaron, however, based on the irregularities experienced on this particular day, decides a more rigorous application of the Burnt Offering regulation is in order. Perhaps the greatest miracle of the story is that after reacting in anger, stating his case, and hearing Aaron's reply, Moses relents and agrees.

Again and again, Moses emerges as a person of singular qualities throughout the stories of Leviticus–Numbers. When zeal is required, Moses has it. When mercy seems necessary, Moses argues for it. Perhaps most difficult of all, when compromise and reversal are in order, Moses is large enough to relent. Rather than Moses betraying a fault of character on such occasions, we may catch a glimpse of one of those characteristics the Scriptures label "divine." Compare the whole tradition of the Lord's "repentance" in the Old Testament (translated "changed his mind" in Exod. 32:14) and the remarkable story of the Messiah's "instruction" by a Canaanite woman in the New (Matt. 15:21–28, a "hearing" that opens the way for the Gentile mission). Flexibility regarding the rules and procedures by which the Lord is worshiped and served is here seen as a "witness to" rather than a "denial of" the character of God.

3. Instructions on Clean/Unclean
Leviticus 11:1–15:33

Having secured some safe space for commerce between Israel's resident Holy One and Israel's unholy people, you might expect the trip to now resume. A sacrificial system with attendant priests is in place. Immediate consumption of God's people is no longer a pressing problem. Why not "head 'em up and move 'em out"?

Well, while we may have settled the issue of animals regarding *sacrifices*, we have not settled the issue of animals regarding *supermarkets*. Yes, we know which animals are appropriate for worship. Yes, we even know what portions of these offerings the priests and others may eat. But what about the eating of animals in general? What items are appropriate in congregational grocery carts? Is one sort of diet appropriate for people in general and another sort of diet appropriate for God's people in particular? Most important, if so, where do you draw the line?

Having established the life of the sanctuary at Israel's center, the priests are now given their instructions for establishing a similar life throughout Israelite society. Here the grand experiment begins. Viewed practically, this ordering of Israel's everyday life is what undergirds and makes possible Israel's ongoing life of worship. Viewed spiritually, this distinguishing between holy and common, clean and unclean, is what enables the glory of the sanctuary to ripple out into the glory of the marketplace, the dining room, even the bedroom!

Several observations.

First, while the Manual of Sacrifice might give the impression that all the priests did was slaughter and sprinkle and eat holy meals, surely the heart of their ministry was the instruction *out in the community*, making clean animals and clean people possible. Like the pastor who visits throughout the week in order to be an effective preacher, like the Sunday school teacher who attends the high school football game on Friday night so that she can attend to her students' needs on Sunday morning, the priest is portrayed in Leviticus *out* of the sanctuary more than *in*: inspecting food-stuffs, examining rashes, and investigating the walls of houses.

Second, it should now be clear that one of the obvious functions of this instruction is to "set apart" the daily life of Israel from the daily lives of surrounding peoples. If someone's food, clothing, or housing is different from ours, we notice and we want to know why. For Israel, then, this "outer" life necessary to maintain its "inner" life of worship thus becomes a primary form of witness, pointing toward the peculiar Lord at its core.

Finally, if and when the sacrificial system breaks down (as it did for both Jews and Christians), some reevaluation of the criteria of holy/common and clean/unclean is in order. If maintaining clean animals and clean hands is no longer the main motivation for priestly instruction, what kinds of sacrifices, and thus what kinds of "cleanliness," are required? Such "application" for today remains the most difficult aspect of the set of regulations that follow, yet *the* area that must be tackled if God's people, in their everyday lives, are yet to be seen as set apart.

FOODS
Leviticus 11:1–47

11:1 The Lord spoke to Moses and Aaron, saying to them: [2] Speak to the people of Israel, saying: From among all the land animals, these are the creatures that you may eat. [3] Any animal that has divided hoofs and is cleft-footed and chews the cud—such you may eat. [4] But among those that chew the cud or have divided hoofs, you shall not eat the following: the camel, for even though it chews the cud, it does not have divided hoofs; it is unclean for you. [5] The rock badger, for even though it chews the cud, it does not have divided hoofs; it is unclean for you. [6] The hare, for even though it chews the cud, it does not have divided hoofs; it is unclean for you. [7] The pig, for even though it has divided hoofs and is cleft-footed, it does not chew the cud; it is unclean for you. [8] Of their flesh you shall not eat, and their carcasses you shall not touch; they are unclean for you.

11:46 This is the law pertaining to land animal and bird and every living creature that moves through the waters and every creature that swarms upon the earth, [47] to make a distinction between the unclean and the clean, and between the living creature that may be eaten and the living creature that may not be eaten.

From Genesis through Leviticus, three different levels of meat consumption are evident, starting with a wide circle, then narrowing down. In Genesis 9, following the flood, human beings are given permission to eat of "every moving thing that lives" on the earth, in the air, in the sea. This is a general command for all the earth's peoples, within which Israel is one family. In Leviticus 1–7, we have just studied animals suitable for the Lord's worship and the priests' consumption: only certain animals at the heart of Israel's herds and flocks, without fault or blemish, in order of decreasing price. Now we are taught a third division of the animals of this world, that between the clean and unclean, marking the boundary line between what the Israelite outside the sanctuary can and cannot eat. The threefold distinction just established between Homo sapiens (among the Israelites who serve as priests, the Israelites who join as worshipers, and all the non-Israelites who are not part of the story) now leads to a similar trifold division in the rest of the animal world (animals for sacrifice, animals for eating, animals to be avoided).

Down through the centuries much ink has been spilled in attempting to unlock the key to these lists' rationale. Some have pointed to hygiene and been intrigued by the higher incidence of disease carried by pork and shellfish. Too bad the current threat on the world market is mad cow disease. Others have posited the animal deities of surrounding peoples and speculated that these distinctions marked a boundary line with pagan practice. Too bad then that the Messiah of God's people was often called "The Lion of Judah" (the lion being "unclean" since it walks about on its paws; Lev. 11:27). Others, perhaps wisely, have simply given up and attributed the selection to God's inscrutable command. The problem with this approach is that we either follow it precisely, every jot and tittle, or not in any way at all.

Possibly a more straightforward rationale goes like this. Central to Israel's life as nomads were its flocks and its herds, animals with cleft hooves, which chew the cud. These necessarily then are the animals required for sacrifice by this people, not so much for the Lord's taste (remember, all the world's animals are the Lord's, and the Lord needs nothing for food; Ps. 50:12–14) as for the people's need (to give something costly and precious, from the center of their lives). Because *these* animals were central to Israel's life, and thus most appropriate for sacrificial offerings, a system of classification was established that bears this sacrificial selection out into the world. Every earthbound animal is measured by the standard of cattle, goats, and sheep, which they knew well. Birds and fish of the sea, which they knew less well, follow less clear-cut criteria (no fish for sacrifices; doves and pigeons considered clean). The whole system thus rumbles back to the mystery of the Lord's election of Israel, a peculiar band of wanderers who knew some of the world's animals, but not some others. The instructions for clean/unclean build into every meal some memory of this selection, even when the days of nomadic wandering are over.

The question for us thus becomes, "What manner of eating might best remind us of our peculiar selection by God?" If Christ himself questions whether any food category in and of itself is unclean (Matt. 15:11), and Peter and Paul follow this with their rejection of any jot-and-tittle continuation of Jewish/Gentile dietary distinctions (proscribing only foods offered to idols, whatever has been strangled, and blood; Acts 15:20), what kinds of food might be labeled clean/unclean for Christians?

Remember, you were slaves. Would a people who remembered that they were slaves, and that it was out of slavery that God called them, refuse to eat the meat of animals that had been raised in inhumane and severely restricted settings, with little freedom to exercise the lives their Creator intended? Israel had been a victim of "mass production" in Egypt. Should this family resist such food today?

Remember, you have been fed with a little. Would a people whose Messiah fed five thousand people with five fishes and two loaves not refrain from eating meats that skewed the balance of the world's foodstuffs (especially Leviticus's sacred cattle) while many in the world go hungry? Many in the church make jokes about vegetarians versus vegans—until a son or daughter reads the Scriptures and becomes one.

Remember, you have been called out of the nations. Would a people who knew they were not *Rome's* or *Babylon's*, but *God's* people not be reluctant to adopt any ethnic menu that marked them more as citizens of the nations than a people set apart by God? Could it be that the Christian's menu might be more restricted, simple, and diverse at the same time?

We can often tell a lot about our neighbor if we're given the opportunity to hear their prayer requests. We may learn even more about our neighbors if we're given the opportunity to peruse their grocery cart (low-fat/junk, generic/brand-name, cost-conscious/extravagant). What would the contents of our cart and the foods of our table reveal about our identity as God's people and the nature of our worship and service?

It is intriguing that a recent study, on the way we modern Christians pick and choose regarding what parts of the tradition we will honor and what parts we will discard, bears the title *Consuming Religion* (see Miller in the bibliography). Those who would strive to understand human behavior at its most basic often think it best to approach members of our community of creatures first and foremost as "consumers," a word whose first provenance is the table. What goes into our mouths does not simply pass through without altering us; it becomes part of these bodies, which have been created by and thus can bear witness to the One who sets us apart. In a culture obsessed with food (simply note the epidemic of food disorders all around us), it seems strange that the church so casually dismisses food choices as a way to remember, bear witness, and remain marked as those with whom God has chosen to dwell. What would happen to church life if the deacons were as careful in their selection of foods for the fellowship table as the elders are careful regarding selection of foods for the Lord's Table? Might the glory at the center of our lives not begin to spread out through the camp?

Note. Anyone who has even the slightest memories from middle school or high school remembers that questions of where to eat and with whom to eat were two of the most loaded issues of each day. Therefore it is no surprise, in a book on Christian practices for teens, that one whole chapter deals with food, especially the difficulty of making "food choices" (Bass and Richter, *Way to Live*). The teenage author sums up much of what we have said regarding Leviticus 11 with these words:

> We all need to eat and drink every day. But food is more than body fuel. It is a gift from God that connects us to the earth and to the needs of others. At the table we share food and our lives. We also thank God, welcome strangers, receive friends, and meet Jesus. Eating together, we become companions [a loaded word!] for life. (65)

CHILDBIRTH
Leviticus 12:1–8

12:1 The LORD spoke to Moses, saying: [2] Speak to the people of Israel, saying: If a woman conceives and bears a male child, she shall be ceremonially unclean seven days; as at the time of her menstruation, she shall be unclean. [3] On the eighth day the flesh of his foreskin shall be circumcised. [4] Her time of blood purification shall be thirty-three days; she shall not touch any holy thing, or come into the sanctuary, until the days of her purification are completed. [5] If she bears a female child, she shall be unclean two weeks, as in her menstruation; her time of blood purification shall be sixty-six days. [6] When the days of her purification are completed, whether for a son or for a daughter, she shall bring to the priest at the entrance of the tent of meeting a lamb in its first year for a burnt offering, and a pigeon or a turtledove for a sin offering. [7] He shall offer it before the LORD, and make atonement on her behalf; then she shall be clean from her flow of blood. This is the law for

her who bears a child, male or female. [8] If she cannot afford a sheep, she shall take two turtledoves or two pigeons, one for a burnt offering and the other for a sin offering; and the priest shall make atonement on her behalf, and she shall be clean.

As eating goes to the heart of our daily lives, so birth goes to the marrow. No event is more necessary for a people's survival. No occasion is more threatening for the persons involved. Here, too, our behavior should reflect our worship; what we do or don't do should witness to our selection by the Lord.

Key to this entire set of regulations is the flow of blood. As there are regulations with respect to the monthly flow of blood (Lev. 15), so there are extraordinary regulations with respect to the flow of blood accompanying birth (12:4). A woman who has had a child is unclean for a set number of days (seven for a male child; fourteen for a female): she shall not be touched. A woman who has had a child must not touch "holy" things for a longer period of time (thirty-three days for a male; sixty-six days for a female): she is cut off from the life of the sanctuary. Again, here, at the most intimate and sacred event of our personal lives, public worship intrudes.

Dare we hazard some comments?

First, the primary focus here is on God. A break has occurred in the womb of our lives. Precious blood has been spilled. Some recognition, some pause, some break in the regular order is required. Men must forgo conjugal relations; women must give up the handling of holy things. One of God's people does not just have a baby and dive back into work or worship. In the birth process, we human beings are privileged to cooperate in one of God's most holy activities: the creation of life, accompanied by the flow of blood. Following this, some proper time and space must be hallowed or set apart, in order for the lines between our lives and God's life to resettle and clarify.

Second, there is no denying the fact that the brunt of this hallowing falls on the woman, especially if she is a woman who's had a female child! While the obvious answer might be the woman's proximity to the blood, the distinction between purification times for male versus female births undermines this easy explanation. We cannot avoid the fact that these regulations were the teachings of male priests directed first and foremost to the male leaders of this society. There can be little if any doubt that the details of Leviticus 12 would be different if female voices had been given an equal say.

Nevertheless, third and finally, it is still incumbent upon us, as males and females, to spin out some modern postpartum practices that might set us apart as worshipers of the Lord. Surely a people who are deeply aware of God's hand in the birth process would be willing to mark this event through the implementation of generous family leave times, for women and for men. Surely congregations who are aware of the holiness of this event would refuse to be critical of new parents who are not instantly back at work or worship, yet stand ready to welcome both parents and newborn with nursery space and workers when the time arrives. Most of all, any people who know the sacredness of any child's birth into this world will be willing to mark this child's arrival by more than just lambs or pigeons on the parents' part: how about sacrifices to grant this child food, healthcare, and education sufficient to become a full servant of the Lord, who gave the child birth?

Even though Mary was yet required to make a purification offering following the birth of Jesus (her offering of birds making clear the lack of wealth on Joseph's part; Luke 2:24; cf. Lev. 12:8), she nevertheless is declared not "unclean" but "favored" of God. It should be clear that participation in the event of birth (an event at which most males will always feel somewhat superfluous!) is not cause for shame, but a call to recognize the Holy One at work, even in the flesh and blood of our lives.

SKIN AND FUNGUS DISEASES
Leviticus 13:1–14:57

At the end of Leviticus 9, there is a sense that everything is in order: the Lord and God's people are in their place; all is right with the world. What immediately follows is an eruption of unholy fire involving Nadab and Abihu, which then must be extinguished, set right, and restored before the life of the community can go on. Here, in Leviticus 13–14, we meet a class of "eruptive" diseases—of the skin, of clothes, of buildings—which likewise, for the sake of the community, must be extinguished, set right, and restored.

As with categories of food, much time and energy have been devoted to determining exactly what this class of diseases might be and why they, of all the diseases possible at that time, were marked as the most threatening for the life of this worshiping community. Clearly, if one of the "diseases" was leprosy, or Hansen's disease, it had to be a leprosy viewed as far more virulent and all-inclusive than this disease is known to be today, invading not only human skin, but garments and interior walls as well! Once more the key seems to be "eruptions" or "breaks" in the given order, whether amid categories of animals, the spilling of blood in childbirth, or eruptions of skin, fabric, or plaster. We hope and pray that God and God's glory might break out in our sanctuaries, our bodies, even our houses. Other eruptions are viewed less charitably. Something or some things drastic must be done.

First the text treats *eruptions of the skin.*

13:1 **The Lord spoke to Moses and Aaron, saying:** [2] **When a person has on the skin of his body a swelling or an eruption or a spot, and it turns into a leprous disease on the skin of his body, he shall be brought to Aaron the priest or to one of his sons the priests.** [3] **The priest shall examine the disease on the skin of his body, and if the hair in the diseased area has turned white and the disease appears to be deeper than the skin of his body, it is a leprous disease; after the priest has examined him he shall pronounce him ceremonially unclean.** [4] **But if the spot is white in the skin of his body, and appears no deeper than the skin, and the hair in it has not turned white, the priest shall confine the diseased person for seven days.** [5] **The priest shall examine him on the seventh day, and if he sees that the disease is checked and the disease has not spread in the skin, then the priest shall confine him seven days more.** [6] **The priest shall examine him again on the seventh day, and if the disease has abated and the disease has not spread in the skin, the priest shall pronounce him clean; it is only an eruption; and he shall wash his clothes, and be clean.** [7] **But if the eruption spreads in the skin after he has shown himself to the priest for his cleansing, he shall appear again before the priest.** [8] **The priest shall make an examination, and if the eruption has spread in the skin, the priest shall pronounce him unclean; it is a leprous disease.**

13:45 **The person who has the leprous disease shall wear torn clothes and let the hair of his head be disheveled; and he shall cover his upper lip and cry out, "Unclean, unclean."** [46] **He shall remain unclean as long as he has the disease; he is unclean. He shall live alone; his dwelling shall be outside the camp.**

The *good news* is that the body of the Israelite is not automatically considered unclean and nonadmissible to the sanctuary, or else glimpsing the Lord's glory might never occur. The *bad news* is that eruptions of the skin do render the body "unclean," requiring something to be done before admission to holy things, one's home, or even the community is allowed (or else the eruption may spread to all). The concern once more is worship and how to preserve the possibility of worship for God's chosen people.

Some observations.

First, while the Bible includes only *visible* eruptions of the body, modern medicine and the diagnostic tools available to us would have to include far more. There are eruptions at the cellular level that, if allowed to grow, can cause eruptions elsewhere. There are eruptions of the internal organs that can prove fatal far more quickly and ruthlessly than eruptions of the skin. There are even eruptions in the biochemistry of the brain that cause good balance, like good skin, to be broken. As an initial move, put us all under the microscope, and we will all contain eruptions. There is no one who is clean, purely. No, not one.

Second, while some movement toward exclusion might be both practical and necessary for the life of the community, complete exclusion not only betrays a false understanding of illness (again, we are all carrying one kind of illness or another), but a wrong-hearted method of protection (preserving the well by casting out the sick). While much of the legislation of Leviticus 13–14 was meant to be restorative (and indeed, the rites of purification take up almost as much space as the rituals for diagnosis), and while all the ministrations of the priest ran the risk of contamination and death (if one accepted the Israelite's view regarding the virulence of these diseases), the division between the sick and the well is not only a false one theologically, but works against the methods of the Good Physician, who came to meet, to touch, and to heal not the well, but the sick.

So, third, the fact that Christ and the early church worked directly to counter this exclusionary impulse calls us to seek to restore the bodies of all who are ill. In a culture that may well be more illness-phobic than the Israelites'; in the midst of a worshiping community where even common cups at communion can prove cause for concern; in a society that, despite its medical sophistication, yet views some diseases as scourges and cause for whispering and distance and exclusion, and views any blotch or wrinkle or imperfection in the skin as justification for injections, surgeries, and complete makeovers—maybe the main message of Leviticus 13–14 for us is its picture of priests willing to go out and examine members of the camp, then work for their restoration. As these priests (and the priestly Jesus) circulated among the people, diagnosing (and healing) those who had bodily eruptions, so God's people today should be out examining the skin, the organs, and the minds of the world's people. Not so much to *cut off*, as to *bring in* the blind, the lame, and the halt, so they might catch a glimpse of God's glory and be made whole. Given a society within which such eruptions were seen as deadly threats, not only to the lives of individuals but also to the saving story of the people as a whole, it is indeed good news that almost as many verses are dedicated to rituals of restoration as prescriptions for exclusion.

Next come eruptions in one's *clothes.*

13:47 Concerning clothing: when a leprous disease appears in it, in woolen or linen cloth, [48] in warp or woof of linen or wool, or in a skin or in anything made of skin, [49] if the disease shows greenish or reddish in the garment, whether in warp or woof or in skin or in anything made of skin, it is a leprous disease and shall be shown to the priest. [50] The priest shall examine the disease, and put the diseased article aside for seven days. [51] He shall examine the disease on the seventh day. If the disease has spread in the cloth, in warp or woof, or in the skin, whatever be the use of the skin, this is a spreading leprous disease; it is unclean. [52] He shall burn the clothing, whether diseased in warp or woof, woolen or linen, or anything of skin, for it is a spreading leprous disease; it shall be burned in fire.

13:59 This is the ritual for a leprous disease in a cloth of wool or linen, either in warp or woof, or in anything of skin, to decide whether it is clean or unclean.

At first glance, this section (Lev. 13:47–59) only confirms the silliness of all these regulations. Leprosy, we know, is highly noncontagious, much less via clothes.

But let us not move too quickly. Not only are some means of transmission not fully understood, but also the notion that bodily eruptions might show up in the clothes is not so far-fetched. If someone is battling depression, where is one of the first places this manifests itself? Look at his clothes. If someone has a strong case of materialism combined with an overfascination with the things of this world, what might you do? Send the priest to inspect her wardrobe. If young people feel insecure inside and desperately want to fit in and be accepted, what are the telltale signs? Examine the labels on their pants, the insignia on their blouses. Did the Israelites really have a less-sophisticated understanding of illness than we?

Finally we read of eruptions in one's *house*.

14:33 The LORD spoke to Moses and Aaron, saying: [34] When you come into the land of Canaan, which I give you for a possession, and I put a leprous disease in a house in the land of your possession, [35] the owner of the house shall come and tell the priest, saying, "There seems to me to be some sort of disease in my house." [36] The priest shall command that they empty the house before the priest goes to examine the disease, or all that is in the house will become unclean; and afterward the priest shall go in to inspect the house. [37] He shall examine the disease; if the disease is in the walls of the house with greenish or reddish spots, and if it appears to be deeper than the surface, [38] the priest shall go outside to the door of the house and shut up the house seven days. [39] The priest shall come again on the seventh day and make an inspection; if the disease has spread in the walls of the house, [40] the priest shall command that the stones in which the disease appears be taken out and thrown into an unclean place outside the city. [41] He shall have the inside of the house scraped thoroughly, and the plaster that is scraped off shall be dumped in an unclean place outside the city. [42] They shall take other stones and put them in the place of those stones, and take other plaster and plaster the house.

14:54 This is the ritual for any leprous disease: for an itch, [55] for leprous diseases in clothing and houses, [56] and for a swelling or an eruption or a spot, [57] to determine when it is unclean and when it is clean. This is the ritual for leprous diseases.

Here, we think, the Israelites' folly turns into madness. What kind of phobia would drive a people to cast out people, burn clothes, and tear down buildings? Surely this is a chapter (Lev. 14:33–57) we can skip over and move past.

But slow down again. Anyone who's read of the dangers of asbestos and radon gas will read this passage with some sense of déjà vu. Anyone who's wrestled with the question of disposal of contaminated wastes and the cleanup of hazardous sites will sense some familiarity as stones and mortar are carted out for burial. Anyone who recognizes the force for good and ill that our primary environment, our homes, play in our lives (physical, emotional, and spiritual) will read with some interest this description of priests going out on home tours, ever vigilant for those spots and blotches that might threaten to separate the dwellers from the God now dwelling in their midst.

Can you imagine a similar deacon-led house inspection today? What would be on the checklist? Negatives: too many square feet for too few people; lack of handicapped access; too many televisions, not enough books. Positives: easily accessible and regularly used devotional materials; guest room for people other than family; cupboards stocked and chairs at table and available for unexpected guests.

It is an intriguing exercise to read Leviticus 13–14 while thinking of some contagion we yet fear, such as nuclear contamination or the Ebola virus. Now the visits of the priests take on an added urgency and risk. Now the precautions and the remedies seem less extreme. Now we begin to see what powers we fear as well as the Power we quickly forget. What if we mounted a body, clothes, and house inspection, searching for signs of the Spirit's eruption in our lives? Would there be sufficient evidence to convict us? Would the blood of one slaughtered bird and the flight of one living bird be sufficient to restore us to fellowship, not just in our sanctuaries, but also in our living rooms, garages, and bedrooms as well? There is a Lord in our midst. Some scrubbing, some ironing, some house clean-ing and renovations are in order.

GENITAL DISCHARGES
Leviticus 15:1–33

15:1 The LORD spoke to Moses and Aaron, saying: [2] Speak to the people of Israel and say to them: When any man has a discharge from his member, his discharge makes him ceremonially unclean. [3] The uncleanness of his discharge is this: whether his member flows with his discharge, or his member is stopped from discharging, it is uncleanness for him. [4] Every bed on which the one with the discharge lies shall be unclean; and everything on which he sits shall be unclean. [5] Anyone who touches his bed shall wash his clothes, and bathe in water, and be unclean until the evening. [6] All who sit on anything on which the one with the discharge has sat shall wash their clothes, and bathe in water, and be unclean until the evening. [7] All who touch the body of the one with the discharge shall wash their clothes, and bathe in water, and be unclean until the evening. [8] If the one with the discharge spits on persons who are clean, then they shall wash their clothes, and bathe in water, and be unclean until the evening. [9] Any saddle on which the one with the discharge rides shall be unclean. [10] All who touch anything that was under him shall be unclean until the evening, and all who carry such a thing shall wash their clothes, and bathe in water, and be unclean until the evening. [11] All those whom the one with the discharge touches without his having rinsed his hands in water shall wash their clothes, and bathe in water, and be unclean until the evening. [12] Any earthen vessel that the one with the discharge touches shall be broken; and every vessel of wood shall be rinsed in water.

15:19 When a woman has a discharge of blood that is her regular dis-charge from her body, she shall be in her impurity for seven days, and who-ever touches her shall be unclean until the evening. [20] Everything upon which she lies during her impurity shall be unclean; everything also upon which she sits shall be unclean. [21] Whoever touches her bed shall wash his clothes, and bathe in water, and be unclean until the evening. [22] Whoever touches anything upon which she sits shall wash his clothes, and bathe in water, and be unclean until the evening; [23] whether it is the bed or anything upon which she sits, when he touches it he shall be unclean until the evening. [24] If any man lies with her, and her impurity falls on him, he shall be unclean seven days; and every bed on which he lies shall be unclean.

15:31 Thus you shall keep the people of Israel separate from their unclean-ness, so that they do not die in their uncleanness by defiling my tabernacle that is in their midst. [32] This is the ritual for those who have a discharge: for him who has an emission of semen, becoming unclean thereby, [33] for her who is in the infirmity of her period, for anyone, male or female, who has a dis-charge, and for the man who lies with a woman who is unclean.

Again, set in context, we have an image of surface calm and goodness, broken by "eruptions." Even the eruptions that are good and lead to new life (ejaculation of semen in procreation, flow of menstrual blood to replenish the womb) require some response on our part prior to reentry to worship. All eruptions, whether normal (regular flow of semen or blood) or abnormal (irregular discharges of semen or protracted flows of menstrual blood), are thus made secondary to God's holy and salutary eruption in our midst.

All one needs to do is turn on the TV to know that genital discharges (though supposedly not talked about or viewed in "polite" company) have been elevated in popular culture as the central events of our lives. How appropriate, then, that these events must be acknowledged, cleaned up, and accounted for prior to reentry into God's sanctuary—where the true life-giving eruption is expected to occur. Leviticus would push us toward "due" reverence, versus "undue" reverence, toward those events that hint at and point toward the creative eruptions that issue from the Lord alone.

Some observations:

First, at last (in contrast to Lev. 12), an equal-opportunity flow/emission! This time *both* female and male are required to monitor their most intimate hygiene. Rather than viewing one gender's fluids as "clean" and the other's "unclean," Leviticus 15 recognizes the life-laden potential of both blood and semen, and calls for some proper recognition when they are spilled. Things we would rather cover over and keep in the dark are brought out into the open and dealt with, whether male or female.

Second, the priests are once again given the unenviable task of distinguishing between "normal" and "abnormal" flows. As mentioned in the section on eruptions of the skin, this undoubtedly forces the priest to make distinctions seldom borne out in real life, where the frequency and duration of such discharges cover a spectrum with no firm boundary in between. This, however, only highlights the overall difficulty of the priest's task, making distinctions "between the holy and the common, and between the unclean and the clean" (10:10) in a world where people's lives (and certainly people's sheets!) are mostly gray.

Third and most provocative, one cannot help but stand amazed at the way this legislation requires the synagogue's and the church's intrusion into even the most intimate areas of God's people's lives! There is indeed no area of our lives so "secular" or "profane" (the reader of Lev. 15 must conclude) that our response to it has no chance of reflecting God's glory. Any culture that grows "casual" in the spilling of seed or blood will quickly become "casual" regarding the gift of life. Likewise, any culture that elevates these "eruptions" to the level of worship will probably prove "casual" regarding the real outpouring that counts—the effusion of God's life-giving presence in worship, which even the ecstasy of sexual union only anticipates.

DISTINGUISHING CLEAN FROM UNCLEAN: SUMMARY COMMENTS

Some summary comments are now in order before we leave this section on the clean and unclean.

On the one hand, we have continually run up against the problems of such "polar" distinctions in the real world. Given the stuff of our sloppy lives—foods to eat; skin, clothes, and houses to maintain; discharges to monitor and clean up—it seems both impossible and foolish to spend much time and energy distinguishing between the clean and unclean in our lives. Better just to confess our uncleanness ("Woe are we, for we are a people of unclean lips who dwell among peoples of unclean lips!") and trust our cleansing to the grace of God ("Wash me and make me clean!").

However, on the other hand, we must be clear that this messiness regarding making distinctions in human life remains whether we are dealing with issues of blood and semen, or issues of marriage, war, and taxes. If there is no place for ethical discussions regarding personal hygiene, there is no room for ethical discussions on love and peace. The great strength of Leviticus 11–15, in fact, rests on its acknowledgment that we "dust creatures" will forever remain creatures who must eat, excrete, and procreate in order to live. Nevertheless, the Lord God has not only chosen to come into our midst, but now also makes provisions to stay in our midst, no matter how messy such residency may prove.

Not only does this call the lie on much of our Christian worship, where we try to pass ourselves off as otherworldly creatures who have no need of food or sex or baths; it also points ahead to another Savior, who was willing to come close to us indeed. If you are going to make yourself available to human beings, you will have to deal with matters of food and blood and bodily fluids. Any good nurse or physician knows this; any good pastor or parishioner ought to. While we might want to skip the reading of Leviticus 11–15 (and certainly avoid any Sunday school lessons or sermons on such topics!), the remarkable good news is that God did not. God comes to live and worship with us, and God makes provisions to continue to live and worship with us, just as we are.

Note. The Christian church has always attracted a strong contingent of folk who would prefer to deal with the spirit and ignore or deny the body. Such "Gnostic" tendencies are met head-on in John by the declaration that "the Word became flesh and lived among us" (John 1:14). It would be hard to imagine a more potent Old Testament parallel to such fleshly affirmation than Leviticus 11–15. This is a God who desires not some disembodied congregation of ethereal spirits to worship and serve him, but rather a God who is working to enable even their foods and fluids and flows to witness to the Lord's tangible presence in their midst.

4. Inauguration of the Day of Atonement
Leviticus 16:1–34

16:1 The LORD spoke to Moses after the death of the two sons of Aaron, when they drew near before the LORD and died. [2] The LORD said to Moses: Tell your brother Aaron not to come just at any time into the sanctuary inside the curtain before the mercy seat that is upon the ark, or he will die; for I appear in the cloud upon the mercy seat. [3] Thus shall Aaron come into the holy place: with a young bull for a sin offering and a ram for a burnt offering. [4] He shall put on the holy linen tunic, and shall have the linen undergarments next to his body, fasten the linen sash, and wear the linen turban; these are the holy vestments. He shall bathe his body in water, and then put them on. [5] He shall take from the congregation of the people of Israel two male goats for a sin offering, and one ram for a burnt offering. [6] Aaron shall offer the bull as a sin offering for himself, and shall make atonement for himself and for his house. [7] He shall take the two goats and set them before the LORD at the entrance of the tent of meeting; [8] and Aaron shall cast lots on the two goats, one lot for the LORD and the other lot for Azazel. [9] Aaron shall present the goat on which the lot fell for the LORD, and offer it as a sin offering; [10] but the goat on which the lot fell for Azazel shall be presented alive before the LORD to make atonement over it, that it may be sent away into the wilderness to Azazel.

16:20 When he has finished atoning for the holy place and the tent of meeting and the altar, he shall present the live goat. [21] Then Aaron shall lay both his hands on the head of the live goat, and confess over it all the iniquities of the people of Israel, and all their transgressions, all their sins, putting them on the head of the goat, and sending it away into the wilderness by means of someone designated for the task. [22] The goat shall bear on itself all their iniquities to a barren region; and the goat shall be set free in the wilderness.

16:29 This shall be a statute to you forever: In the seventh month, on the tenth day of the month, you shall deny yourselves, and shall do no work, neither the citizen nor the alien who resides among you. [30] For on this day atonement shall be made for you, to cleanse you; from all your sins you shall be clean before the LORD. [31] It is a sabbath of complete rest to you, and you shall deny yourselves; it is a statute forever. [32] The priest who is anointed and consecrated as priest in his father's place shall make atonement, wearing the linen vestments, the holy vestments. [33] He shall make atonement for the sanctuary, and he shall make atonement for the tent of meeting and for the altar, and he shall make atonement for the priests and for all the people of the assembly. [34] This shall be an everlasting statute for you, to make atonement for the people of Israel once in the year for all their sins. And Moses did as the LORD had commanded him.

Just when you might begin to think things are covered (what food to eat, what clothes to wear, what to do when things "erupt"), the story apparently jumps back—to the story of Nadab and Abihu, the sons of Aaron who brought fire before the Lord (Lev. 16:1). What was the point of Leviticus 11–15 and all the regulations regarding clean versus unclean in between? Here is one attempt at an answer.

Without these intervening chapters, the Day of Atonement might seem unnecessary. As long as the members of the priestly family did not commit some heinous mistake (like that of Nadab and Abihu), the sins of the people might be covered. Armed with the Manual of Sacrifice, the life of God's people might roll on for perpetuity, whether in the wilderness or at home in the land.

However, anyone who has been paying attention to Leviticus 11–15 is by now quite nervous, if not completely overwhelmed. How am I to know if I inadvertently swallowed a swarming insect while out chasing the sheep? What if a person with a flow of blood or a house with a spot in its plaster has gone unnoticed by the priest? What if some nocturnal emission has occurred and I don't know it, yet walk into the sanctuary with my Grain Offering? Even without the fire of Nadab and Abihu, a dread begins to fall on God's people. Once more it becomes doubtful whether having a Holy Lord this close is a wise idea or not.

Right at this point, an additional means of atonement is made available. On one day of each year, Yom Kippur, the Day of Atonement, the priest enters the Holy of Holies and makes atonement for the sanctuary and all the sins of the priests and people. Not *in place* of the other sacrifices and intervening regulations, but *in addition* to these, an extraordinary means of grace is given.

There is much that needs to be said.

Once a year. Up to this point, all sacrifice is "occasional," motivated either by an outbreak of praise or by the need for atonement in the life of an individual or group. Now a communal sacrifice is built into the calendar forever (v. 29). This makes it clear that no matter whether it is a good year or a bad year, the priests and the people are making extra efforts or coasting, there is a natural accumulation of "unholiness" in the lives of God's people that requires a cleansing. Like the Prayer of Confession built into every weekly service; like the command to pray, "Forgive us our debts, as we forgive our debtors," every day; this is an acknowledgment of who we are and who God is. Without some *regular* provision for forgiveness, we are without hope.

Some particulars. (1) *The stripping, washing, and clothing of the priest.* While the priest must be clothed appropriately for all sanctuary service, special provisions are required on this day. As the technician is suited up and hosed down in order to handle radioactive fuel rods; as the child is scrubbed and jacketed for first communion; so the priest must be specially prepared for this encounter with power. (2) *The parting of the curtain.* On all other days, the service of the sanctuary takes place "outside the veil." This day is the only day when the priest is allowed into the inner sanctum, the Holy of Holies. Here we walk on holy ground. We edge up close enough to feel the breath from God's nostrils. Meticulous care and proper timing are absolutely necessary. (3) *Offerings for the priest, the sanctuary, and the people.* Atonement is not a need of the laity alone. Indeed, the largest of the offerings, the bull, is necessary *for the priest* in order to approach the Lord. In the presence of God, all distinctions between human beings cease. When invited into the Lord's private study, even the priest whispers, "But who can endure the day of his coming, and who can stand when he appears?" (Mal. 3:2). (4) *One goat driven out.* Though a quick death seems more humane than a desert banishment, and though the lack of specificity regarding the identity of Azazel only adds to the foreboding, the use of a scapegoat can only be seen as an accommodation to our own all-too-human and lethally specific evil. In the absence of an animal substitute, surely we would find fellow human beings, indeed, next-door neighbors to send out. The human proclivity for scapegoating is as old as the Hittites and as recent as the desire to repatriate all illegal immigrants. This harsh concession to our bloodlust keeps such practices in check. (5) *The cloud of incense.* Even with the washing and preparation, even given the splashings of blood from bull and goat, even with the utmost care in timing and procedure, when push comes to shove, the Lord, even on this day, is encountered in a cloud (v. 13). Though Moses is privileged to see the Lord as God passes by, and the people are granted the experience of seeing the Lord's glory in the camp, not even the high priest on the Day of Atonement can see the Lord and live. Yes, even Aaron, even here, sees through a glass darkly rather than face-to-face.

Centrality for Judaism and Christianity. Both Judaism and Christianity recognize something so fundamental here that it must somehow be continued. For the Jews, Yom Kippur remains the highest of holy days, though the offerings of bulls and goats have been replaced by offerings of prayer and the reading of Scripture. For the Christians, the Day of Atonement becomes linked, step-by-step, with the once-for-all sacrifice of Christ. Again, some particulars: (1) *The stripping, washing, and clothing of the priest.* The baptism of Jesus by John takes on an added dimension if viewed as the first step in his preparation for offering up his life and vocation as an atoning offering to God ("The next day he [John] saw Jesus coming toward him and declared, 'Here is the Lamb of God who takes away the sin of the world!'" John 1:29). The priest is not only preparing to approach the altar, but also to place himself upon it. (2) *The parting of the curtain.* An annual transit for priests alone now becomes a perpetual passing through for all, thanks to the rending of the curtain accomplished in Jesus' death (Matt. 27:51). Standing next to Aaron, you can almost hear the fabric ripping. A "new and living way" has been opened through the curtain, thanks to the costly work of the priestly Christ (Heb. 10:19–20). (3) *Offerings for the priest, the sanctuary, and the people.* While the priest required a sacrifice (the largest sacrifice!) to gain entry to the Holy of Holies, Jesus entered "not with the blood of goats and calves, but with his own blood, thus obtaining eternal redemption" (Heb. 9:12). The former sacrifice that demonstrated the lack of distinctions between people, ordained and lay, now reveals the true distinction between this one human being and all others. (4) *One goat driven out.* As in Hebrews (13:11–13) and in the words of familiar hymns, it is no accident that Jesus is crucified outside the city walls: "There is a green hill far away, outside a city wall, where our dear Lord was crucified, who died to save us all" (C. F. Alexander). Like the goat selected for Azazel, Jesus submits to his selection as the one who will carry all the people's sins—of priests, of people, of sanctuary—outside the camp ("and the LORD has laid on him the iniquity of us all"; Isa. 53:6). (5) *The cloud of incense.* Only in relation to the clouds of incense in the Holy of Holies does the astounding clarity of Christ's revelation become clear. What was withheld from the eyes of even the high priest on the holiest of days has now been made clear to us all: "And the Word became flesh and lived among us, and we have seen his glory, the glory as of a father's only son, full of grace and truth" (John 1:14).

It cannot be stressed too much that with Leviticus 16 a bridge has been crossed. Before this chapter, an elaborate and rich set of offerings was set in place for both the spontaneous outpouring of praise and for sins entered into inadvertently or unknowingly. Now a day is set aside every year where peace is restored to the camp through the actions of the priest in the sanctuary and the penance of the people outside ("You shall deny yourselves"; Lev. 16:29). "All the iniquities of the people of Israel, and all their transgressions, all their sins" (16:21) are hereby covered and set right. The story may now continue; the march draws ever nearer, just as when the liturgist stands before the congregation and declares, "Friends, I ask you to believe the good news of the gospel," and they reply, "In Jesus Christ, we are forgiven!"

5. Instructions on Holiness
Leviticus 17:1–27:34

From the drama of the Day of Atonement, we plunge back into rules and regulations. What is the relationship between this chapter and what came before? More particularly, what is the relationship between the instructions on clean versus unclean in Leviticus 11–15 and the instructions regarding holiness ahead?

On the one hand, there are some obvious differences between the two, most notably with respect to terminology. As hard as it may be for us to understand, the language of clean/unclean focused primarily on matters of ritual preparedness, whether a person was fit (by the food she had eaten, the clothes she had worn, the current state of her skin and monthly cycles) to join in the worship of God. Like the person who prepares himself for communion, or the officer getting ready for ordination, the focus is on the sanctuary and its purity, culminating in the procedures for that highest of all sanctuary days, the Day of Atonement.

Now the word "all" appears repeatedly in the Lord's instructions to Moses and Aaron ("all the people," Lev. 17:2; "all the congregation," 19:2). The introductions look up from the tent of meeting to remember the days in Egypt and to anticipate the days in Canaan (18:3). A phrase appears, which multiplies and repeats itself: "I am the LORD your God" (18:2). The goal is no longer limited to the desire to approach God in the sanctuary, but also the hope of reflecting God out in the world: "You shall be holy, for I the LORD your God am holy" (19:2). These and other considerations have won this section the designation "H" (standing for Holiness Code) versus the designation "P" (Priestly Code) pointing toward presumed differences in authorship and intent.

On the other hand, however, the differences are not always so distinct, and especially in the early going, there are clear links in the topics that are covered. Chapter 11 deals with foods that should and should not be eaten.

Chapter 17 deals with the slaughter of animals, rules clearly related to the eating to follow. Chapter 15 covers the topic of genital discharges, events connected with our sexuality, though beyond individual control. Chapter 18 covers sexual behavior more generally, especially with regard to the partners we should or should not choose. Chapter 16 describes the great Day of Atonement. Chapters 23 and 25 describe the full calendar of Israel's festivals, including a repetition of the Day of Atonement as placed in its proper sequential location. These instructions, though different, are like the two images of a face divided in the middle by the line where two mirrors join: you need both images to make the face whole; one without the other leads to distortions.

Perhaps it is best to describe this shift as a change in *tone* and *scope* and *hope*. Regarding *tone*, it is almost as if the first, immediate fear of annihilation is passing. Sacrifices have been proposed, categories of clean/unclean established, and the Day of Atonement, with an ordained priest, set in motion. Slowly, gradually, priest and people begin to be assured that this new arrangement—a God who tabernacles with God's people—may miraculously work out.

So, regarding *scope*, after this first run-through and initial attempt at resolution, while still in camp and before the march begins, the focus of this incarnational, God-with-us work moves out beyond the sanctuary, through the camp, and even out into the world. Now the holiness experienced at the center overflows into the boundaries, with God's people's holiness now serving as a witness to the Holy God in their midst.

The *hope* thus spreads out like an overflowing cup, or oil running down Aaron's beard, or bread broken to feed five thousand, until the dream emerges of uncovering, or witnessing to holiness in all of life. In these chapters we thus encounter some of the most extravagant dreams that God's people were ever given: one which was mined by Jesus to sum up all the Law and the Prophets—love of neighbor; and another that is frequently tapped today to give voice to the revolutionary, world-changing response the visitation of God's Holiness should inspire—the Year of Jubilee.

"Boring," you say. "Tedious," you protest. Yes, for sure—at first glance. But could it be that just as we, with Aaron, have entered the Holy of Holies of God's presence on the Day of Atonement, so we now, in the following chapters, enter the Holy of Holies of God's dreams for God's people through the Holiness Code? Might Israel, might Christ's church, truly become holy as our Lord is Holy? This is the possibility these chapters will flesh out, detail by detail.

HOLINESS REGARDING ANIMALS
Leviticus 17:1–16

17:1 The Lord spoke to Moses: ² Speak to Aaron and his sons and to all the people of Israel and say to them: This is what the Lord has commanded. ³ If anyone of the house of Israel slaughters an ox or a lamb or a goat in the camp, or slaughters it outside the camp, ⁴ and does not bring it to the entrance of the tent of meeting, to present it as an offering to the Lord before the tabernacle of the Lord, he shall be held guilty of bloodshed; he has shed blood, and he shall be cut off from the people. ⁵ This is in order that the people of Israel may bring their sacrifices that they offer in the open field, that they may bring them to the Lord, to the priest at the entrance of the tent of meeting, and offer them as sacrifices of well-being to the Lord. ⁶ The priest shall dash the blood against the altar of the Lord at the entrance of the tent of meeting, and turn the fat into smoke as a pleasing odor to the Lord, ⁷ so that they may no longer offer their sacrifices for goat-demons, to whom they prostitute themselves. This shall be a statute forever to them throughout their generations.

17:10 If anyone of the house of Israel or of the aliens who reside among them eats any blood, I will set my face against that person who eats blood, and will cut that person off from the people. ¹¹ For the life of the flesh is in the blood; and I have given it to you for making atonement for your lives on the altar; for, as life, it is the blood that makes atonement. ¹² Therefore I have said to the people of Israel: No person among you shall eat blood, nor shall any alien who resides among you eat blood. ¹³ And anyone of the people of Israel, or of the aliens who reside among them, who hunts down an animal or bird that may be eaten shall pour out its blood and cover it with earth. ¹⁴ For the life of every creature—its blood is its life; therefore I have said to the people of Israel: You shall not eat the blood of any creature, for the life of every creature is its blood; whoever eats it shall be cut off.

In the Manual of Sacrifice, animals appropriate for sacrifices have been specified. In the section on clean/unclean animals, the world's creatures have been divided into the edible and inedible. Now we move to a prior and more practical question: "How do animals go from living creatures to food?" This is not a topic most modern churchgoers confront. The dirty work is left to others. At most, we choose whether we want ours "rare" or "medium." What cues for holiness might we find here?

Every meal is an offering. As noted in the Manual of Sacrifice, the people of Israel knew their animals. It was the parishioner, not the priest, who slaughtered the Burnt Offering or Sacrifice of Well-Being at the entrance to the tent of meeting. Therefore, the topic at hand is not how to get one's cattle to the butcher, but rather where and to whom all butchering should be directed.

The answer here is simple, yet radical: all animals must be butchered at the tent of meeting. Why? So that all meat might be received as from the hands of God. Remember, at the Sacrifice of Well-Being (the sacrifice that now provides the pattern for all proper butchering), certain parts are first offered to God so that the remainder may be returned to priest and parishioner by the Lord as host. Now, every ox or lamb or goat that is eaten shall so be first received. Wherever you are, inside the camp or outside, when the time comes to sit down for dinner, bring your animal first to the tent of meeting, then back home. That way, the meal might first be "sanctified" by worship.

Any cattle-farmer would be stupefied by the all-inclusive nature of this proscription. "Surely you don't mean *every* cow or goat or lamb?" And yet this is just what this instruction requires. God knows God's people well. Let them slaughter their cattle in their stockyards, and they begin to think of the meat as being their own. Let them kill a sheep or goat on the hillside, and they may offer a thigh or leg to a local deity (like the "goat-demons") just to play it safe. Let them turn the slaughter over to somebody else and purchase it shrink-wrapped in the deli, and soon they will forget where food comes from, how costly it is to prepare, and thus to whom it should all be "offered up" before we partake.

Obviously, here we enter a dream (a theme we'll find repeating itself frequently in the Holiness Code). While this method of slaughter may have worked temporarily while Israel was still in camp, once they were on the road, and (even more!) widely scattered in the land, this legislation had to be either overthrown (cf. Deut. 12:15) or modified (maybe with a symbolic offering of the *first* of the cattle and the flocks, a preliminary offering that sanctifies the rest; cf. Lev. 27:26).

Nevertheless, here we catch a glimpse of just how holy God dreams of God's people becoming. A people with such respect for life might find such reverence reflected in places other than the dinner table. A people with this constant orientation toward God would never forget whose hand provides all creatures food "in due season" (Ps. 104:27). A people grounded in such practice would never give thanks for their meat to Winn Dixie or the Golden Corral or any other worldly power without first sanctifying it with a blessing—directed to whom? To the Lord God, from whom all blessings flow.

The blood is life. If the first instruction required the transport of many cattle, sheep, and goats, the next instruction adds an essential step to any "processing." Before any meat is eaten, it must be bled. No blood may be consumed by God's people because the blood of any creature "is its life" (Lev. 17:14).

This is *not* first and foremost a "biological" consideration. If so, we might simple overturn it by saying, "The DNA is its life." No, blood has been claimed by God as the agent of atonement in the Manual of Sacrifice, as this chapter reminds us (v. 11). Therefore, any blood spilled casually is not only an affront to the animal for which this blood was life, but also an affront to the Lord who has deemed it to be an instrument for saving life.

We begin to get the picture. Every time the Israelites sat down to dinner, they thought of the life of the sanctuary. Every time they raised a piece of meat to their lips, they remembered the life of the animal that had given its life at the entrance and on the altar of the tent of meeting. Every time they missed some of the redness they might have desired in their steak, they remembered not only the blood of the creature that now gave them life, but also the blood on the altar through which their reconciliation with God became visible. Blood is not a substance to be used for nourishment of our bodies because it has already been set apart as a substance to point toward the salvation of souls (for Jews and, even more, for Christians: "without the shedding of blood there is no forgiveness of sins"; Heb. 9:22).

Suppertime thus became an act of worship for the Jew, as surely as drinking water (a reminder of baptism) and breaking bread (a reminder of communion) should be for the Christian. Holiness is spreading out of the sanctuary and into the homes and restaurants of God's people. Not just the words we say, not just the acts of service we perform, but the very foods we eat are claimed as ways of remembering and witnessing the presence of a forgiving God in our midst.

They shall be cut off. Clearly, these instructions are not just a matter of etiquette. Violations are met with the harshest sentence next to death itself: being cut off from the life of the community and the life of worship, which is indeed life itself. Our instructions then have moved from questions of who might enter the sanctuary to who might remain in the community. The stakes, especially in the small, everyday actions of our lives, could not be higher.

We can only speculate how our modern, casual approach to the slaughter of animals and the consumption of blood has affected our lives as a community. A society that simply outsources food production to industry should not be surprised to discover brutality and bloodthirst showing up in other areas of its life. Although the synagogue early on wrestled with accommodating these regulations to life away from and without the Temple (cf.

Deut. 12:21), it still debates rules for kosher slaughter today. The church originally held on to the prohibition against consuming blood (Acts 15:1–20), yet only certain "sects" of the church do so today (note the Jehovah's Witness prohibition of the use of blood for transfusions). We may think our shrink-wrapped steaks and veal and mutton are signs of civilization. But a society that grows overefficient at killing animals will surely also become equally efficient at slaughtering human beings. As Jacob Milgrom makes clear: "A credo that purports to curb the inbruted nature of man is doomed to failure unless rooted and remembered in a regularly-observed ritual, one which will intrude into the home, adhere to the family table, and impinge daily on the senses, all the while penetrating the mind and conditioning the reflexes into habitual patterns of behavior" (quoted in Bailey, *Leviticus–Numbers*, 213).

Martin Marty cites the rabbinical story regarding Ba'al Shem Tov, founder of the Hasidic tradition of Judaism. After his death, one of his followers was seen to shake his head whenever he witnessed this rabbi's successors slaying an animal for kosher meat. One of these slaughterers finally protested: "Why do you shake your head? Have I not said the prayers? Have I not sharpened the knife on the whetstone to the highest keenness to reduce as much as possible the pain of the animals? What then is lacking?" Then the disciple replied, "When the Ba'al Shem Tov would sharpen the knife, he moistened the stone with his tears" (*Context*, March 1, 1995, 5).

HOLINESS IN SEXUAL RELATIONS
Leviticus 18:1–30

18:1 The LORD spoke to Moses, saying: [2] Speak to the people of Israel and say to them: I am the LORD your God. [3] You shall not do as they do in the land of Egypt, where you lived, and you shall not do as they do in the land of Canaan, to which I am bringing you. You shall not follow their statutes. [4] My ordinances you shall observe and my statutes you shall keep, following them: I am the LORD your God. [5] You shall keep my statutes and my ordinances; by doing so one shall live: I am the LORD. [6] None of you shall approach anyone near of kin to uncover nakedness: I am the LORD.

18:19 You shall not approach a woman to uncover her nakedness while she is in her menstrual uncleanness. [20] You shall not have sexual relations with your kinsman's wife, and defile yourself with her. [21] You shall not give any of your offspring to sacrifice them to Molech, and so profane the name of your God: I am the LORD. [22] You shall not lie with a male as with a woman; it is an abomination. [23] You shall not have sexual relations with any animal and defile yourself with it, nor shall any woman give herself to an animal to have sexual relations with it: it is perversion. [24] Do not defile yourselves in any of these ways, for by all these practices the nations I am casting out before you have defiled themselves. [25] Thus the land became defiled; and I punished it for its iniquity, and the land vomited out its inhabitants. [26] But you shall keep my statutes and my ordinances and commit none of these abominations, either the citizen or the alien who resides among you [27] (for the inhabitants of the land, who were before you, committed all of these abominations, and the land became defiled); [28] otherwise the land will vomit you out for defiling it, as it vomited out the nation that was before you. [29] For whoever commits any of these abominations shall be cut off from their people. [30] So keep my charge not to commit any of these abominations that were done before you, and not to defile yourselves by them: I am the LORD your God.

Food and sex. It does not get much more basic than this (with the exception of "power," which in some way follows in Lev. 19). A Holy God requires a holy people. Not just in the sanctuary, but also in the supermarket and in the bedroom.

Given the general lack of interest in Levitical instructions regarding food, it is interesting how high runs the interest in Levitical instructions regarding sex, at least in the arena of public debate. With the exception of one verse in chapter 19 (v. 18, quoted by Jesus) and the second half of chapter 25 (the Year of Jubilee, also quoted by Jesus, but by only some of his followers), Leviticus 18 may be the most quoted chapter in the book today. More accurately, many quote (literally, and with little if any context) this one verse: "You shall not lie with a male as with a woman; it is an abomination" (18:22).

This may well tell us more about *us* than about *Leviticus*.

First, most of the chapter concerns proper boundaries *within* families rather than proper boundaries *between* genders or creatures. Surely Leviticus accurately recognizes that the gravest threat to holiness in the camp is what goes on *within* the tents of families rather than *between* the tents of men, women, or animals next door. In those days and ours, it is *within* the family circle that proper affections between son and mother or brother and sister-in-law are most apt to blur and go astray. Would that we were as vigilant regarding *incest* (where one partner may be coerced, intimidated, and silenced) as we seem to be regarding *homosexuality* (where the sex is often consensual).

Second, *every* section of chapter 18 requires interpretation in order to apply. One example will suffice. Nowhere in the list of forbidden family connections do we find a prohibition against sex between a man and his sister or a man and his daughter. Why? Because Leviticus 18 is not really concerned with incest per se, but rather with the proper protection of the boundaries distinguishing one male's domain from another's (note the refrain, "It is your father's nakedness," "It is your own nakedness," "It is your brother's nakedness"). If we would broaden these instructions to include boundaries protecting the spheres of daughters and of sisters, we must do so by interpretation and application. Surely the same must be said of verse 22.

Last, it's strange that instructions that would connect with the *many* are leaped over in order to focus on instructions that apply only to the *few*. Why is there no church discussion on the need for marital abstinence during the time of a spouse's menstruation (v. 19)? Why is a man crossing boundaries with a relative's *wife* (v. 20), a crossing that receives the same penalty as homosexual activity (cf. 20:13 and 20:10), so much less interesting than crossing boundaries with a relative's *husband*? Why is sacrificing one's children to Molech (v. 21)—or any of the lesser gods who control and threaten our lives and dreams and hopes—seen as "irrelevant" to our lives today, but not verse 22? Dare we say it? In a country overrun by pets—that often receive better food, medical care, and burials than most of the world's children—might not proper boundaries between human beings and animals (v. 23) prove to be a decidedly fruitful topic for discussion in our congregations today? In summary, stated briefly, if we cannot "simply" apply chapter 25 of Leviticus to our lives today (a chapter to which Jesus refers repeatedly in his ministry), neither can we do so with Leviticus 18 (a chapter to which he does not).

So, let us regroup. Let us be aware that the stakes are high ("Otherwise the land will vomit you out for defiling it"; 18:28). And let us walk through chapter 18, slowly.

First, to state the obvious, the holiness sought in our bedrooms flows out of the holiness we have been given in the sanctuary. As stated before, the entire impetus of Leviticus arises from the Lord's decision to come and live intimately in the midst of God's people. Here a new chapter in God's relationship with Israel is established, one fraught with boundless potential for good and for ill. Sound familiar? While human sexual relations can never claim to participate in the power and possibilities of this fundamental relationship, certainly they should reflect and incorporate some of its characteristics. Just as great harm can come from improvisations in intimate encounters with the Lord (e.g., Nadab and Abihu), so great harm can come from "improvisations" in intimate encounters with one another. The relationship and the encounters are given for life; improperly handled, they can lead to death (interpersonally, biologically, and spiritually). Both synagogue and church, then, are rightly concerned with questions of human sexuality. Here, more than most places, we model or fail to model our intimate relationship with God.

Second, the primary way Leviticus 18 tries to deal with this area of potential holiness or defilement is through the proper delineation of boundaries. Just as worship is guarded by clarity regarding who approaches the Lord when and where and for what purpose, so such holy discernment is held up as the way to derive good rather than ill from food and from sex (the failure to do so for *both* of these is labeled "an abomination" in 20:13, 25). The priests of Leviticus are not so much concerned with attitude ("Do you *really* want to approach the Lord?") as with arrangement ("Are you the proper person in the proper place for the proper function with respect to the Lord?"). We should not be surprised, then, that they bring this same kind of tangible, referential concern to sex (who, when, for what?). Surely, this is a perspective to which we in our culture should listen ("But I *really* love him [or her]!" the daily soap opera proclaims).

Certainly there are problems with such "externality." Jesus himself pointed out one: you can cross boundaries in your *thoughts* as well as your *actions* ("I say to you that everyone who looks at a woman with lust has already committed adultery with her in his heart"; Matt. 5:28). Another is equally obvious: simply maintaining boundaries does not guarantee good rather than ill with regard to sex. No one need search far to find abusive sexual relationships that fit all the Levitical codes!

Nevertheless, as we strive for some good order in worship, so we should strive for some good order in sexual relationships. Leviticus simply argues that as there are proper boundaries in our relationship in the sanctuary (priest here, parishioner there), so there are proper boundaries in our sexual relations with one another (brother here, sister-in-law there). These are boundaries we ignore at our own peril.

So, third, how does Leviticus 18 draw the lines, and how should we?

For the first time in Leviticus, a criterion *outside* the worship practice of Israel comes to the fore. While food boundaries were defined primarily on the basis of sanctuary worship (the foods appropriate for sacrifice providing the model for what is appropriate to eat), Leviticus 18 begins and ends with references to the sexual practices of other nations: "You shall not do as they do in the land of Egypt, where you lived, and you shall not do as they do in the land of Canaan, to which I am bringing you" (18:3); "Do not defile yourselves in any of these ways, for by all these practices the nations I am casting out before you have defiled themselves" (18:24). The boundary line here, then, runs primarily between the sexual relations practiced by others—within the family (vv. 6–18), with regard to menstrual cycles (v. 19), with respect to neighbors (v. 20), with regard to same-gender sex (v. 22), and with respect to sex with animals (v. 23)—and sexual relations practiced by Israel. As the sanctuary relationship between God and God's people was unique and distinctive, the argument seems to go, so the sexual relationships among God's people should be unique and distinctive. (This may help to explain the strange insertion of the prohibition of sacrificing children to Molech, v. 21, in this otherwise exclusively "sexual" chapter. Distinctive worship, distinctive sex.)

The questions for us thus become: How do the sexual relations we practice set us off from the culture around us and point toward the distinctive worship at our core? Do we recognize proper boundaries for sex and affection within our families, boundaries that make clear that our deepest needs for intimacy have been fulfilled by God (vv. 6–18)? Do we demonstrate proper restraint and concern in the timing of our conjugal relations, showing due reverence for the cycles of life and rebirth as shown forth in our God-given and God-calibrated bodies (v. 19)? Do we truly love our neighbor enough to maintain proper boundaries between the intimacies appropriate for them and the intimacies appropriate for us (v. 20)? Do we recognize the link between crossing boundaries in sexual devotions and sanctuary devotions, especially with regard to our children (v. 21)? How do we determine proper boundaries for same-gender sex in a culture so enthused or repulsed by this kind of activity that those caught across this boundary have no one to instruct them regarding choices of abstinence, monogamy, or promiscuity (v. 22)? If actions *and* thoughts have consequences, and if simply maintaining boundaries is *not* enough, what *would* a Christian approach to animals look like, and what would make it distinctive in our world (v. 23)? Though it will satisfy few and enrage many, the key here seems to be restraint: a proper, disciplined restraint in this area of our lives, reflective of similar restraint in our relationship with God. As we know not to cross certain boundaries in our approach to God, so we will refrain from crossing similar boundaries in our approaches to one another, especially those of a sexual nature.

All those who would call such an approach fuzzy or worse are called to pay attention. First, there are boundaries we would observe that Leviticus does not. The prime example here would be polygamy, marriage to several partners, practiced with no censure in other parts of the Scriptures (though being married to two sisters simultaneously is prohibited; v. 18!).

Apparently, while the Levitical priests were concerned about *whom* you married, they were not concerned with *how many* you married—much to our chagrin. We may well want to add some other boundaries, some rather distinctive boundaries of our own. Second, there are boundaries in Leviticus that the Scriptures themselves dispute. One example here is the practice of levirate marriage, the obligation of a brother to marry the wife of his deceased brother, laid down as law elsewhere in the Old Testament (Deut. 25:5–10) and used for argument in the New (Matt. 22:23–29). What then do we do with Leviticus 18:16: "You shall not uncover the nakedness of your brother's wife; it is your brother's nakedness" (cf. 20:21)? Be clear. If the Bible itself continues its discussion of boundaries (as will become even clearer in the latter chapters of Numbers), so must we.

However, in conclusion, to all those who would thus say that Leviticus 18, and any sexual boundary-drawing, are irrelevant or harmful or non-Christian, we go back to where we started. As the Lord desires holiness in the sanctuary, so the Lord desires holiness in kitchen and bedroom. One of the main ways we witness to the holiness of the sanctuary is through the meticulous observation of proper boundaries (*"You* shall bring it to the entrance of the tent of meeting; . . . then *the priest* shall turn the whole into smoke on the altar"; 1:3, 9). In order to spread this witness to the bedroom, we must be willing to exercise similar restraint in our sexual practice ("None of *you* shall approach anyone *near of kin* to uncover nakedness: I am the LORD"; 18:6).

Yes, these boundaries may sometimes shift (as Christians and Jews have shifted boundaries *even in the sanctuary!*). But such shifting is never done without peril. Why? Because these boundary lines are often the difference between life and death: "You shall keep my statutes and my ordinances; by doing so one shall live: I am the LORD" (18:5). Because these boundary lines are one of the main things that set us apart from others, and thus enable our witness to our neighbors: "You shall not do as they do in the land of Egypt, where you lived, and you shall not do as they do in the land of Canaan, to which I am bringing you" (Lev. 18:3). Because these boundary lines in our everyday lives are faithful ways of reminding us whose we are in our worship lives: "Speak to the people of Israel and say to them: I am the LORD your God" (18:2).

No, sex is not holy in and of itself, any more than food is holy. But sex and food, properly handled, can keep us in touch with the One who is holy. Every day of our lives.

Note. It goes without saying that the seriousness with which we approach boundaries in the bedroom ("We ought to throw the whole lot out of the church!"), compared to the casualness with which we approach boundaries in the sanctuary ("Who wants to read the Scripture lesson today?"), only shows how far from the biblical world we have come. Certainly it is right and proper for the church to recognize the power for good and ill in our approach to human sexuality. But where, oh where is the church's recognition of the power for good and ill in our approach to God? In our hierarchies of power, we have become more like the world, rather than distinctive from the world. In our discussions of homosexual practice, we are more consumed with how people approach one another, than with how they approach God. The people of Leviticus were overwhelmed by the power of the God who had come to dwell in their midst. On this basis, they then tried to draw out boundary lines in their lives. As long as the church discusses sexuality based solely on preferences and genetics and nature/nurture, we might as well let others take our place at the table. We will have nothing truly distinctive to offer.

HOLINESS IN ALL OF LIFE
Leviticus 19:1–37

19:1 The LORD spoke to Moses, saying: [2] Speak to all the congregation of the people of Israel and say to them: You shall be holy, for I the LORD your God am holy. [3] You shall each revere your mother and father, and you shall keep my sabbaths: I am the LORD your God. [4] Do not turn to idols or make cast images for yourselves: I am the LORD your God. [5] When you offer a sacrifice of well-being to the LORD, offer it in such a way that it is acceptable on your behalf. [6] It shall be eaten on the same day you offer it, or on the next day; and anything left over until the third day shall be consumed in fire. [7] If it is eaten at all on the third day, it is an abomination; it will not be acceptable. [8] All who eat it shall be subject to punishment, because they have profaned what is holy to the LORD; and any such person shall be cut off from the people. [9] When you reap the harvest of your land, you shall not reap to the very edges of your field, or gather the gleanings of your harvest. [10] You shall not strip your vineyard bare, or gather the fallen grapes of your vineyard; you shall leave them for the poor and the alien: I am the LORD your God. [11] You shall not steal; you shall not deal falsely; and you shall not lie to one another. [12] And you shall not swear falsely by my name, profaning the name of your God: I am the LORD. [13] You shall not defraud your neighbor; you shall not steal; and you shall not keep for yourself the wages of a laborer until morning. [14] You shall not revile the deaf or put a stumbling block before the blind; you shall fear your God: I am the LORD. [15] You shall not render an unjust judgment; you shall not be partial to the poor or defer to the great: with justice you shall judge your neighbor. [16] You shall not go around as a slanderer among your people, and you shall not profit by the blood of your neighbor: I am the Lord. [17] You shall not hate in your heart anyone of your kin; you shall reprove your neighbor, or you will incur guilt yourself. [18] You shall not take vengeance or bear a grudge against any of your people, but you shall love your neighbor as yourself: I am the Lord. 19 You shall keep my statutes. You shall not let your animals breed with a different kind; you shall not sow your field with two kinds of seed; nor shall you put on a garment made of two different materials. [20] If a man has sexual relations with a woman who is a slave, designated for another man but not ransomed or given her freedom, an inquiry shall be held. They shall not be put to death, since she has not been freed; [21] but he shall bring a guilt offering for himself to the Lord, at the entrance of the tent of meeting, a ram as guilt offering. [22] And the priest shall make atonement for him with the ram of guilt offering before the Lord for his sin that he committed; and the sin he committed shall be forgiven him. [23] When you come into the land and plant all kinds of trees for food, then you shall regard their fruit as forbidden; three years it shall be forbidden to you, it must not be eaten. [24] In the fourth year all their fruit shall be set apart for rejoicing in the Lord. [25] But in the fifth year you may eat of their fruit, that their yield may be increased for you: I am the Lord your God. [26] You shall not eat anything with its blood. You shall not practice augury or witchcraft. [27] You shall not round off the hair on your temples or mar the edges of your beard. [28] You shall not make any gashes in your flesh for the dead or tattoo any marks upon you: I am the Lord. [29] Do not profane your daughter by making her a prostitute, that the land not become prostituted and full of depravity. [30] You shall keep my sabbaths and reverence my sanctuary: I am the Lord. [31] Do not turn to mediums or wizards; do not seek them out, to be defiled by them: I am the Lord your God. [32] You shall rise before the aged, and defer to the old; and you shall fear your God: I am the Lord. [33] When an alien resides with you in your land, you shall not oppress the alien. [34] The alien who resides with you shall be to you as the citizen among you; you shall love the alien as yourself, for you were aliens in the land of Egypt: I am the Lord your God. [35] You shall not cheat in measuring length, weight, or quantity. [36] You shall have honest balances, honest weights, an honest ephah, and an honest hin: I am the Lord your God, who brought you out of the land of Egypt. [37] You shall keep all my statutes and all my ordinances, and observe them: I am the Lord.

The drive for holiness in all parts of Israel's life now gathers speed and overflows. Like the child who has learned to read and now pores over every written word she passes, like the young person freshly in love who searches for signs of his beloved in tree and cloud and water, like the congregation that works to make everything just right for the return of a beloved pastor, so Moses' instructions now break the bonds of sacrifice and food and sex, to bounce around and off every aspect of Israel's existence. The concern is truly no longer just a holy sanctuary, but also a holy people. The goal moves beyond mere preservation toward the overflow of God's goodness to neighbor and alien. Any order or structure apparent in other portions of Leviticus disappears altogether, as God's people dare to dream of lives as potent, sanctified, and ever spreading as the smoke of their Burnt Offerings.

It is small wonder then that Jesus plucked a verse out of this white hot chapter when asked to cite those instructions preeminent over all ("One of the scribes came near and . . . asked him, 'Which commandment is the first of all?'" Mark 12:28). It is no surprise then that out of the two references given to Leviticus in the Common Lectionary, both of them come from this chapter, indeed both ending with the same verse: "But you shall love your neighbor as yourself: I am the LORD" (Lev. 19:18).

First I present a walk-through of this cornucopia of holy possibilities, then some summary comments.

Verses 1–3. The motivation for all these laws is the same. As God is "holy" (in other words, "distinct," "set apart," "wholly other"), so should God's people be "holy." Remember, *the* thing that makes Israel distinct from all the other nations is its chosenness ("In this way, we shall be distinct, I and your people, from every people on the face of the earth"; Exod. 33:16; cf. a similar distinction made by God with regard to cattle, in Exod. 9:4). The only way to make this chosenness visible to others (who are excluded from the glory of God's sanctuary and thus from this firsthand experience of God's presence) is through that glory lived out in this people's lives (a kind of "reflected" light, if you will). The juxtaposition is both perplexing and profound, driving the motivation for Israel's most basic laws even deeper than that given in the Ten Commandments: "You shall be holy" (Lev. 19:2). "You shall each revere your mother and father" (v. 3). "For I the LORD your God am holy" (v. 2). "Do not turn to idols or make cast images for yourselves" (v. 4). This is no utilitarian argument, but an argument grounded in the gracious election of God.

Verses 5–8. So that no one might think that the "worship" laws have now been superseded by the "living" laws, an elaboration on the rules for the Sacrifice of Well-being is here inserted, specifying a three-day statute of limitations on the eating of the proscribed meats and grains. Clearly, God's true desire is for both extravagant sacrifice in the sanctuary and the overflowing of justice and righteousness outside (cf. Amos 5:21–24). Or better, God and Leviticus 19 make no distinction between the two.

Verses 9–10. One cannot read these verses without thinking of Ruth and Boaz (Ruth 2). However, this instruction on gleaning is more than just a look forward (to coming days when Israel might be dependent on others' largesse) or a look backward (when the lack of such mercy led to their out-cry in Egypt). This is a glimpse into the heart of Israel's God, whose cups and feasts and harvests are always overflowing with enough to supply us and the vulnerable in our midst. As God is bounteous and merciful to Israel, so should Israel be to others (cf. this pattern with that in Deut. 15, where God's giving is linked with the open-handedness of God's people; vv. 7–18).

Verses 11–14. Clearly, at their core, these laws echo the Ten Com-mandments (Do not steal, swear falsely, profane the name of the Lord). But at every turn, they up the ante. Holding a laborer's wages until the morning may be the same as stealing (v. 13). Reviling the deaf or taking advantage of the blind may edge onto murder (v. 14). Here we observe a drive to go beyond legality toward holiness, continued by Jesus in the Ser-mon on the Mount ("Blessed are those who hunger and thirst for righ-teousness, for they will be filled"; Matt. 5:6).

Verses 15–16. Not only should we not do harm to our neighbors, but also we should strive to deal with them with justice. Whether rich or poor, they should be the recipients of just judgments (cf. Jas. 2). Again, the motivation is obvious, if not explicitly stated: as God has been impartially just with you, so you should be with one another.

Verses 17–18. Even if Jesus had not lifted these verses out as one half of his summary of the law (the other coming from Deut. 6:5), we should know that here we are on truly holy ground. From the requirement to do justice, we now arrive at the challenge to love. Such love cannot coexist with hate in one's heart. Such love cannot turn a blind eye to a neighbor's wrongdoing, but reproves only on the basis of love. Such love leaves vengeance and grudges and seeks for our neighbor what we all so covet for ourselves. Here indeed is a sacrifice whose aroma is pleasing to our God.

Verse 19. Curiously, a law that seems to obliterate distinctions (there's only one kind of person in the world: my neighbor) is followed by one that desires to keep distinctions—on the farm, in the fields, on one's back. The good order established by the priests in previous chapters is here pre-served from disruption for technology's sake. Though this antimixing bias undoubtedly reflected Israel's antimixing stance vis-à-vis sacrifices, foods, and life among the nations, in our age of cloning and synthetics, it ought to give us pause. How do we move so quickly and easily from one instruction we still accept as gospel (v. 18) to one we so cavalierly and resolutely disre-gard (v. 19)? Here we touch on a distinction that finally moves beyond the bounds of Leviticus–Numbers and out into the broader themes of Scripture as a whole: maintaining holiness *negatively* (through separating and not mixing) and maintaining holiness *positively* (through the pursuit of love).

Verses 20–22. Though it is impossible to ignore this instruction's tacit acceptance of slavery, and though we might wish that it protected the life of a slave whether her papers had been filed or not, at least some movement toward drawing boundaries around the sexual use of slaves here begins (in contrast to the previous chapter!). Like the gleanings left in their fields and vineyards, these are "gleanings only" from the fields of justice. But Israel's harvest of holiness, grounded in the holiness of its God, grows ever outward, from the poor and the alien (v. 10) toward the slave (v. 20). What may have been expected, at worst, and overlooked, at best, is now classified a "sin."

Verses 23–25. Instructions that might be seen simply as "practical" (three years for trees to establish themselves) are transformed into something holy (when all the fruit of the fourth year is "set apart," in other words, taken to the sanctuary in praise). As in the Offering of First Fruits four chapters ahead (Lev. 23), the restraint of the arborist, when it comes to harvest and consumption, is another means of receiving all good gifts as from the Lord. Give, and it shall be given back to you—tenfold!

Verses 26–32. An intriguing series of paired instructions follow, contrasting the ways of God's people with the ways of others. God's people refrain from eating anything with its blood (Lev. 17), while others practice augury and witchcraft (maybe through the use of animals and their blood). God's people distinguish themselves (if they're male!) by letting the hair on their temples and beards grow long (think of Samson and modern-day Hasidics), while others gash and tattoo their flesh to tap other powers (like the prophets of Baal; 1 Kgs. 18) or show their membership in other groups (like gangs, movie stars, and others today). Others, in desperation, may make their daughters prostitutes, even in the name of worship (perhaps referring to the temple prostitution so prevalent in the time of the divided monarchy), but God's people keep the Sabbaths, and reverence the sanctuary (rest and restraint versus excess). Others go out and seek mediums or wizards (or experts of every size and shape), but God's people rise up before the aged and defer to the old (even in their own congregations!).

Do you see the pattern? Do you begin to feel how holiness spreads its tent out? Look at a people's food and faces, their worship and their wizards. Watch what they *do*, and just as important, what they *don't* do—every day, in little things and large. If you pay attention, and if you compare their lives to others, you may catch a glimpse of the God who has a claim on them. "I am the Lord, I am the Lord, I am the Lord your God," goes the refrain (vv. 28, 30, 31, 32).

Verse 33. God's people had already been instructed to love their neighbors as themselves (v. 18). Now they are instructed to love their aliens, their nonslave and non-Israelite neighbors, as themselves, even treating them as fellow citizens (talk about immigration reform)! This is holiness on the grand scale, the kind that inspired a later rabbi to push even further: "But I say to you, Love your enemies and pray for those who persecute you" (Matt. 5:44).

Verse 35. But to close out these instructions, grand gestures may not come up every day, and love is terribly difficult to measure, so if you want to be holy, no fingers on the scales, no escape clauses in the contracts, no obscene profits in the balance sheets. From hair to "hin" (v. 36), from two kinds of seed to two kinds of neighbors, from treatment of mother and father to the poor and the alien, the deaf and the blind, witches and wizards—this is what holiness looks like, in the sanctuary and out.

Some summary observations.

The whole of life. Surely the most exhilarating aspect of Leviticus in general, and the Holiness Code in particular, is the desire to claim all of life for God, or better, to show forth God's claim on the whole of our lives. Here is no division between the sacred and the secular. Here is no distinction between behavior in worship and behavior at work. God's people have experienced the Lord's holiness in the sanctuary. Now this same holiness has become as a fire in them that has to get out, to spread out—through the camp and through the world. That this dream, in final form, may well have come to the Israelites while they were in exile, makes its claims all the more astounding. They dreamed not only of return and restoration, but also of something brand-new: a life that in its grandest and most trifling details would show forth the glory of God.

Dos and don'ts. The fact that this life is bounded with dos and don'ts might make some deem it "artificial" and "legalistic." This was exactly the diagnosis of Jesus toward the lives of the scribes and Pharisees of his day. However, the only thing that makes such instruction "artificial" and "legalistic" is the loss of the vital connection between an encounter with a holy and living God and the desire to show forth such holiness with our lives. If this material is simply read through from the beginning of Leviticus to this point, it is clear that a tide is swelling. This is no attempt to gain a distant God's attention or to impress one's powerful neighbors. This is just a sketchbook for a holy people who are overwhelmed by the gracious proximity of their Holy God. Listen to question 86 of the Heidelberg Catechism and its answer: "Q. 86. Since we are redeemed from our sin and its wretched consequences by grace through Christ without any merit of our own, why must we do good works? A. Because just as Christ has redeemed us with his blood, he also renews us through his Holy Spirit according to his own image, so that with our whole life we may show ourselves grateful to God for his goodness and that he may be glorified through us; and further, so that we ourselves may be assured of our faith by its fruits and by our reverent behavior may win our neighbors to Christ" (*Book of Confessions*, 4.086).

A matter of character. While there may be some parts of this sketchbook that we would amend and restrict or enlarge, as Jesus did (giving sight to the blind, hearing to the deaf, and expanding love even to the enemy), nothing can relieve us from the scope of the project. The goal here is nothing less than the living out of God's character in the world. This is not just words; it is also actions. This is not just in church; it is also in the fields and market. This is not just for when people are watching; it is also for when they are not or don't even care. We do not deal falsely. Why? Because God has not dealt falsely with us. We love. Why? Because God first loved us. We strive to be holy in all of our life. Why? Because God is holy, and the world belongs to God, and we are privileged to be called God's people. We are indeed in the Holy of Holies. Worship and living don't get much better than this. To quote a more recent confession: "In gratitude to God, empowered by the Spirit, we strive to serve Christ in our daily tasks and to live holy and joyful lives, even as we watch for God's new heaven and new earth, praying, 'Come, Lord Jesus!'" (A Brief Statement of Faith, lines 72–76, *The Book of Confessions*, 10.4).

PENALTIES FOR VIOLATION OF HOLINESS
Leviticus 20:1–27

20:1 **The Lord spoke to Moses, saying: ² Say further to the people of Israel: Any of the people of Israel, or of the aliens who reside in Israel, who give any of their offspring to Molech shall be put to death; the people of the land shall stone them to death.**

20:6 **If any turn to mediums and wizards, prostituting themselves to them, I will set my face against them, and will cut them off from the people. ⁷ Consecrate yourselves therefore, and be holy; for I am the Lord your God. ⁸ Keep my statutes, and observe them; I am the Lord; I sanctify you. ⁹ All who curse father or mother shall be put to death; having cursed father or mother, their blood is upon them. ¹⁰ If a man commits adultery with the wife of his neigh-**

bor, both the adulterer and the adulteress shall be put to death. [11] The man who lies with his father's wife has uncovered his father's nakedness; both of them shall be put to death; their blood is upon them. [12] If a man lies with his daughter-in-law, both of them shall be put to death; they have committed perversion, their blood is upon them. [13] If a man lies with a male as with a woman, both of them have committed an abomination; they shall be put to death; their blood is upon them. [14] If a man takes a wife and her mother also, it is depravity; they shall be burned to death, both he and they, that there may be no depravity among you. [15] If a man has sexual relations with an animal, he shall be put to death; and you shall kill the animal. [16] If a woman approaches any animal and has sexual relations with it, you shall kill the woman and the animal; they shall be put to death, their blood is upon them.

20:22 You shall keep all my statutes and all my ordinances, and observe them, so that the land to which I bring you to settle in may not vomit you out. [23] You shall not follow the practices of the nation that I am driving out before you. Because they did all these things, I abhorred them. [24] But I have said to you: You shall inherit their land, and I will give it to you to possess, a land flowing with milk and honey. I am the LORD your God; I have separated you from the peoples. [25] You shall therefore make a distinction between the clean animal and the unclean, and between the unclean bird and the clean; you shall not bring abomination on yourselves by animal or by bird or by anything with which the ground teems, which I have set apart for you to hold unclean. [26] You shall be holy to me; for I the LORD am holy, and I have separated you from the other peoples to be mine. [27] A man or a woman who is a medium or a wizard shall be put to death; they shall be stoned to death, their blood is upon them.

Just as soon as the high point is reached—a vision of God's holiness flowing out into every niche and cranny of our everyday lives—it is seen as unattainable, at least for some. "Further" instructions are necessary: a listing of punishments required for the most heinous violations. In contrast to the God who has drawn near, given instruction, and been revealed in the glory of the sanctuary, we are now introduced to a God who promises to "set my face against" any and all perpetrators, and "cut them off" from dwelling among God's people—by stoning, by burning, or by barrenness.

First, we must not pretend that this is the only place we encounter this side of God in the Scriptures. A theme of blessings and curses is built into God's covenantal relationship with us ("For I the LORD your God am a jealous God, punishing children for the iniquity of parents, to the third and the fourth generation of those who reject me, but showing steadfast love to the thousandth generation of those who love me and keep my commandments"; Exod. 20:5–6). Not only will God "myself" cut off violators elsewhere in Leviticus–Numbers (the holy fire that burns sacrifices in Leviticus ends up burning mostly people in Numbers!), but such excisions are also a strong part of the New Testament story ("If your right hand causes you to sin, cut it off and throw it away; it is better for you to lose one of your members than for your whole body to go into hell"; Matt. 5:30).

A radical dream has been invoked. The dream is that God's people might be holy even as God is holy (cf. Matt. 5:48, "Be perfect, therefore, as your heavenly Father is perfect"). Radical dreams require radical methods to keep them going (eventually as radical as the cross!). In order for God's dream to come true—the dream of a holy God dwelling in the midst of a holy people—not only may the lives of doves and cattle be required, but also the lives of men, women, and participating animals (Lev. 20:15–16) as well.

Second, just as you can tell the values and character of a parent by monitoring what behavior provokes her sternest discipline (is it biting, or fighting, or failure to tell the truth?), so we can discern the values and the character of God by observing what actions invoke the strongest response. Clearly the severity of the response diminishes as we proceed through chapter 20: from God's direct action (in vv. 3, 5, 6); to directives that those found guilty "shall be put to death" (vv. 10, 11, 13, 15, 16; v. 14 specifies death by burning; cf. death by stoning in v. 27); to more ambiguous instructions that they shall be "cut off in the sight of their people" (v. 17) or simply "be subject to punishment" (vv. 17, 19, 20). Although we might be most offended by sex with animals, it is instructive to note what is most offensive to God, or better, what is deemed most disruptive to the relations of God's community.

At the top is worship of Molech (whom we have already encountered, in 18:21), more specifically, through "giving" our children to Molech, a god other than our God. While this giving up most likely referred to the practice of child sacrifice (cf. Lev. 18:21), and while child sacrifice to any god is elsewhere strictly forbidden (Deut. 18:10), the key to reprehensibility here is the offering up to Molech rather than God. Indeed, every good parent's dream is that her children might somehow offer themselves up to God's service, a dream that is acted out tangibly in the Scriptures (e.g., Hannah with Samuel, 1 Sam. 1) and legislated for in Leviticus (see later discussion regarding the redemption of one's firstborn, in Num. 3). The theme is thus improper worship in the most basic sense, turning over what's most precious, the community's children, to the service of the wrong gods. Rename Molech "Wealth" or "Fame," "Power" or "Privilege," "War" or "Government"—all gods to whom we may sacrifice sons and daughters—and this first order of business should give us pause.

Next, consultation with mediums and wizards represents a turning away from proper divine and human authorities (God, Moses and Aaron, the priests) to acknowledge other powers and seek other advice. Here is the same pairing we met in the last chapter: where others are portrayed as turning to mediums and wizards, God's people rise before the old and defer to the elderly (Lev. 19:31–32). It is not the stance of listening that is repugnant, but rather listening to the wrong authorities. A people who curse their mothers and fathers (20:9), and thus repudiate the authority of those traditions that have gone before (including Leviticus's instructions), will soon be seeking out every broker and personal trainer and feel-good therapist who comes along. At the top, bad worship. Next in line, bad instruction.

Last but not least, we arrive at the kind of behaviors with which we might have started: turning to the wrong members of our family, neighborhood, or the animal kingdom for companionship. Here the punishments for the behaviors described two chapters before are spelled out in gory and graphic detail. Suffice it to say, regarding these further instructions, it is not sex itself that is bad, but sex channeled into improper channels (see the discussion on Lev. 18). Bad worship and bad instruction bear the fruit of improper relations.

So third, in summation, it should now be obvious that all these selected offenses have at their heart a sin of turning: turning away from God's worship, turning away from proper authorities, turning away from proper human relationships. When such things happen, the relationship at the core of this community threatens to fall apart. The loss of this relationship is worse than death itself, for the individual, and even more for the community. God—through the exodus, the descent of God's glory, and the gift of these instructions—has consecrated, set apart, made holy this people. This, and this alone, is what marks them off as distinctive from all the nations about them ("You shall be holy to me; for I the LORD am holy, and I have separated you from the other peoples to be mine"; 20:26). Lose this, and you've lost everything. Thus the vehemence of the threat!

Yet it must immediately be said that this threat to "cut off" is one that the Lord finally (after invoking it once in the exile) backed away from. Not because God's people kept their focus (there's a story in the Scriptures for almost every violation here listed!), but because God kept God's promise (to stay with God's people). Though sin always, at its heart, involves a turning away from God, and though such turning is most reprehensible (indeed, only possible) for those to whom God has already turned in grace, the story of Leviticus–Numbers, and the story of the gospel, finally reveals a God who refuses to set "my face" and "cut off" God's people. Indeed, it is at this very point (of steadfast love and mercy) that God's holiness might be said to burn the brightest ("For I am God and no mortal, the Holy One in your midst, and I will not come in wrath"; Hos. 11:9). Surely then, something similar to this, in addition to the right relations already listed, should set God's people apart from the nations, as they have already been set apart by God.

Note. A word on separation. It is a curious paradox, throughout Leviticus–Numbers, that those things from which Israel would separate itself are also the things most essential for its survival. The Lord God's immediate presence, a source of instant annihilation for those who maintain no separation, is also their only true source of life. Blood, from which they maintain a distance so as to remain clean for worship, is also the substance with which the priest splatters the altar to render it clean for sacrifice. Could it be that one of the remaining paradoxes (past the exile) is to begin to see the nations as Israel's greatest threat and Israel's greatest hope? Israel is separated from the nations only so it can learn to be a blessing to the nations, and in this connection, it will find hope. We will deal with this theme at the end of our study, especially as we examine the tension between stability in Leviticus and movement in Numbers, but some opening shot is appropriate here.

HOLINESS OF PRIESTS
Leviticus 21:1–24

21:1 **The Lord said to Moses: Speak to the priests, the sons of Aaron, and say to them: No one shall defile himself for a dead person among his relatives, ² except for his nearest kin: his mother, his father, his son, his daughter, his brother; ³ likewise, for a virgin sister, close to him because she has had no husband, he may defile himself for her. ⁴ But he shall not defile himself as a husband among his people and so profane himself. ⁵ They shall not make bald spots upon their heads, or shave off the edges of their beards, or make any gashes in their flesh. ⁶ They shall be holy to their God, and not profane the name of their God; for they offer the Lord's offerings by fire, the food of their God; therefore they shall be holy. ⁷ They shall not marry a prostitute or a woman who has been defiled; neither shall they marry a woman divorced from her husband. For they are holy to their God, ⁸ and you shall treat them as holy, since they offer the food of your God; they shall be holy to you, for I the Lord, I who sanctify you, am holy. ⁹ When the daughter of a priest pro-**

fanes herself through prostitution, she profanes her father; she shall be burned to death.

21:16 **The LORD spoke to Moses, saying:** [17] **Speak to Aaron and say: No one of your offspring throughout their generations who has a blemish may approach to offer the food of his God.** [18] **For no one who has a blemish shall draw near, one who is blind or lame, or one who has a mutilated face or a limb too long,** [19] **or one who has a broken foot or a broken hand,** [20] **or a hunchback, or a dwarf, or a man with a blemish in his eyes or an itching disease or scabs or crushed testicles.** [21] **No descendant of Aaron the priest who has a blemish shall come near to offer the LORD's offerings by fire; since he has a blemish, he shall not come near to offer the food of his God.** [22] **He may eat the food of his God, of the most holy as well as of the holy.** [23] **But he shall not come near the curtain or approach the altar, because he has a blemish, that he may not profane my sanctuaries; for I am the LORD; I sanctify them.** [24] **Thus Moses spoke to Aaron and to his sons and to all the people of Israel.**

The requirements placed upon a people in whose midst the Lord is dwelling are stringent. The requirements placed upon those who would dare to approach God as leaders in worship are even more so: "They shall be holy to their God, and not profane the name of their God; for they offer the LORD's offering by fire, the food of their God; therefore they shall be holy" (21:6).

As a member of the cabinet must expect more rigorous background checks than a member of the congress; as an assistant to a surgeon must be extra clean to draw near the place of incision; as a community offers up its best resources and best young people to that occupation it deems most critical for the viability of its future (what would it be today: economic planning, technological innovation, military preparedness?); so God in Leviticus instructs Moses to tell the priests: only the best will do. Such holiness was poured upon them in the rites of ordination enumerated in Leviticus 8. Now such holiness must be maintained—through the living out of priestly lives, day by day.

Some observations regarding priestly holiness.

First, in Leviticus 21 it quickly becomes clear that holiness is maintained primarily by *not* doing certain things: *not* attending one's wife's funeral, verse 4 (revealing the strange hierarchy of priestly obligation in Israel; parents and children, but not spouses); *not* shaving one's head, verse 5 (perhaps here with reference to non-Israelite rites of mourning rather than merely to matters of hairstyle; cf. 19:27–28); *not* marrying certain types of women, verse 7 (especially those which the stipulations of Lev. 18 have pronounced "unclean"). Regardless of how we evaluate the specifics, these instructions reveal both the origins of holiness as gift (and thus something more to be protected than enhanced) as well as the impossibility of earning such status by meritorious conduct (casting some doubt over the whole topic of "qualifications" for church office!). The priest in Israel "earned" the privilege of serving the Lord in the sanctuary primarily by being born into the house of Aaron, not by showing any particular facility at either sacrifice or instruction. It thus stands essentially at odds with any "meritocracy" for priestly service that is not grounded first and foremost in the prior selection of God. (Perhaps this is why there's little "priestly" parallel to the "prophetic" tradition of protest from Moses, Jeremiah, and others: "Why me, Lord?")

Second, while the requirements for priests are strict (funerals of only nearest kin, no shaving of beards, no marriage to either prostitutes or divorcées), the requirements for chief priests are even more so: he may marry only "a virgin of his own kin," verse 14; cannot even dishevel his hair, verse 10; may not attend any funerals, even of mother and father, verse 11. Surely all these regulations were meant to flesh out the priest's single-minded loyalty to God alone, a loyalty that took precedence over all other personal and familiar obligations (cf. Jesus' words in Nazareth, "Who are my mother and my brothers?" Mark 3:33; and the whole tradition of priestly celibacy, being "married" to the church alone). The precious privilege of living one's life in hands-on service to a holy God requires an extravagant response on the person's part. Costly sacrifice, in Leviticus, is not a matter for animals alone. (Thus not only sacrificial animals, but also sacrificial priests were to be "treated" as holy; v. 8.)

Third, while some of these requirements are picked up by Jesus and applied to the sacrifices demanded of all disciples ("Follow me, and let the dead bury their own dead"; Matt. 8:22), the motivation for such prescriptions has shifted from questions of ritual cleanliness (at least the *initial* reason for the priests' staying away from funerals) to those of ultimate loyalty ("No one who puts a hand to the plow and looks back is fit for the kingdom of God"; Luke 9:62). Thus, at the same time that Jesus may ask all disciples to forgo the funerals of mother and father if these things get in the way of following, fellowship with prostitutes (Matt. 21:32), contact with the dead (Mark 5:41), and baptisms of eunuchs (Acts 8, considered unqualified for priestly service due to deficiencies in the testicles; Lev. 21:20)—these are all seen, by Jesus and the early church, as ways of drawing nearer, versus shutting oneself off from, the presence of God and God's kingdom.

We must then move from a discussion of Levitical proscriptions to our own discussions of what proper requirements for Christian leadership might be. Should they be defined positively as well as negatively (cf. 1 Tim. 3)? Should they include restrictions on money and power, as well as sex? What blemishes of the heart (versus the skin, the limbs, or the genitals) might preclude one from such office? What is the proper balance between loyalty to the family and loyalty to the church? How does a community hold up strict requirements for those who would assume leadership, yet recognize ordination as a gift to individuals who are always in some sense unclean? Everybody's skin has a blemish, if you look closely enough. Everybody's limbs are unequal, if measured carefully enough. We are all blind and lame to some degree when it comes to our calling from God, especially those whose vision and gait are the strongest. Surely things only get murkier when we move beneath the skin ("For the LORD does not see as mortals see; they look on the outward appearance, but the LORD looks on the heart"; 1 Sam. 16:7).

Israel, by these regulations, was striving resolutely to be the kind of community that offered up its "best" for the priesthood, just as it did for its sacrifices ("From the sheep or goats, your offering shall be a male without blemish"; Lev. 1:10). Surely such a weighting of service to the Lord, versus service to other powers, is to be commended. Even Leviticus's emphasis on maintaining a holiness given, rather than acquiring holiness through skills (moral, technical, or educational), has much to teach us.

But chapter 21's restriction of the priesthood to members of one family, one gender, and one method of assessing wholeness presents basic problems for application. Surely any who believe Jesus Christ to be the perfect model for priesthood and the perfect Lamb for sacrifice will have to approach this chapter more as a launching than a landing point. Compared to the clear-skinned, perfectly proportioned, scabless candidates for priesthood proposed here, Isaiah proposes another kind of offering altogether: "So marred was his appearance, beyond human semblance. . . . He had no form or majesty that we should look at him, nothing in his appearance that we should desire him. . . . As one from whom others hide their faces he was despised, and we held him of no account" (52:14; 53:2–3).

HOLINESS OF OFFERINGS
Leviticus 22:1–33

22:1 **The LORD spoke to Moses, saying: 2 Direct Aaron and his sons to deal carefully with the sacred donations of the people of Israel, which they dedicate to me, so that they may not profane my holy name; I am the LORD. 3 Say** to them: If anyone among all your offspring throughout your generations comes near the sacred donations, which the people of Israel dedicate to the LORD, while he is in a state of uncleanness, that person shall be cut off from my presence: I am the LORD.

22:10 No lay person shall eat of the sacred donations. No bound or hired servant of the priest shall eat of the sacred donations; [11] but if a priest acquires anyone by purchase, the person may eat of them; and those that are born in his house may eat of his food.

22:17 The LORD spoke to Moses, saying: [18] Speak to Aaron and his sons and all the people of Israel and say to them: When anyone of the house of Israel or of the aliens residing in Israel presents an offering, whether in payment of a vow or as a freewill offering that is offered to the LORD as a burnt offering, [19] to be acceptable in your behalf it shall be a male without blemish, of the cattle or the sheep or the goats. [20] You shall not offer anything that has a blemish, for it will not be acceptable in your behalf.

22:31 Thus you shall keep my commandments and observe them: I am the LORD. [32] You shall not profane my holy name, that I may be sanctified among the people of Israel: I am the LORD; I sanctify you, [33] I who brought you out of the land of Egypt to be your God: I am the LORD.

Now that the holiness of the sanctuary has spread out to the smallest details of everyday life, the focus shifts back to the central activities of the priests. Like the hostess checking rooms in expectation of an honored guest, or the trail guide going over procedures before a hike begins, the Lord instructs Moses to instruct Aaron further in two key areas of the sacrificial system: first, who gets to eat the designated food from the sacrifices, and second, what kinds of animals qualify.

Regarding who gets to eat, two different restrictions are spelled out.

First, no priest who has become unclean through any action (intentional or unintentional) shall eat of the proscribed food—unless this priest has been purified by ritual actions (washing with water, v. 6) and the requisite passage of time (after sunset, v. 7). Clearly, the holiness of these offerings, necessary for them to be effective, is ever under threat, especially by the hands of those by whom they are most closely handled. So a sort of liturgical hygiene, far more rigorous than any merely biological hygiene, is required. Although this stands in tension with many of the debates in church history that tried to disconnect the sanctity of the sacrament from the sanctity of the celebrant (look up the Donatist controversy in a church history dictionary), it helps to remind us of a problem that is equally destructive: a preacher preaching forgiveness while estranged from his wife; a prophet railing against injustice while underpaying her clerical staff; a church officer urging sacrificial giving when he makes no regular pledge. Holy gifts can be threatened by unholy recipients. Great care is in order.

Second, regarding restrictions, no one outside the priest's family (except for "purchased" servants, v. 11!) should be allowed to eat the designated food. Part of this instruction is practical (protecting the priest's portion from encroachment by others); part of it is theological (reserving this "set apart" food for those who had been "set apart" themselves, and their families). Two countermovements in sharing are thus set in motion: one is an exciting largesse (as the eating of the food is now spread out to include family and servants, similar to the "house" baptisms in the New Testament); the other is a provocative restriction (keeping this food for priests and family only, though other parts of the sacrifice were not so reserved; see Lev. 3). Such regulations are questioned within the Scriptures themselves (e.g., the story of David's use of the Bread of Presence for his troops, in 1 Sam. 21, later quoted by Jesus in Mark 2:26), and such practices of restriction continue to be topics in the church today (the "fencing" of the table to exclude the nonbaptized). Yet Leviticus 22 reminds us that an approach to God and the things of God should never be made lightly or casually or without recognizing the claims that such gifts make on the recipients. Set-apart food requires set-apart people, back then and also now.

The other major section of Leviticus 22 concerns animals acceptable as offerings. Here the expanded criteria for priests (Lev. 21) are now applied to the animals: no blemished, blind, injured, or maimed animals; none with discharges, itches, or scabs; none with testicles bruised, crushed, torn, or cut. While the value placed on obviously "imperfect" life versus ostensibly "perfect" life should be as repugnant to us regarding animals as it was for human beings (Lev. 21), the more practical import is obvious. Don't give your *seconds* to God (be they time, talents, or money) and keep the *firsts* for yourself. Such behavior undoubtedly began as soon as sacrifices were instituted in the wilderness and remained a favorite target for prophets long afterward ("Cursed be the cheat who has a male in the flock and vows to give it, and yet sacrifices to the Lord what is blemished; for I am a great King, says the LORD of hosts, and my name is reverenced among the nations"; Mal. 1:14).

Leviticus 22 closes with a motivational summary that is impressive in its thoroughness. The proper motivation for all this care regarding offerings is finally detached from any factor resident in the worshipers, such as the hope for better crops, families, or national success. "I am the LORD," "I am the LORD," "I am the LORD," God reminds Moses three times (vv. 31

and 32). Again, it is the holy presence of God that requires such careful obedience on the part of God's people. A Holy Lord has chosen to dwell in the midst of an unholy people. Only the Lord's presence has any hope of setting them apart. All the activities of "setting apart" that have now been laid down (including those just cited for setting apart offerings) serve only one central function: to remind them that they are set-apart people of a set-apart God.

Note. Even amid this seemingly coldhearted analysis of acceptable and unacceptable animals, the compassion of Israel toward its most prized creatures is evident. "When an ox or a sheep or a goat is born, it shall remain seven days with its mother, and from the eighth day on it shall be acceptable as the LORD's offering by fire. But you shall not slaughter, from the herd or the flock, an animal with its young on the same day" (vv. 27–28). Would that we consumers of veal and lamb and other meats demonstrated such compassion today.

HOLINESS OF FESTIVALS
Leviticus 23:1–44

Introduction

Having pushed the response to God's holy presence down to the tiniest niches of kitchen and bedroom, there is little space left to expand other than outward: out into space (the Holiness of Land, Lev. 25); and out into time (the Holiness of Festivals, Lev. 23). In many ways this is the most radical step of them all.

While the loss of Israel's land might jeopardize its ability to preserve any rituals of field and hearth, and the loss of Israel's Temple might make impossible the rituals of altar sacrifices, as long as Israel was alive, and day succeeded night, time was available to be sacrificed, sanctified, set apart. So, while God's presence with Israel first created a crisis that was spatial (Holy God/unholy people), God's presence with this people now blossoms into a possibility that is "timeless," or better, "time-full."

Here is a response to God's presence accessible to all God's people, anywhere: the prisoner in his cell (some think true Sabbath observance was born in Babylon); the parent overwhelmed by her duties (resting from work in the home is often far more radical than resting from work in the office); and the executive traversing time zones by airplane (though this poses a new, Levitical problem as to when the Sabbath begins).

Every week, every month, every year now becomes a "camp" wherein God's holy presence might be manifest, through the observance of festivals pegged to this God's saving acts. At various stages in this people's journey, the Lord's holy presence with them was revealed. Now these singular revelations are built into a holy calendar so that their benefits might spread forward throughout time and space.

The Sabbath
Leviticus 23:1–3

> 23:1 **The Lord spoke to Moses, saying:** [2] **Speak to the people of Israel and say to them: These are the appointed festivals of the Lord that you shall proclaim as holy convocations, my appointed festivals.** [3] **Six days shall work be done; but the seventh day is a sabbath of complete rest, a holy convocation; you shall do no work: it is a sabbath to the Lord throughout your settlements.**

Before enumerating the annual festivals, the sole weekly festival is cited. The priority of this festival is made clear not only by its position in the Ten Commandments ("Remember the sabbath day, and keep it holy"; Exod. 20:8), and not only by its priority in this listing (ahead of all the rest), but also by its linkage to the "rest" or sabbath of God in the creation, long before all the other events toward which the festivals of Israel point ("For in six days the Lord made heaven and earth, the sea, and all that is in them, but rested the seventh day"; Exod. 20:11). As the Lord marked time, so God's people will mark their time. As the Lord has consecrated and set apart this time, so God's people will consecrate and set apart this time. Weekly Sabbath observance thus becomes a way of spreading the holiness of God's character out into the world; it is a regular way of reminding God's people just who it is that has taken up residence in our camp: the Holy Lord, Creator of us and all that is.

Several observations about this hallowed day might be made.

1. *The radical nature of this sacrifice.* While money may be replaced (though not easily), and even life replenished (on the level of herd and field, though not on the level of particular cow or ear of grain), time is essentially a nonrenewable resource: once it's gone, it's really gone. Thus to give up one day out of seven to rest in God's saving presence was, is, and ever shall be a radical statement, whether for food-to-mouth wanderers in the desert, subsistence farmers in Palestine, or busy executives and volunteers today. Although most argue that the

requirements for animal sacrifice (though not other sacrifices!) have been set aside in Christ, and though Jesus was more than willing to enter the Scriptures' own wrestling with the proper motivation and thus the proper observation of the Sabbath (cf. Jesus' assertion that the Sabbath was made for humankind, in Mark 2:27), Jesus never denies the need to set aside time for God (as evidenced by his own patterns of prayer and Sabbath observance; Mark 6:2). Indeed, early on, the Christian community "set aside" the first day of the week, Sunday, as a way to remember the new creation God had made possible in Christ's resurrection (though the history of how this was coordinated with or set in contrast to the Jewish Sabbath is complicated). If God's creation of the world can inspire radical sacrifice, how about our "new creation" in Christ (2 Cor. 5:17)?

2. *Holy day versus holy days.* The purpose of a weekly Sabbath was not to make one day more holy than the others. As the offering of first sheep and first grains marked all of the flock and all of the field as belonging to God, so the setting aside of this last day (or first for Christians) claimed all of the week's time as God's. Once more we see how sacrifice does not so much reposition God as reposition us. By regularly setting aside one day out of seven, we are trained to experience all of our days as set apart by God.

3. *Public testimony.* While matters of food and sex may be visible only to one's closest acquaintances, the setting aside of one day out of seven will not go long unnoticed, by one's neighbors, one's teammates, and one's employer. Thus, Sabbath observance (more than sacrifice, circumcision, or dietary restrictions) became the most public way Israel demonstrated that it was a nation "holy" to God. A person who will not work one day out of seven stands out in a crowd, even more in a corporation. Why would you do such a thing? "Because the Lord God, holy is God's name, has chosen to dwell in my camp."

Spring Festivals
Leviticus 23:4–22

> 23:4 **These are the appointed festivals of the Lord, the holy convocations, which you shall celebrate at the time appointed for them. ⁵ In the first month, on the fourteenth day of the month, at twilight, there shall be a passover offering to the Lord, ⁶ and on the fifteenth day of the same month**

is the festival of unleavened bread to the Lord; seven days you shall eat unleavened bread. [7] On the first day you shall have a holy convocation; you shall not work at your occupations. [8] For seven days you shall present the Lord's offerings by fire; on the seventh day there shall be a holy convocation: you shall not work at your occupations.

23:9 The Lord spoke to Moses: [10] Speak to the people of Israel and say to them: When you enter the land that I am giving you and you reap its harvest, you shall bring the sheaf of the first fruits of your harvest to the priest. [11] He shall raise the sheaf before the Lord, that you may find acceptance; on the day after the sabbath the priest shall raise it.

23:15 And from the day after the sabbath, from the day on which you bring the sheaf of the elevation offering, you shall count off seven weeks; they shall be complete. [16] You shall count until the day after the seventh sabbath, fifty days; then you shall present an offering of new grain to the Lord.

23:22 When you reap the harvest of your land, you shall not reap to the very edges of your field, or gather the gleanings of your harvest; you shall leave them for the poor and for the alien: I am the Lord your God.

As in other matters, the neat order of this Levitical summary belies a complex history of evolution underneath. Why does the New Year festival, Rosh Hashanah, fall in the seventh month? Is the calendar lunar or solar, grounded in agriculture or grounded in history? Where are the names for the months found elsewhere in the Scriptures (Nisan, Abib, etc.), and where are some missing festivals (like Hanukkah and Purim)? Most of all, how do we harmonize this list of festivals with lists found in other places in the Bible (Exod. 23 and 34; Deut. 16; as well as the schedule connected to the offerings of these festivals in Num. 28–29)?

While such questions are beyond the scope of this study, some brief comments may be helpful before we proceed to specific festivals.

The basic pattern in Leviticus 23 is clear. Two festivals are located in the spring, in connection with the first and second harvests of the agricultural season. One festival is located in the fall, in connection with the final harvest and ingathering. These provide the main pattern to which attendant special days are attached (e.g., the Festival of Trumpets, vv. 23–25). Over this basic template, then, other patterns are laid. The most important is the history of Israel's story (exodus, wandering, conquest), about which we will say more. Perhaps more traumatic is the history of Israel's exile (the source of those missing names). Other history followed later (Hanukkah and Purim), and thus shows up in no listing in the first books of the Scriptures. Whether shifts from first to seventh months have more to do with the history of Israel's journey from Egypt to Palestine ("This month shall mark for you the beginning of months; it shall be the first month of the year for you"; Exod. 12:2), or the adaptations and after-shocks of its captivity (Babylon began its New Year in the spring, not the fall)—such adjustments are not as important as the way the Levitical priests now claim the entire order for God. As they focus on the individ-ual farmer and ask how this farmer's worship might claim even the calen-dar of seedtime and harvest as a place where God's holiness is at work, their journey of reinterpretation begins.

We begin with the two major festivals located in the spring: the Festi-val of Unleavened Bread and the Festival of Weeks.

The Festival of Unleavened Bread. In the first month of the year, marked by the harvest of Israel's first crop of the season (barley), the first harvest of God's gracious choosing took center stage: the exodus from Egypt. This began midmonth with that most foundational of all the cere-monies, the Passover, celebrating the "passing over" of the angel of death in Egypt. This was followed by a seven-day Festival of Unleavened Bread, which both began and ended with "holy convocations," including both the cessation of work and the offering of sacrifices (more in Num. 28). Attached to this festival, in Leviticus, is another foundational celebration from Israel's "settled" days in the Promised Land: the Offering of First Fruits, familiar from the ancient credo in Deuteronomy ("A wandering Aramean was my ancestor"; 26:5). Israel's first beginnings as a nation thus become attached to Israel's first harvests as a people, building into the annual cycle a memory of their first planting and harvest by the hands of the Lord: "Your right hand, O LORD, shattered the enemy" (Exod. 15:6); "You brought them in and planted them on the mountain" (Exod. 15:17).

The Festival of Weeks. Several weeks after the first sheaf of barley was waved (v. 11), the first of the wheat harvest (the new grain) came in. This led to the counting off of fifty days (Pentecost, *pente* being Greek for fifty) from the time of the elevation offering to the beginning of the Festival of Weeks (vv. 15–16). This festival was also marked by cessation from work and offering sacrifices. Perhaps it was the similarity between this time period (stretching between first and later harvests) and the time between Israel's first Passover and its arrival at Mount Sinai in the wilderness (Exod. 19:1) that led to this festival's association with the giving of the law. As the Festival of Unleavened Bread celebrated the "first fruit" of God's gracious provision to Israel, the exodus, so this second early harvest was slowly transformed into a celebration of a second early fruit, the law.

Here several observations are in order.

1. *Setting apart time for God.* As certain animals, people, and practices have already been set apart for God, this attempt to extend the sphere of holiness is now applied to time. Though the clearest and most fundamental marker remains the weekly observance of Sabbath, the year now is subject to the same partitioning. The weekly patterns of sacrifice and witness practiced as Sabbath are now extended to the arrival and passing of the seasons.

2. *Giving thanks to God as Lord of the harvest.* From the beginning, however, something more radical than claiming time for God is at work. Deep down in the transformation of these festivals rests the claim that the same Lord who orders the agricultural seasons has also ordered the seasons of Israel's life. The Lord who has set up tent in Israel's midst is not just along for the ride. As has been made evident in the past, and as is to be trusted in the future, this God is Lord of the harvest, whether the crop is barley and wheat, or exodus and law.

3. *Transformed calendar, transformed people.* The very evolution of this calendar captures the character of a God who is always "on the move." As Israel's experience moved from that of wandering slaves, to settled farmers, to scattered exiles, so its calendar shifted from celebrations linked with agriculture to convocations linked with sacred nurture. Jesus' transformation of Passover in the Lord's Supper and the Holy Spirit's transformation of Pentecost in the upper room thus mark nothing "new" in the transformation of God's people's annual festivals. As Jesus said, the festivals are there to serve humankind, not vice versa, by helping humankind remember who is numbering our days. "So teach us, Lord," we might paraphrase Psalm 90, "to count our days as you do that we may gain wise hearts and holy lives."

Fall Festivals
Leviticus 23:23–44

23:23 The Lord spoke to Moses, saying: 24 Speak to the people of Israel, saying: In the seventh month, on the first day of the month, you shall observe a day of complete rest, a holy convocation commemorated with trumpet blasts. 25 You shall not work at your occupations; and you shall present the Lord's offering by fire.

23:26 The Lord spoke to Moses, saying: 27 Now, the tenth day of this seventh month is the day of atonement; it shall be a holy convocation for you: you shall deny yourselves and present the Lord's offering by fire; 28 and you shall do no work during that entire day; for it is a day of atonement, to make atonement on your behalf before the Lord your God.

23:39 **Now, the fifteenth day of the seventh month, when you have gathered in the produce of the land, you shall keep the festival of the LORD, last-
ing seven days; a complete rest on the first day, and a complete rest on the
eighth day.** [40] **On the first day you shall take the fruit of majestic trees,
branches of palm trees, boughs of leafy trees, and willows of the brook; and
you shall rejoice before the LORD your God for seven days.** [41] **You shall keep
it as a festival to the LORD seven days in the year; you shall keep it in the seventh month as a statute forever throughout your generations.** [42] **You shall
live in booths for seven days; all that are citizens in Israel shall live in booths,**
[43] **so that your generations may know that I made the people of Israel live in
booths when I brought them out of the land of Egypt: I am the LORD your
God.** [44] **Thus Moses declared to the people of Israel the appointed festivals
of the LORD.**

After the early, springtime harvests of barley and wheat, the summer set
in. Months of higher temperatures and lower rainfall accompanied the
ongoing task of tending the later crops (such as olives and grapes). At the
end of this time (which, viewed differently, marked the beginning of
another), the time of final harvests and ingathering arrived. In the Levitical script, this festival moved forward in three steps:

1. *The Festival of Trumpets.* Though every month was marked by a Festival of the New Moon (Num. 10:10; 28:11), this seventh month, due
   to its other associations (below), became the most important of them
   all. Like them, it was marked off with "trumpet blasts" (Lev. 23:24; cf.
   Num. 10:10) and a summons to "complete rest" (Lev. 23:24).
2. *The Day of Atonement.* The details of this great day have already
   been discussed (Lev. 16). Its location here, amid the fall festivals,
   highlights its function as a time for looking back on the fruits of the
   season now past, and ahead to the season now at hand.
3. *The Festival of Booths.* These two special days are now enclosed by
   the third and final required pilgrimage festival, marked by a holy convocation at its beginning and end. Although its link with earlier agricultural festivals is evident (here the waving of grain has been replaced
   with the waving of branches from leafy trees), its transformation to a
   national festival is explicit: "You shall live in booths for seven days . . .
   so that your generations may know that I made the people of Israel
   live in booths when I brought them out of the land of Egypt" (v. 42).
   The final chapter of the annual agricultural cycle is thus linked with
   the final chapter in the saving history of God's people: their sojourn in
   the wilderness before their entry into the Promised Land.

Looking back now over the full cycle of annual festivals, several ʌ
vations may be helpful:

1. *A sacred reckoning.* If you add up the days set aside for Sabbath (52),
   add in the movable festivals of the New Moon (12), and the holy convocations and special days of the three great festivals (6), you end up
   with 70 out of 365 days, almost 20 percent of one's days "set aside" for
   rest, sacrifice, and remembrance. Again, for any people, this marks a
   radical response to God's grace. For a people often living by the nar-
   rowest of margins, it is a statement and a dream of radical proportions.
2. *A fundamental claim.* It is one thing to testify to patterns evident to
   everyone: the advent of new moons (the basis of the Jewish calendar), or the solstices and equinoxes of the sun (the basis for locating
   Easter and other movable feasts of the Christian calendar). It is quite
   another to attach to these universal occasions more particular events
   that are claimed as even more foundational: the leading out of a
   people from Egypt; the birth, death, and resurrection of a Jew from
   Nazareth. The calendar thus becomes a means of distinguishing
   between the holy and the common, the sacred and the profane.
3. *An essential witness.* Again, though personal habits of food and
   dress are noticeable to one's neighbors, such extravagant patterns of
   work and rest become quite public protests, which may well set one
   off (sociologically, economically, and religiously) from one's neighbors. Although such observance can lead to problems (as Jews and
   Christians try to coordinate calendars, as technology allows us to
   ignore the cycles of sun and moon, and as we move from a position
   of majority to minority in our culture), it also provides one highly
   tangible way to witness to the Lord at the heart of our camp.

Note. As Israel's compassion toward vulnerable animals showed up in
the last chapter (Lev. 22:27–28), so its compassion toward vulnerable people shows up here: "When you reap the harvest of your land, you shall not
reap to the very edges of your field, or gather the gleanings of your harvest; you shall leave them for the poor and for the alien: I am the LORD
your God" (23:22). Though this prohibition against hoarding the harvest
has already been noticed in Leviticus 19, it shows up again in this chapter
on festivals. Why? First, lest it be forgotten. Second, so that Israel's life
outside the festivals does not undermine its life within them. Third,
because Israelites see themselves as set-apart gleanings among the nations,
whom the Lord God has set apart and saved.

Holiness of Lamp and Bread
Leviticus 24:1–9

24:1 **The LORD spoke to Moses, saying:** [2] **Command the people of Israel to bring you pure oil of beaten olives for the lamp, that a light may be kept burning regularly.** [3] **Aaron shall set it up in the tent of meeting, outside the curtain of the covenant, to burn from evening to morning before the LORD regularly; it shall be a statute forever throughout your generations.** [4] **He shall set up the lamps on the lampstand of pure gold before the LORD regularly.** [5] **You shall take choice flour, and bake twelve loaves of it; two-tenths of an ephah shall be in each loaf.** [6] **You shall place them in two rows, six in a row, on the table of pure gold.** [7] **You shall put pure frankincense with each row, to be a token offering for the bread, as an offering by fire to the LORD.** [8] **Every sabbath day Aaron shall set them in order before the LORD regularly as a commitment of the people of Israel, as a covenant forever.** [9] **They shall be for Aaron and his descendants, who shall eat them in a holy place, for they are most holy portions for him from the offerings by fire to the LORD, a perpetual due.**

After listing the occasions when the Lord's presence with God's people would be best remembered and experienced, two tangible reminders of the Lord's constant presence in the camp are established. On the days when no trumpets are blowing, no bulls being slaughtered, no sheaves being waved, how are we to know and trust that God is yet with us? At night, look for the light of the lamp perpetually burning in God's tent. During the day, see the twelve loaves of bread set out on the Lord's table.

The lamp. Fire, and the light which accompanies it, had been the sign of the Lord's presence for Moses at his call (Exod. 3) and the people at the mountain (Exod. 19). It, along with a pillar of cloud by day, had been the primary sign of God's nocturnal accompaniment in their wanderings since Egypt (Exod. 13:21). In the journey yet ahead, the fire that had smoldered within the cloud when the sanctuary was first completed (Exod. 40:38) and had appeared to the people on the day when sanctuary worship first began (Lev. 9:24)—that same fire would now simmer in the midst of the cloud over the sanctuary every evening, assuring God's people they were still on the right path (Num. 9:15).

Fire and light, then, from a lamp filled with pure oil, were the perfect symbols of God's perpetual presence all through every night. A people thereby trained to think of light as evidence of God's presence thus celebrated the appearance of light as the first act of God in creation ("Then God said, 'Let there be light'"; Gen. 1:3) and the first new act of God in the advent of the Messiah ("The light shines in the darkness"; John 1:5). In turn, they sought such illumination from other sources of God's presence in their lives ("Your word is a lamp to my feet and a light to my path"; Ps. 119:105) and used care of lamps as a perfect picture of readiness for the Lord's approach ("Ten bridesmaids took their lamps and went to meet the bridegroom"; Matt. 25:1).

Whether transformed into the seven-branched menorah of later tradition, or the flesh-and-blood incarnation of the Messiah, the promise of a light that will not be extinguished is a promise at the heart of both Jewish (the Jewish celebration of Hanukkah) and Christian hope ("The darkness did not overcome it"; John 1:5). Only in the final kingdom to come will such lamps no longer be needed "for the Lord God will be their light, and they will reign forever and ever" (Rev. 22:5).

The bread. While light is chosen as the best sign of the Lord's presence at night, twelve loaves of bread are selected as the best sign of God's presence in the sanctuary during the day. Here too a practice begins that has influenced both Jews and Christians as we seek to find signs of the Lord's presence in our midst. What is the widow of Zarephath asked to offer to Elijah so that she may know that the Lord lives? A morsel of bread (1 Kgs. 17:8–16). What is used as the main material for miraculous feedings in both Old and New Testaments, when evidence of the Lord's presence is needed? Loaves of bread (2 Kgs. 4:42–44; cf. Mark 8:1–9).

Twelve loaves of bread become the proper symbols of the twelve tribes of Israel living their lives as holy sacrifices for a perpetually present Lord ("When anyone presents a grain offering to the LORD, the offering shall be of choice flour"; Lev. 2:1). One loaf of bread becomes the proper symbol for a single faithful Jew sent to achieve a similar task in the New Testament ("While they were eating, he took a loaf of bread"; Mark 14:22). Bread, then, whether common or showbread ("You shall place them in two rows, six in a row, on the table of pure gold"; Lev. 24:6), whether produced in the land or given from the sky ("Then the LORD said to Moses, 'I am going to rain bread from heaven for you'"; Exod. 16:4), thus becomes one of the central symbols of the Lord's presence with God's people ("Give us this day our daily bread"; Matt. 6:11). In the vernacular, "sharing bread with those in need" also becomes one of the central actions with which to test the people's proper response.

PUNISHMENT FOR BLASPHEMY
Leviticus 24:10–23

24:10 **A man whose mother was an Israelite and whose father was an Egyptian came out among the people of Israel; and the Israelite woman's son and a** certain Israelite began fighting in the camp. [11] The Israelite woman's son blasphemed the Name in a curse. And they brought him to Moses—now his mother's name was Shelomith, daughter of Dibri, of the tribe of Dan— [12] and they put him in custody, until the decision of the Lord should be made clear to them. [13] The Lord said to Moses, saying: [14] Take the blasphemer outside the camp; and let all who were within hearing lay their hands on his head, and let the whole congregation stone him. [15] And speak to the people of Israel, saying: Anyone who curses God shall bear the sin. [16] One who blasphemes the name of the Lord shall be put to death; the whole congregation shall stone the blasphemer. Aliens as well as citizens, when they blaspheme the Name, shall be put to death. [17] Anyone who kills a human being shall be put to death. [18] Anyone who kills an animal shall make restitution for it, life for life. [19] Anyone who maims another shall suffer the same injury in return: [20] fracture for fracture, eye for eye, tooth for tooth; the injury inflicted is the injury to be suffered. [21] One who kills an animal shall make restitution for it; but one who kills a human being shall be put to death. [22] You shall have one law for the alien and for the citizen: for I am the Lord your God. [23] Moses spoke thus to the people of Israel; and they took the blasphemer outside the camp, and stoned him to death. The people of Israel did as the Lord had commanded Moses.

In a world now so filled with signs of the Lord's presence, you would think that everything that is said, and everything that is done would make clear a constant awareness of this guest who is close by. Unfortunately, that is not the case, then or now.

Suddenly, in the midst of all these rules and regulations, the first action since the inauguration of Israel's worship in chapters 8–10 occurs. As Nadab and Abihu lit unholy fire to wave before the Lord, now two residents of the camp light the fires of interpersonal conflict and go at it.

At first glance, there is nothing unusual here. Surely an encampment this big—motionless in the desert, filled with peoples of different tribes and even different ethnic stock (half-Israelite/half-Egyptian, a disturbingly "necessary" detail?)—had seen more than a few scuffles as the sanctuary was built and the law laid down. But in the tussle of the fight, something other than a fist is thrown. The Name of the Lord, that personal name, which is not even to be used for blessings and bar mitzvahs, is lifted up—in a curse. Sadly, there's little need for a sound track of this scene.

What is surprising is that no immediate remedy is in sight. Despite the details of the instructions that have gone before ("nor shall you put on a garment made of two different materials"; 19:19), the earlier prohibition of "wrongful" use of the Lord's name and reviling God (Exod. 20:7; 22:28), and the decree that cursing father or mother is a capital offense

(Lev. 20:9), the penalty for using the Lord's proper name in a curse has not been specified. Maybe it was a sin that the Levitical priests could not imagine. Maybe it is an example of the way instruction must grow and adapt to the ever-creative propensities of God's people. Regardless, the offender is impounded, without parole, awaiting a decision "of the LORD."

All too quickly that decision comes, leading the offender out for a "laying on of hands" outside the camp, then an opportune lesson on the seriousness of injuries between humans ("eye for eye, tooth for tooth") and between humans and animals (restitution, "life for life"), then a clatter of stones, death, and silence. The moral of the story? "The people of Israel did as the LORD had commanded Moses" (24:23).

What can we say?

First, we must recognize that the major offense is not the fight with one's neighbor, but the blasphemy against God. Can you imagine? Here are people who know that words from our mouths are as deadly as blows from our fists (cf. Jas. 3 on the deadly power of the tongue). Here are people who have learned that due reverence toward God precedes proper respect for the neighbor (note how the commandment regarding misuse of God's name precedes the commandment regarding murder in Exod. 20). Here are people who know that you first settle how you stand and speak to God, and then ask how you stand with or lie with, speak or don't speak to your neighbor (see Lev. 19).

Once more, the severity of the response to the Israelite's words in comparison to actions (itself a modern distinction!) only shows how distant from Leviticus we live our lives. It is indeed right to worry over our feeding of the hungry and our assault on the poor, but how much do we worry over our words toward God? Leviticus 24 teaches us that we should so worry, deeply—or else our relationship with God will suffer violence, and our relationships with our fellow human beings will do the same.

Second, the words of the blasphemer pollute not only the person who abuses the Lord's name, but everyone who hears it. This is the reason that all those who hear this must lay their hands on the head of the perpetrator. Like laying hands on a sin offering, the sin of those who have heard must be returned upon the head of the sinner. Sin, in the Scriptures, is seldom an individual matter. Its effects ripple out into the entire community. Surely this should give us pause as we blithely uphold the notion of "free speech" but not "free actions," as if the destructive power of speech, especially God-directed speech, cannot affect us or our neighbors.

Third, and equally difficult, the lex talionis (law of retaliation) attached to this story functioned initially to restrain violence. Why not put this man's father and this man's mother, Shelomith, to death? They raised him. Why not include the other combatant who provoked this outcry? Isn't he too responsible? Why not include all those charged with inculcating a reverence for the divine name within the children of this community? No! If someone injures an eye, only an eye will be jeopardized. If someone takes a life, only one life shall be required. If someone utters a blasphemy, only the blasphemer will be disciplined. In a society where vengeance could sometimes spread across several clans and many generations, the judgment of one-for-one can be seen, at first, as merciful.

Fourth, as argued earlier regarding sacrifice, the motivation for such costly procedures (slaughtering cattle, stoning blasphemers) was not a callous disregard for life, but indeed a purposeful attempt to act out the preciousness of life: animal life, human life, the "life" of the relationship between a people and their God. Anyone who blasphemes, no matter how important, shall be put to death. Anyone who kills, no matter how "expendable" the victim, shall be put to death. Anyone who kills an animal, for whatever purpose, shall make restitution, life for life. This is the heart of this instruction. Life in this world, whether between human beings or between human beings and God, is too precarious and too precious a gift to treat lightly. When the community is threatened by blasphemy or murder, something costly must be done.

Nevertheless, fifth and finally, how do we square this law and this story with the new law of Jesus to turn the other cheek (Matt. 5:38–42) and the Gospel story of the crucifixion of Jesus on the same charge as our Israelite: blasphemy (Mark 14:64)?

We begin by pointing out that Jesus does not simply replace the actions required in Leviticus ("eye for eye, tooth for tooth") with no actions of his own. It isn't that the slapping of a person's cheek requires no response, but the challenge is to make the cheek offered your own. Jesus took life and assaults on life seriously. He just replaces the costly retaliations of Leviticus with responses more costly still.

So, what happens when you move up from questions of eyes and teeth to matters of life and death itself? What happens if the tooth, the eye, and the life required become not those of the sinner, but, voluntarily, those of the sinned against?

Now the Gospel story shifts the law onto another plane entirely: the one accused of blasphemy is led outside the camp and executed. Only it is not just his death that sanctifies the Lord's name, as with the death in Leviticus, but his death and his resurrection. By taking upon himself the consequences of our own blasphemies, Christ lifts the Name higher than ever before.

This leaves us not with answers, but with a challenge. How can we, who follow this Christ, duly recognize the deadly work of actions and words—for human life, for animal life, and for the life of our ongoing relationship with God? What costly retaliations might we propose that follow the Lord's command and Jesus' example?

HOLINESS OF LAND
Leviticus 25:1–55

Introduction

At first glance, the two year-long observances listed in this chapter might appear to be additional festivals for marking time. As the week and year have been hallowed by their partitioning into certain "holy seasons," this glorious project now extends out into decades and centuries (for those who like orders of ten) or Sabbaths and Jubilees (for those who like orders of seven).

However, from the beginning, even while the periods for these celebrations are designated by units of time, the holy gaze of the resident Lord in these passages is directed more at earth than eons, more at dirt than decades, more at soil than centuries. Indeed, the commands contained herein begin with an imperative whose object is not human at all: "When you enter the land that I am giving you, *the land* shall observe a sabbath for the LORD" (v. 2). As we began with Leviticus seeking to expand the holiness of the Lord upward, with the ascending smoke of the Burnt Offering, so we end with Leviticus seeking to extend God's holiness downward, into the very dirt upon which God's people walk and work and worship.

The Sabbatical Year
Leviticus 25:1–7

> 25:1 The LORD spoke to Moses on Mount Sinai, saying: ² Speak to the people of Israel and say to them: When you enter the land that I am giving you, the land shall observe a sabbath for the LORD. ³ Six years you shall sow your field, and six years you shall prune your vineyard, and gather in their yield; ⁴ but in the seventh year there shall be a sabbath of complete rest for the land, a sabbath for the LORD: you shall not sow your field or prune your vineyard. ⁵ You shall not reap the aftergrowth of your harvest or gather the grapes of your unpruned vine: it shall be a year of complete rest for the land. ⁶ You may eat what the land yields during its sabbath—you, your male and

female slaves, your hired and your bound laborers who live with you; [7] for your livestock also, and for the wild animals in your land all its yield shall be for food.

While, as with dietary restrictions, many and various utilitarian rationales for the Sabbath year have been adduced (e.g., the increased productivity of soil allowed to lie fallow), the seven-year marking of this observance, like the seven-day marking of the weekly Sabbath, is essentially an attempt to extend the holy character of the Lord to the land, as well as the people and animals in this camp. As the Lord rested on the seventh day, so the land will be allowed to rest for the seventh year. Like a child mimicking a parent's daily habits—shaving, sewing, cutting the grass—people, animals, and land in Israel are called to mimic their Creator in work and in rest.

A demonstration of trust. Like the double dose of manna on the sixth day, which proves sufficient to cover the Sabbath (Exod. 16), so the yield of the land in the sabbatical year will prove sufficient sustenance for twelve months long ("You may eat what the land yields during its sabbath"; v. 6). Here, in a radical way, the Israelites are required to demonstrate that they trust divine providence as much as they trust human productivity. Put away the hoses, close up the factories, shut off the computers. One year out of seven, let the Lord alone provide, as for the birds of the air (Matt. 6).

An act of compassion. Repeatedly the Israelites are informed that they are blessed to be a blessing (Gen. 12). They have been chosen to be God's holy people so that they might share the benefits of their election with others. Here, as elsewhere, the Sabbath rest is extended not only to slaves and hired hands (it's *not* just a year off for the bosses!), but also to the land itself. Would that *we* were as diligent in sharing our blessings with *humus* as we are with *humans*!

A witness for others. As tangible a witness as it may be to close up shop and put away your tools once a week, how much more dramatic (and terrifying!) it would be to close up and put away for an entire year! The fact that arguments over what people were to do with this time never surfaced (in comparison with such arguments over what to do on the Sabbath day) makes it doubtful that this observance was ever practiced with any regularity. The fact that we consider such observances only for teachers and preachers and other "nonessential" laborers today makes it doubtful that it ever will. But if you want a model for costly discipleship, extravagant mercy, and extraordinary witness, one need look no further than the Sabbath year.

The Year of Jubilee
Leviticus 25:8–55

> 25:8 You shall count off seven weeks of years, seven times seven years, so that the period of seven weeks of years gives forty-nine years. ⁹ Then you shall have the trumpet sounded loud; on the tenth day of the seventh month—on the day of atonement—you shall have the trumpet sounded throughout all your land. ¹⁰ And you shall hallow the fiftieth year and you shall proclaim liberty throughout the land to all its inhabitants. It shall be a jubilee for you: you shall return, every one of you, to your property and every one of you to your family. ¹¹ That fiftieth year shall be a jubilee for you: you shall not sow, or reap the aftergrowth, or harvest the unpruned vines. ¹² For it is a jubilee; it shall be holy to you: you shall eat only what the field itself produces. ¹³ In this year of jubilee you shall return, every one of you, to your property.
>
> 25:23 The land shall not be sold in perpetuity, for the land is mine; with me you are but aliens and tenants. ²⁴ Throughout the land that you hold, you shall provide for the redemption of the land.

The astounding thing about Leviticus is this. As soon as its instructions have launched one untenable practice (all slaughtering at the sanctuary, no blemishes on the priests, one Sabbath year every seven), it proposes another, still more extravagant! There is a prodigality to the law in Leviticus that is found nowhere else in Scripture, except for Jesus' "fulfilling" of the law in the Gospels (Turn the other cheek, love your enemies, don't let your left hand know what your right hand is giving). Such confidence, such effusiveness, such breadth of dreaming can again be attributed to one thing and one thing only: an immediate and overwhelming experience of a Creator God come home to dwell. If the Lord of the Universe can set up tent in our campground, all things—even Jubilees—are possible. If the Lord of the Universe has not, cannot, and will not set up tent in our campground, we'll be lucky to be generous with even the change in our pockets.

First, a description of what this dream imagined; second, its implications for us.

While allowing the land to rest is laudable, simply repeating this observance proves insufficient for true rest, true restoration, true wholeness or peace to appear. Human beings are too busy developing land, buying and selling lots, and placing liens against themselves and their time, for a simple rest to lead to restoration. At the heart of Jubilee (whose name is derived from the "ram" that provides the horn marking its beginning) is the proclamation of "liberty": for the land (through release of all mortgages, liens, etc.) and for the Hebrew people (through release from all slavery and hired service). All the Israelites were commanded to return to their home plots, rest a year, and start over.

At its heart, then, the Jubilee Year's purpose was no different, though far broader, than all the other Levitical legislation. Its goal was to preserve the marks of this people who had been set apart by God. As they had been set free from Egypt, so they should remain free in the Promised Land. As you could tell that these people belonged to the Lord by the way they ate and dressed, as you could tell that these people belonged to the Lord by the way they marked their calendars, so you could now tell that these people belonged to God by the way they handled their purses, their paychecks, and their property. Every fifty years everybody returned to where they started, to demonstrate they remained aliens and tenants, though "free" aliens and tenants, on the land that now and forever belonged to God (v. 23).

Here is a dream that creates great possibilities and, given human nature, engenders great problems.

The possibilities. What would it be like to belong to a church or a synagogue where the people were united more by God's redemption than they were differentiated by neighborhood, income, and possessions? What would it be like to be in a denomination that was as eager to act on issues of minimum wages (for hourly employees), maximum salaries (for CEOs clergy), and equalization of resources for small and large congregations? What would it be like to go to a world gathering of Christians where freedom from monetary debt was taken as seriously as freedom from spiritual debt?

Without some method for restoration (and the Jubilee's method is about as simple as they come!), the tangible signs of our liberty in the Lord always threaten to get lost under the distinctions of our day-to-day existence: slave or free, owners or renters, creditors or debtors. In our day of affluenza, conspicuous consumption, and gross disparities of wealth and economic power, this is more true than ever.

The Jubilee was an attempt not only to reenact the experience of Israel's original exodus, but also an experiment in building its marks into the boundary lines and property markers of its day-to-day existence. Like a story that's been told so many times that its plot line has weakened, like a song that's been embellished so many times that its tune has lost its thread, so God's people, once settled, always threatened to lose their coherence in God. The camp had to be restored, the family lines retraced, deep down as the dirt.

The problems. The very key to the dream's success, grounding the restoration in the particularities of the land, must also stand as one of the main "practical" reasons for its failure. Not only does this restrict such practice to those in on the original "purchase," but it also led to a complex series of maneuvers that filled most of Leviticus 25 with additional legislation (if you bought a piece of land in the forty-eighth year, what should its price be in comparison to the same plot bought in the second year?). Like many clear and simple inspirations (Give God your best, rest on the seventh day, love your neighbor as yourself), Jubilee instruction collided with the human propensity for finding loopholes and using good legislation for bad ends. While there were periodic revivals of the practice of Sabbath and Passover (read the stories of 1–2 Kings), the same cannot be said of the Jubilee Year (with the exception of some of its principles, like the sanctity of ancestral lands; see the story of Naboth the Jezreelite, 1 Kgs. 21).

Thus, when Jesus stood in Nazareth and read Isaiah 61, which in turn quoted Leviticus 25, he was raising the sound of the Jubilee trumpet once more in the hearing of God's people, proclaiming a year of liberty and release made present in him (Luke 4:18–21). Viewed in one way, Jesus on that day simply joined a long line of prophets calling God's people back to a holy practice long ago discarded as "impractical." Viewed another way, Jesus—placing this day alongside the overall trajectory of his life, death, and resurrection—now grounded Jubilee practice not in the landscapes of Palestine, but in the scenes of a new kingdom, where even the Son of Man has no land to call his own.

The scary thing about this is that Jesus' dream is therefore not a reduction of the dream given in Leviticus 25 or its projection onto a "spiritual" plane. Instead, now every year becomes a Jubilee Year. Now it's no longer just a question of property and debt reduction, but traveling, and traveling "light," with no bread, no bag, no money in their belts (Mark 6:8). Now Jubilee is not so much a matter of looking backward (toward the original distribution of the land), but forward (to a kingdom where there is land enough for all). The "redemption" bought by this man spreads out in such a way that it calls for everyday debt reduction ("Give us this day . . . And forgive us our debts, as we also have forgiven our debtors"; Matt. 6:11–12), sharing of all possessions (Acts 4), and liberation for the nations as well as the people of Israel (note the distinction between slaves *from the nations* and those not yet redeemed *from Israel*; Lev. 25:44–46).

When the Lord drew near to the Israelites as they camped by Mount Sinai in the wilderness, God's presence inspired a dream in God's people of a world where the Lord's holiness might shine as brightly through sales of property as it did through sounds of prayer. If the Lord has drawn even closer in the life, death, and resurrection of Jesus of Nazareth, can Christians dream of any less?

Note. Besides such real-life issues as land reparations and debt forgiveness, Leviticus 25 also addresses the issue of charging interest to members of the family: "Do not take interest in advance or otherwise make a profit from them, but fear your God; let them live with you" (v. 36). Surely, the interpretation of these verses was no easier for Levitical priests in the past that for lien officers and loan sharks today. However, it continues to be curious how some of the verses of Leviticus are quoted repeatedly while others show up in no lectionaries or liturgies at all. Again, how would the politics of the church be affected if every quote from Leviticus 18 were necessarily accompanied by a quote from Leviticus 25?

CLOSING REWARDS AND PUNISHMENTS
Leviticus 26:1–46

26:1 **You shall make for yourselves no idols and erect no carved images or pillars, and you shall not place figured stones in your land, to worship at them; for I am the LORD your God.** [2] **You shall keep my sabbaths and reverence my sanctuary: I am the LORD.** [3] **If you follow my statutes and keep my commandments and observe them faithfully,** [4] **I will give you your rains in their season, and the land shall yield its produce, and the trees of the field shall yield their fruit.** [5] **Your threshing shall overtake the vintage, and the vintage shall overtake the sowing; you shall eat your bread to the full, and live securely in your land.** [6] **And I will grant peace in the land, and you shall lie down, and no one shall make you afraid; I will remove dangerous animals from the land, and no sword shall go through your land.** [7] **You shall give chase to your enemies, and they shall fall before you by the sword.** [8] **Five of you shall give chase to a hundred, and a hundred of you shall give chase to ten thousand; your enemies shall fall before you by the sword.** [9] **I will look with favor upon you and make you fruitful and multiply you; and I will maintain my covenant with you.** [10] **You shall eat old grain long stored, and you shall have to clear out the old to make way for the new.** [11] **I will place my dwelling in your midst, and I shall not abhor you.** [12] **And I will walk among you, and will be your God, and you shall be my people.** [13] **I am the LORD your God who brought you out of the land of Egypt, to be their slaves no more; I have broken the bars of your yoke and made you walk erect.**

26:14 **But if you will not obey me, and do not observe all these commandments,** [15] **if you spurn my statutes, and abhor my ordinances, so that you will not observe all my commandments, and you break my covenant,** [16] **I in turn** will do this to you: I will bring terror on you; consumption and fever that waste the eyes and cause life to pine away. You shall sow your seed in vain, for your enemies shall eat it. [17] I will set my face against you, and you shall be struck down by your enemies; your foes shall rule over you, and you shall flee though no one pursues you. [18] And if in spite of this you will not obey me, I will continue to punish you sevenfold for your sins. [19] I will break your proud glory, and I will make your sky like iron and your earth like copper. [20] Your strength shall be spent to no purpose: your land shall not yield its produce, and the trees of the land shall not yield their fruit.

26:40 But if they confess their iniquity and the iniquity of their ancestors, in that they committed treachery against me and, moreover, that they continued hostile to me— [41] so that I, in turn, continued hostile to them and brought them into the land of their enemies; if then their uncircumcised heart is humbled and they make amends for their iniquity, [42] then will I remember my covenant with Jacob; I will remember also my covenant with Isaac and also my covenant with Abraham, and I will remember the land. [43] For the land shall be deserted by them, and enjoy its sabbath years by lying desolate without them, while they shall make amends for their iniquity, because they dared to spurn my ordinances, and they abhorred my statutes. [44] Yet for all that, when they are in the land of their enemies, I will not spurn them, or abhor them so as to destroy them utterly and break my covenant with them; for I am the Lord their God; [45] but I will remember in their favor the covenant with their ancestors whom I brought out of the land of Egypt in the sight of the nations, to be their God: I am the Lord. [46] These are the statutes and ordinances and laws that the Lord established between himself and the people of Israel on Mount Sinai through Moses.

There have been times in the book of Leviticus where one wonders if it can get any better than this: a holy encampment of God's people with the glory of the Lord residing squarely in their midst. But soon this camp will need to start moving. And soon thereafter, they have hopes of entering the land. As incentive, perhaps, and as warning, for sure, the people of Israel now receive a vision of faithful life in the land of promise, and then (taking up three times the space!) a nightmare of unfaithful life, first in the land of promise, then in the despair of exile.

Vision of the faithful life. The law as given in Leviticus has always been primarily a guide toward expanding the glorious holiness of the Lord out through the camp into the world. When done correctly, it leads not only to avoidance of sin and pollution, but also to the abundance of life lived in the presence of God.

The vision here described seems almost Edenic in its bounty. Crops abound, people multiply, fears subside. The Lord not only dwells in the people's midst, but also walks, as God did with Adam and Eve, "among" them (v. 12). No longer cowering in servitude to the Egyptians or, out of shame, before their God, these happy people, whose yokes have been taken from them, now walk "erect" (v. 13). Here is a snapshot picture of the Aaronic benediction incarnate: the Lord not abhorring, but looking with favor upon God's people, and granting them peace (Num. 6:26).

Sadly, this priestly pattern for the hope of life well-lived on this earth is repeated elsewhere in Scripture only in apocalyptic sections, where the hope of a new heaven and a new earth supersede any program to construct such a vision here and now (cf. Mic. 4; Rev. 21). If the church, as God's people, wants to dream, here's the blueprint.

Vision of the exiled life. Strangely, few portions of Scripture sound as "modern" as some of those found in the second two-thirds of Leviticus 26: "I will make your sky like iron and your earth like copper" (v. 19). "Though you eat, you shall not be satisfied" (v. 26). "The sound of a driven leaf shall put them to flight" (v. 36).

If someone wanted to put words to the life of an elderly person imprisoned in an inner-city ghetto; a sated and yet bored resident in some posh, cul-de-sac development; or a refugee of the latest genocide in some easily ignored foreign country, here it is, in spades (cf. Deut. 28). Sadly, it is easier for us to describe with power the life of exile than the life of promise.

Here, before Israel's journey resumes, Leviticus traces out its whole unholy history: backward (to Eden) and forward (past the settlement and on into exile). Uncannily, its metaphors encompass all our destructive journeys, whether individual ("Your strength shall be spent to no purpose"; v. 20), or communal ("Ten women shall bake your bread in a single oven"; v. 26), or global ("Then the land shall enjoy its sabbath years as long as it lies desolate"; v. 34). Throwing aside or pushing down underneath all psychological, sociological, economical, political, or ecological explanations for such trajectories, Leviticus proposes this cosmic pattern: people who abhor the instructions of the Lord will find themselves abhorred as well. From the pleasing odors of the burnt offerings at Leviticus's beginning, we end with the smell of rotting carcasses at its end (vv. 30–31).

Prospect of redemption. However, any God who can dream up a Year of Jubilee cannot finally leave even a rebellious people without hope. A trait of God's character that Moses glimpsed in Exodus ("The LORD, the LORD, a God merciful and gracious, slow to anger, and abounding in steadfast love and faithfulness"; 34:6), which we will see acted out again and again in Numbers, also finally flares up even here.

"But," Leviticus 26:40 begins, "but if they confess their iniquity and the iniquity of their ancestors, . . . turn, . . . then I will remember" (vv. 40, 41, 42). Even though God's people have "abhorred my statutes," yet "for all that" God will not "abhor them so as to destroy them utterly and break my covenant with them" (vv. 43–44). Why? "For I am the LORD their God" (v. 44).

We have caught many glimpses of the Lord's holiness so far in our journey: annihilating sacrifices, protecting the holiness of the Name, dreaming dreams that burst all bounds of the human imagination and all possibilities of human fulfillment; but here we catch a glimpse of holiness far more profound. What would such holiness look like reflected in the lives of God's people?

FINAL INSTRUCTIONS REGARDING REDEMPTION
Leviticus 27:1–34

27:1 **The LORD spoke to Moses, saying:** [2] **Speak to the people of Israel and say to them: When a person makes an explicit vow to the LORD concerning the equivalent for a human being,** [3] **the equivalent for a male shall be: from twenty to sixty years of age the equivalent shall be fifty shekels of silver by the sanctuary shekel.** [4] **If the person is a female, the equivalent is thirty shekels.** [5] **If the age is from five to twenty years of age, the equivalent is twenty shekels for a male and ten shekels for a female.** [6] **If the age is from one month to five years, the equivalent for a male is five shekels of silver, and for a female the equivalent is three shekels of silver.** [7] **And if the person is sixty years old or over, then the equivalent for a male is fifteen shekels, and for a female ten shekels.** [8] **If any cannot afford the equivalent, they shall be brought before the priest and the priest shall assess them; the priest shall assess them according to what each one making a vow can afford.**

27:26 **A firstling of animals, however, which as a firstling belongs to the LORD, cannot be consecrated by anyone; whether ox or sheep, it is the LORD's.** [27] **If it is an unclean animal, it shall be ransomed at its assessment, with one-fifth added; if it is not redeemed, it shall be sold at its assessment.** [28] **Nothing that a person owns that has been devoted to destruction for the LORD, be it human or animal, or inherited landholding, may be sold or redeemed; every devoted thing is most holy to the LORD.** [29] **No human beings who have been devoted to destruction can be ransomed; they shall be put to death.** [30] **All tithes from the land, whether the seed from the ground or the fruit from the tree, are the LORD's; they are holy to the LORD.** [31] **If persons wish to redeem any of their tithes, they must add one-fifth to them.** [32] **All tithes of herd and flock, every tenth one that passes under the shepherd's**

staff, shall be holy to the LORD. [33] **Let no one inquire whether it is good or bad, or make substitution for it; if one makes substitution for it, then both it and the substitute shall be holy and cannot be redeemed.** [34] **These are the commandments that the LORD gave to Moses for the people of Israel on Mount Sinai.**

In Leviticus 25 we saw how the initial Jubilee legislation blazed up with glory and then devolved into a convoluted discussion of prorated purchase prices. So here, the initial flame of dedicatory sacrifices (encountered in the Manual of Sacrifice in Lev. 1–7) now leads to a complex method of buying one's way out of one's obligations. The initial dream may be wearing thin. The time for march is drawing nigh.

What happens if someone, like Hannah, following her initial vow to offer her son as thanksgiving to the Lord (1 Sam. 1:22), has second thoughts? Maybe the farm is failing and Samuel's hands are needed in the field. Maybe a subsequent vision has convinced her that Samuel can serve the Lord as effectively at home as in the temple. Regardless, a dedicatory vow she has made now stands to be reversed. What is the appropriate price?

A demonstration of mercy. First one must recognize all of Leviticus 27 as an accommodation to human fickleness. From the beginning, apparently, the Lord has known that our talk often outdistances our walk. In foxholes, delivery rooms, and other places of crisis (where God's glory seems particularly evident), promises are made that we find ourselves unable to keep. Rather than forcing us into a lifetime of guilt and regret, and the potential dissolution of our relationship with God, the Lord initiates a series of substitute motions that provide us a tangible way to save face.

The costs are high, usually the assessed value of the person, animal, or property plus 20 percent. All offertory animals (v. 9) and objects devoted to destruction (v. 28: those things and people [!] necessarily dedicated to God following *ḥerem* or "holy war") are off-limits.

But even within this watered-down legislation, subsequent discounts are possible (v. 8), depending on the priest's assessment of what the giver can give (to the roles of surgeon, diagnostician, and mason, we now add priestly appraiser!). The Lord is indeed a merciful Lord.

A snapshot of values. Just as you can tell what work we most value, based on comparisons of annual salaries, so you can see what the Israelites (and God?) most valued based on comparisons of "redemptive" costs (females usually half the price of males; children and old folks, 70–90% less).

Perhaps here more than anywhere else in Leviticus, the humanness of Israel's response is exposed. Not only does such pricing contradict this people's previous legislation (19:32, urging respect and deference toward the elderly), but it also goes a long way toward explaining the reaction to Jesus' radical restructuring of "prices" later ("On the way they had argued with one another who was the greatest. . . . Then he took a little child and put it among them"; Mark 9:34, 36).

Watch out when people break out calculators in church! Before long, some categories of people will be marked as "Premium Value" in the work of the kingdom, and others as "Bargain Basement." Though this instruction's intentions may be gracious, its effects may be deadly.

A glimpse of the cross. Nevertheless, even here, in this most human of Leviticus's 27 chapters, we can discern a foretaste of God's overarching purposes. Anticipating the fact that our initial enthusiasms fizzle, that we make promises we cannot keep, and that the relationship established at the beginning of Leviticus will one day fall apart, the Lord sets in place a method of redemption that will one day prove salvific: substitutionary sacrifice, the ability to substitute one price for another.

What happens when all of humankind should be "devoted to destruction" due to our rejection of a gift even greater than that of God's glory in the sanctuary? Not even *all* our lives *plus 20 percent* are sufficient to pay this vow: "No human beings who have been devoted to destruction can be ransomed" (27:29).

Thank the Lord that Leviticus 27 was *not* God's final word (or Word) on redemption. The story is moving forward. It's time to march.

B. Instructions for the March "in the Wilderness"
Numbers 1:1–10:10

Though it feels like ages have passed since Israel's exodus from Egypt in Exodus 14, we now find it has only been one year and one month: "on the first day of the second month, in the second year after they had come out of the land of Egypt" (v. 1). It took Israel approximately three months of traveling to get from Egypt to Sinai (Exod. 19:1). It will take them one month to present their preparatory offerings and participate in their pre-march Passover before they resume their journey (Num. 7; 9). That leaves nine months (an appropriate, developmental period!) for the gestation and the birth of Israel's corpus of instructions and awe-filled worship, including the construction of all the tabernacle materials and the ordination of the priests. All things considered, and despite the turgid nature of Leviticus, things are moving along at a clip (three months' journey, nine months' preparation), at least, for now.

But before the journey can begin in earnest, before a group sets out on a hike, before an expeditionary force heads out to battle, a reckoning must be made to see who is here. This is a *precautionary* measure, to keep track of any who might get lost along the way (like the teacher counting heads before a field trip, or a sergeant numbering troops before an assault). This is a *sobering* measure, reminding everyone of the dangers that lie ahead ("everyone in Israel able to go to war"; v. 3). Most of all, this is an *encouraging* measure, boosting the confidence of all those who set out (who can feel lonely in a crowd of 600,000?). Yet even in this seemingly universal and all-too-human exercise, the particularity of this people, their Lord, and their mission is evident.

6. Taking the First Census
Numbers 1:1–54

1:1 The LORD spoke to Moses in the wilderness of Sinai, in the tent of meeting, on the first day of the second month, in the second year after they had come out of the land of Egypt, saying: ² Take a census of the whole congregation of Israelites, in their clans, by ancestral houses, according to the number of names, every male individually; ³ from twenty years old and upward, everyone in Israel able to go to war. You and Aaron shall enroll them, company by company. ⁴ A man from each tribe shall be with you, each man the head of his ancestral house. ⁵ These are the names of the men who shall assist you: From Reuben, Elizur son of Shedeur. ⁶ From Simeon, Shelumiel son of Zurishaddai. ⁷ From Judah, Nahshon son of Amminadab. ⁸ From Issachar, Nethanel son of Zuar. ⁹ From Zebulun, Eliab son of Helon. ¹⁰ From the sons of Joseph: from Ephraim, Elishama son of Ammihud; from Manasseh, Gamaliel son of Pedahzur. ¹¹ From Benjamin, Abidan son of Gideoni. ¹² From Dan, Ahiezer son of Ammishaddai. ¹³ From Asher, Pagiel son of Ochran. ¹⁴ From Gad, Eliasaph son of Deuel. ¹⁵ From Naphtali, Ahira son of Enan. ¹⁶ These were the ones chosen from the congregation, the leaders of their ancestral tribes, the heads of the divisions of Israel. ¹⁷ Moses and Aaron took these men who had been designated by name, ¹⁸ and on the first day of the second month they assembled the whole congregation together. They registered themselves in their clans, by their ancestral houses, according to the number of names from twenty years old and upward, individually, ¹⁹ as the LORD commanded Moses. So he enrolled them in the wilderness of Sinai.

1:44 These are those who were enrolled, whom Moses and Aaron enrolled with the help of the leaders of Israel, twelve men, each representing his ancestral house. ⁴⁵ So the whole number of the Israelites, by their ancestral houses, from twenty years old and upward, everyone able to go to war in Israel— ⁴⁶ their whole number was six hundred three thousand five hundred fifty. ⁴⁷ The Levites, however, were not numbered by their ancestral tribe along with them. ⁴⁸ The LORD had said to Moses: ⁴⁹ Only the tribe of Levi you shall not enroll, and you shall not take a census of them with the other Israelites. ⁵⁰ Rather you shall appoint the Levites over the tabernacle of the covenant, and over all its equipment, and over all that belongs to it; they are to carry the tabernacle and all its equipment, and they shall tend it, and shall camp around the tabernacle. [51] When the tabernacle is to set out, the Levites shall take it down; and when the tabernacle is to be pitched, the Levites shall set it up. And any outsider who comes near shall be put to death. [52] The other Israelites shall camp in their respective regimental camps, by companies; [53] but the Levites shall camp around the tabernacle of the covenant, that there may be no wrath on the congregation of the Israelites; and the Levites shall perform the guard duty of the tabernacle of the covenant. [54] The Israelites did so; they did just as the LORD commanded Moses.

The scandal of particularity. It would have been easier on storytellers and commentators (not to mention lay readers!) if Numbers 1 had simply read: "Then lots of folks got ready to travel." However, the Holy Scriptures, and the Holy God they reveal, resolutely refuse such shortcuts.

From the beginning this has been a particular story about particular people ("Now the LORD said to Abram"; Gen. 12:1). Later missions will begin with equally personal gatherings ("As Jesus passed along the Sea of Galilee, he saw Simon and his brother Andrew casting a net into the sea—for they were fishermen"; Mark 1:16). The reader of this story in Numbers is forced to slow down and stumble over the pronunciation of some very particular Hebrew names (though it's still a cakewalk in comparison to Chronicles!).

Why? The reader of this story must remember who these people are: the descendants of the tribes of Jacob, to whom this same Lord had made promises. The reader of this story must see that none of the twelve tribes has been left out, even if it takes splitting Joseph's tribe into two (v. 10) to make up for the tribe of Levi, now dedicated to the tabernacle (vv. 48–54). Most important, the reader of this story must learn to trust that even or especially *in the wilderness*, this is a Lord who counts sheep down to the last one: not 600,000; not 603,000; but 603,550. Scan through your congregational roll. Watch out for fellow Christians' names in the local newspaper. Pray daily, by name, for mission personnel overseas. The Lord works through particular people to do God's particular work, yesterday, today, and forever.

The cost of census. Not only does this census take up a lot of ink (54 verses versus Genesis 1's 31!), it comes at a cost (note the "ransom" required for all such registrations in Exod. 30:11–16). There is good reason for this. Elsewhere in Scripture it becomes clear what kind of people love to take a census: kings (David in 2 Sam. 24, Augustus in Luke 2). Why? Because it is the best way to mobilize a people for the king's battles, either through active conscription or taxation. "Watch out!" the Bible seems to say. "Be careful when kings or congregations start counting numbers." This is the first step toward tyranny, coercion, and a return to the slavery of Egypt.

However, what makes Numbers 1 unique is that this is a census requested by God. This is remarkable. This is unusual (some would argue that the next divine census awaits the end of Revelation). Surely the Lord has no need for such enumeration. Certainly the Lord knows the risks of such headcounts. Given all this, we must push further.

The cost of the battle ahead. Like reading the names of those who embarked from England on the eve of D-Day, there is an ominous overtone, a sense of foreboding hanging over this census in Numbers 1 (as those who skip to Num. 26 will discover). This generation is a doomed generation. Another costly census lies ahead. Out of the 603,550 persons in this first census, only two will be among the 601,730 persons in the second. For all the military preparedness so evident in Numbers 1, they faced a threat none of them could imagine. It goes back to the matter of who has come to reside in their midst, and whether their primary threat comes from *without* or *within*.

However, before we get to Numbers 26, Numbers 1 makes it clear that the first generation was not a faceless generation to the Lord. As they know their animals, so God knows this flock. No Lord who is able to number the hairs on our heads can then prove unable to count the sheep in God's own flock, even if such lack of knowledge would be desirable.

A certain air of pathos thus hangs over Numbers 1. The Lord requests a census in order to remember. At the end of the story, it will be important not only to list those who have made it, but to remember those who have not, and all the costs along the way. Otherwise, this will prove to be a story for winners only, a gospel solely for those who succeed. As the Lord "brakes" for this processional, so should we.

7. Instructions for Camp and March
Numbers 2:1–34

2:1 The Lᴏʀᴅ spoke to Moses and Aaron, saying: ² The Israelites shall camp each in their respective regiments, under ensigns by their ancestral houses; they shall camp facing the tent of meeting on every side.

   2:17 The tent of meeting, with the camp of the Levites, shall set out in the center of the camps; they shall set out just as they camp, each in position, by their regiments.

   2:32 This was the enrollment of the Israelites by their ancestral houses; the total enrollment in the camps by their companies was six hundred three thousand five hundred fifty. ³³ Just as the Lᴏʀᴅ had commanded Moses, the Levites were not enrolled among the other Israelites. ³⁴ The Israelites did just as the Lᴏʀᴅ had commanded Moses: They camped by regiments, and they set out the same way, everyone by clans, according to ancestral houses.

It is not enough for the Lord to number the people. Now they must be ordered and arranged, both to order the camp in its resting and to arrange it for the day of march. The same Lord who delights in ordering days and nights (Gen. 1) now takes joy in the arrangement of God's people, both to sit and to move.

God's people at rest. When God's people gather in camp, it is a thing of beauty: twelve tribes arranged in four groups of three each—East, South, West, and North. Viewed one way, the arrangement marks the four corners of the earth, reminding those in the camp that their Lord is a cosmic Lord, managing on the *microlevel* the same as God has managed on the *macrolevel*. Viewed another way, the arrangement marks the fundamental way this community must be ordered: all in equal proximity to the tent of meeting at its center. At one time this tent was set up outside the camp (Exod. 33:7). Now, before the march, it is clear that it belongs in the center, with each of the tribes "facing the tent of meeting on every side" (Lev. 2:2). Like the many pictures of the twelve disciples gathered at the table, with Christ at the center, this camp is a thing of beauty and proper orientation. Would that similar care were taken in the arrangement of our homes and congregations and communities!

God's people on the move. As pretty as this snapshot may be when everybody holds still, it also is made clear that this is an arrangement conducive to movement: "They shall set out first" (v. 9), "second" (v. 16), "third" (v. 24), and "last" (v. 31) on the march. This is a camp and a people ordered in their sitting and in their rising, in their "going out" and their "coming in" (Ps. 121:8). Again, would that we could say the same for the architecture of our houses, our sanctuaries, and our communities. You can tell that these are God's people by the way they eat, dress, and now, arrange their camp, both for fellowship and for following. This is a people whom God has created and ordered *both* to be at rest and on the move.

8. Enrollment of the Levites
Numbers 3:1–4:49

3:1 This is the lineage of Aaron and Moses at the time when the LORD spoke with Moses on Mount Sinai. ² These are the names of the sons of Aaron: Nadab the firstborn, and Abihu, Eleazar, and Ithamar; ³ these are the names of the sons of Aaron, the anointed priests, whom he ordained to minister as priests. ⁴ Nadab and Abihu died before the LORD when they offered unholy fire before the LORD in the wilderness of Sinai, and they had no children. Eleazar and Ithamar served as priests in the lifetime of their father Aaron. ⁵ Then the LORD spoke to Moses, saying: ⁶ Bring the tribe of Levi near, and set them before Aaron the priest, so that they may assist him. ⁷ They shall perform duties for him and for the whole congregation in front of the tent of meeting, doing service at the tabernacle; ⁸ they shall be in charge of all the furnishings of the tent of meeting, and attend to the duties for the Israelites as they do service at the tabernacle. ⁹ You shall give the Levites to Aaron and his descendants; they are unreservedly given to him from among the Israelites. ¹⁰ But you shall make a register of Aaron and his descendants; it is they who shall attend to the priesthood, and any outsider who comes near shall be put to death. ¹¹ Then the LORD spoke to Moses, saying: ¹² I hereby accept the Levites from among the Israelites as substitutes for all the firstborn that open the womb among the Israelites. The Levites shall be mine, ¹³ for all the firstborn are mine; when I killed all the firstborn in the land of Egypt, I consecrated for my own all the firstborn in Israel, both human and animal; they shall be mine. I am the LORD.

3:40 Then the LORD said to Moses: Enroll all the firstborn males of the Israelites, from a month old and upward, and count their names. ⁴¹ But you shall accept the Levites for me—I am the LORD—as substitutes for all the firstborn among the Israelites, and the livestock of the Levites as substitutes for all the firstborn among the livestock of the Israelites. ⁴² So Moses enrolled all the firstborn among the Israelites, as the LORD commanded him. ⁴³ The total enrollment, all the firstborn males from a month old and upward, counting the number of names, was twenty-two thousand two hundred seventy-three.

4:46 All those who were enrolled of the Levites, whom Moses and Aaron and the leaders of Israel enrolled, by their clans and their ancestral houses, ⁴⁷ from thirty years old up to fifty years old, everyone who qualified to do the work of service and the work of bearing burdens relating to the tent of meeting, ⁴⁸ their enrollment was eight thousand five hundred eighty. ⁴⁹ According to the commandment of the Lord through Moses they were appointed to their several tasks of serving or carrying; thus they were enrolled by him, as the Lord commanded Moses.

As the Lord has carefully arranged the tribes *in general*, so God here commences the arrangement of the Levites *in particular*. Moses and Aaron were both of the tribe of Levi. From Aaron's sons come the priests (ordained and installed in Lev. 8–10). From the rest of the Levitical clans come the Levites (whose duties, purpose, and arrangement will be spelled out here). Though these chapters are particular and detailed in the extreme ("Over the table of the bread of the Presence they shall spread a blue cloth, and put on it the plates, the dishes for incense, the bowls, and the flagons for the drink offering; the regular bread shall also be on it; then they shall spread over them a crimson cloth, and cover it with a covering of fine leather, and shall put its poles in place"; 4:7–8), this very "excessiveness" has something to say.

Priorities for the march. While we might set aside a special squadron to guard the nuclear missiles or the travelers' checks, the priority in this camp is for "the things of God." The time for moving the tabernacle fast approaches. Since great care was taken in its construction, great care must be taken in its transport. Every peg and cord must be accounted for. Every utensil has its proper method of packing. So involved and precious is this labor that an entire tribe is set aside for its service. First, we might ask why we don't expend efforts to make our sanctuaries and the gospel they proclaim "portable." Second, would we take such care with their transmittal if we did?

Memorial of the exodus. The setting aside of the Levites for tabernacle service is meant to remind the Israelites of their being set aside by God in the exodus. As the Lord had required the lives of the Egyptians but not the Israelites, so legislation was set in place ever afterward to require the firstborn of Israel "for the Lord" (Exod. 13:1–2). However, since those freely dedicated for such service could be redeemed by payment (Lev. 27), those required for consecration were now individually "redeemed" (one for one) by the Levites (with an extra payment for the 273 left over; Num. 3:44–51). The Levites thus became a living reminder of the cost not only of humans drawing close to God ("Any outsider who comes near shall be put to death"; Num. 3:10), but also the cost of God's drawing near to human beings. When God sets up tent in the middle of camp, something must be done: if not the sacrifice of the firstborn, then the dedication of a tribe of people in their stead. Later, this set-apart people is called the church ("But you are a chosen race, a royal priesthood, a holy nation, God's own people"; 1 Pet. 2:9).

Accommodation by God. Seating arrangements are a hot topic throughout the Bible ("Declare that these two sons of mine will sit, one at your right hand and one at your left, in your kingdom"; Matt. 20:21) and throughout our lives (from sitting next to the window to pews in the sanctuary). If people sweat over the arrangements of a dinner with the president, how much more will they sweat over the camping arrangements of a people with their God!

Numbers 3–4 can thus be read *negatively* as a claim to power by the descendents of Aaron, who wanted the entrance to the tent of meeting for themselves and reserved the other sides for the tribes of Levi. Or, these chapters can be read *positively* as indicating the Lord's willingness, here in Israel's infancy, to step in and settle incipient disputes before they become dangerous. Like the parent who arranges seating in the car before the trip begins, or the captain who arranges accommodations in a ship before the voyage begins, the Lord of Numbers deigns to stoop down, call out names, assign pegs and poles to the people in God's flock before the march begins.

Jesus reminded the disciples that such arrangements in the kingdom should be left to God: "To sit at my right hand and at my left, this is not mine to grant, but it is for those for whom it has been prepared by my Father" (Matt. 20:23). Could it be that such seating charts await *the end* because we have never been comfortable or never agreed with the seats given at *the beginning*? The Lord is getting everything *and everyone* in order for this march.

9. Further Instructions #1
Numbers 5:1–6:27

In a pattern we have already seen and will see repeated throughout this journey, the time for instruction is never over. Previous topics of conversation require additions. New issues arise within the lives of God's people.

ON UNCLEAN PERSONS
Numbers 5:1–4

5:1 The LORD spoke to Moses, saying: ² Command the Israelites to put out of the camp everyone who is leprous, or has a discharge, and everyone who is unclean through contact with a corpse; ³ you shall put out both male and female, putting them outside the camp; they must not defile their camp, where I dwell among them. ⁴ The Israelites did so, putting them outside the camp; as the LORD had spoken to Moses, so the Israelites did.

Over many chapters in the middle of Leviticus, the categories of clean versus unclean have been elaborately defined. Now the Israelites continue their preparation for the march by "purifying" the camp. Clearly it makes no sense to clean swords and boots without also examining the people who are carrying and wearing them.

As stated earlier (Lev. 11–15), though we may and should vigorously protest the criteria by which such categories are determined, and though we must be ever distrustful toward those who would take such discrimination in their own hands, this was Israel's way of embodying in themselves their being "set apart" by God. Only those with "clean hands" and "clean hearts," in this sense, are ready for the hike now ahead.

Who then are the persons that need to be put out of our camp before the march begins? Jesus gave several lists of the kind of persons not fit for this journey: "No one who . . . looks back is fit for the kingdom of God"

(Luke 9:62). If the attention has shifted to fitness for the trip, and if the choice is between people dropping out now or after God's people are on the move, some pretrip screening and testing may be appropriate. Of course, part of the "running joke" of Numbers is the growing awareness that, before the trip is over, everyone (save a very elect few) will prove themselves unfit for the march. Thus they all, in some quite basic way and by their own action or inaction, will be properly designated as "outside the camp."

ON CONFESSION AND RESTITUTION
Numbers 5:5–10

> 5:5 The LORD spoke to Moses, saying: ⁶ Speak to the Israelites: When a man or a woman wrongs another, breaking faith with the LORD, that person incurs guilt ⁷ and shall confess the sin that has been committed. The person shall make full restitution for the wrong, adding one fifth to it, and giving it to the one who was wronged. ⁸ If the injured party has no next of kin to whom restitution may be made for the wrong, the restitution for wrong shall go to the LORD for the priest, in addition to the ram of atonement with which atonement is made for the guilty party. ⁹ Among all the sacred donations of the Israelites, every gift that they bring to the priest shall be his. ¹⁰ The sacred donations of all are their own; whatever anyone gives to the priest shall be his.

Uncleanness is not the only hazard to effective marching on the part of God's people. Wrongs done to others break faith with the Lord and require confession and restitution toward one's neighbor (cf. the Reparation Offerings in Lev. 4–5).

Although such breaches in community might be tolerated in camp, they cannot be allowed to continue once on the road. Now is the time to settle up, even if there's no "next of kin" (v. 8). Now is the time to square accounts, with respect to both secular and sacred donations (vv. 9–10). Now is the time, above all, for unity of purpose. Any internal squabbles can lead to disaster. A breakdown in trust between neighbors reflects and breeds distrust between the wrongdoer and God. Similar to the disencumbering required before coming to the altar ("when you are offering your gift at the altar, if you remember that your brother or sister has something against you"; Matt. 5:23), confession and restitution must precede the breaking of camp.

Even in the wilderness, even when resources are scarce and supplies tight, confession and restitution are not matters for words alone. Restoration must be in full plus 20 percent of whatever has been taken from the offended. How much more effective would our charge and benediction be every Sunday, and how much more potent our recess out of the sanctuary, if preceded by words and actions such as this?

ON A JEALOUS SPOUSE
Numbers 5:11–31

5:11 The LORD spoke to Moses, saying: ¹² Speak to the Israelites and say to them: If any man's wife goes astray and is unfaithful to him, ¹³ if a man has had intercourse with her but it is hidden from her husband, so that she is undetected though she has defiled herself, and there is no witness against her since she was not caught in the act; ¹⁴ if a spirit of jealousy comes on him, and he is jealous of his wife who has defiled herself; or if a spirit of jealousy comes on him, and he is jealous of his wife, though she has not defiled herself; ¹⁵ then the man shall bring his wife to the priest. And he shall bring the offering required for her, one-tenth of an ephah of barley flour. He shall pour no oil on it and put no frankincense on it, for it is a grain offering of jealousy, a grain offering of remembrance, bringing iniquity to remembrance. ¹⁶ Then the priest shall bring her near, and set her before the LORD; ¹⁷ the priest shall take holy water in an earthen vessel, and take some of the dust that is on the floor of the tabernacle and put it into the water. ¹⁸ The priest shall set the woman before the LORD, dishevel the woman's hair, and place in her hands the grain offering of remembrance, which is the grain offering of jealousy. In his own hand the priest shall have the water of bitterness that brings the curse. ¹⁹ Then the priest shall make her take an oath, saying, "If no man has lain with you, if you have not turned aside to uncleanness while under your husband's authority, be immune to this water of bitterness that brings the curse. ²⁰ But if you have gone astray while under your husband's authority, if you have defiled yourself and some man other than your husband has had intercourse with you," ²¹ —let the priest make the woman take the oath of the curse and say to the woman—"the LORD make you an execration and an oath among your people, when the LORD makes your uterus drop, your womb discharge; ²² now may this water that brings the curse enter your bowels and make your womb discharge, your uterus drop!" And the woman shall say, "Amen. Amen." ²³ Then the priest shall put these curses in writing, and wash them off into the water of bitterness. ²⁴ He shall make the woman drink the water of bitterness that brings the curse, and the water that brings the curse shall enter her and cause bitter pain. ²⁵ The priest shall take the grain offering of jealousy out of the woman's hand, and shall elevate the grain offering before the LORD and bring it to the altar; ²⁶ and the priest shall take a handful of the grain offering, as its memorial portion, and turn it into smoke on the altar, and afterward shall make the woman drink the water. 27 When he has made her drink the water, then, if she has defiled herself and has been unfaithful to her husband, the water that brings the curse shall enter into her and cause bitter pain, and her womb shall discharge, her uterus drop, and the woman shall become an execration among her people. 28 But if the woman has not defiled herself and is clean, then she shall be immune and be able to conceive children. 29 This is the law in cases of jealousy, when a wife, while under her husband's authority, goes astray and defiles herself, 30 or when a spirit of jealousy comes on a man and he is jealous of his wife; then he shall set the woman before the LORD, and the priest shall apply this entire law to her. 31 The man shall be free from iniquity, but the woman shall bear her iniquity.

If breaches among neighbors threaten the cohesion of the march, how much more so divisions within marriages! Again, what is interesting is how little attention is given to the provisions of the march (swords and spears, cattle and oxen, food and drink) and how much attention is given to the relationships among the troops. If the relationship between Israel and the Lord and relationship between Israelite and Israelite are maintained, Numbers seems to assume, this march will be successful. If not, it will surely fail.

Nevertheless, the harshness of the procedure here described ("He shall make the woman drink the water of bitterness that brings the curse"; v. 24); its limitation to suspect wives and not husbands ("if any man's wife goes astray and is unfaithful to him"; v. 12); and the ease with which this entire ordeal may be induced ("if a spirit of jealousy comes on him"; v. 14) are causes for grave concern and hesitation. How can we, so painfully aware of the hidden abuses modern husbands are already dealing out upon their wives, in any way endorse the wisdom of such public abuse?

The deadliness of jealousy. The best thing that can be said about this instruction is that it at least recognizes that something must be done. Jealousy is as much a part of the human heart as the cholesterol and plaque we so assiduously measure. Moreover, once present, it shall find some out: through destructive behavior directed toward the spouse, toward the person himself, or toward the community at large.

Again, relationships are so critical for this journey that something must be done. We cannot simply stare at our shoes and hope it will pass, as we so often do when we are confronted with such possibilities in conversations at a church supper or in a church parking lot. Better to resolve such conflict publicly, immediately, and following some sort of orderly procedure, than simply label it a "private matter" that we hope works itself out.

Place it in God's hands. As heinous as this particular procedure was and is ("Now may this water that brings the curse enter your bowels and make your womb discharge, your uterus drop!" v. 22), it must at least be credited with taking the decision out of the hands of a single male, or even a roomful of males, with the power to accuse and convict. The very fact that this particular problem of the heart was lifted out of the other instructions and given extra space and an elaborate ordeal is an indication that God's people knew they were messing with judgments beyond their ken.

Anyone who has ever tried to adjudicate between the partners of a splintering marriage knows that the waters of bitterness and curses are as apt to reveal the truth of such secrets as hours of counseling and referrals. We are wading in deep waters here. While harmony of husband and wife is as necessary for this journey as food and water, it may well take a greater miracle of God to produce the former than the latter.

The Lord as jealous husband. All under, above, and through this painstaking and pains-making ordeal, Israel undoubtedly hears the echoes of another story: a people suspected of unfaithfulness toward their Lord and thus liable for an ordeal (Exod. 20:5; Jer. 8:14). All through the prophetic materials, Israel is portrayed as the harlot, making room for God's role as the jealous spouse (e.g., Hos. 2). In fact, before Israel reaches the Promised Land, this breach of relationship shall be acted out by the vast majority of this first generation that remains ("Thus Israel yoked itself to the Baal of Peor"; Num. 25:3).

However, if the Lord responds to such jealousy, finally, not with an ordeal (at least, not a *terminal* one), but with mercy, how could any man (or woman) so forgiven justify such subsequent action toward another ("Should you not have mercy on your fellow slave, as I had mercy on you?" Matt. 18:33)? Surely as we laid the Levitical treatment of lepers alongside Jesus' treatment of the same, we must place this procedure for dealing with supposed unfaithfulness beside Jesus' ordeal in John 8 ("Jesus bent down and wrote with his finger on the ground. When they kept on questioning him, he straightened up and said to them, 'Let anyone among you who is without sin be the first to throw a stone at her'"; vv. 6–7).

Given these theological and practical problems with the ordeal proposed in Numbers, it goes without saying that this particular procedure for rectifying marital jealousy is one that must be abandoned. But that leaves us with this question, "How *will* the church point toward the miracle of forgiveness before the march begins—between husbands and wives, one servant and another, the people and their God?" This is not a question any serious travelers can or should long ignore.

ON NAZIRITES
Numbers 6:1–21

6:1 The Lord spoke to Moses, saying: ² Speak to the Israelites and say to them: When either men or women make a special vow, the vow of a nazirite, to separate themselves to the Lord, ³ they shall separate themselves from wine and strong drink; they shall drink no wine vinegar or other vinegar, and shall not drink any grape juice or eat grapes, fresh or dried. ⁴ All their days as nazirites they shall eat nothing that is produced by the grapevine, not even the seeds or the skins. ⁵ All the days of their nazirite vow no razor shall come upon the head; until the time is completed for which they separate themselves to the Lord, they shall be holy; they shall let the locks of the head grow long. ⁶ All the days that they separate themselves to the Lord they shall not go near a corpse. ⁷ Even if their father or mother, brother or sister, should die, they may not defile themselves; because their consecration to God is upon the head. ⁸ All their days as nazirites they are holy to the Lord.

After all the stipulations for "ordinary" holiness that have gone before, it is a wonder that some few in the camp, before embarking, would want to set themselves off further "for the Lord." Ordinary diet, hairstyles, and neighborly contacts were not sufficient for these few. They wanted to do more!

Requirements for Nazirites. In reality, there were no areas of restriction for the Nazirites that the ordinary Israelite did not also "mark off." The "setting apart" of the Nazirites just went further.

While the ordinary Israelite forswore the eating of certain foods, the Nazirite added to this list drink (wine and all grape products, perhaps the choicest of the Promised Land's fruits that these refugees anticipated; see the grape cluster in Num. 13:23). While the ordinary Israelite marked himself by refusing to round off the forelocks or trim the beard (Lev. 19:27), the Nazirite let all his hair grow (perhaps as a way of "remembering" the "wildness" of the wilderness, where such grooming was undoubtedly a luxury). While the ordinary Israelites were obligated to follow certain procedures following contact with a corpse (Num. 19), and the priests were forbidden to come near any corpse except those of closest kin (Lev. 21), the Nazirites forswore contact even with the corpse of father and mother (perhaps to make clear who their true parent was).

The Nazirite law was thus a last-minute provision for those who wanted to go further in their dedication and response. In an age more filled with loopholes than extra hoops through which to leap (especially in relation to God's service!), the existence of Numbers 6 is cause for thanksgiving.

The contributions of Nazirites in Scripture. Throughout the biblical story, God reserves a place for those dedicated few who desire to go further. Whether it is a Samson (Judg. 13) or Samuel (1 Samuel) in the Old Testament, or John the Baptist (Matt. 3) in the New, at crucial times more extravagant and dedicated leadership is necessary. Here provisions are made for people willing to pay this higher price, even if, as is the case in this chapter, it is for a limited time ("After that [the ceremony marking the end of the Nazirite's temporary vow] the nazirites may drink wine"; v. 20).

The fulfillment of the Nazirite vow. For this very reason, it is highly significant that when the Lord's Messiah comes, he comes not as a Nazirite (marked off by the peculiar vows he or his parents have made), but as a Nazarene (marked off simply by the lowly locale of his upbringing). While he might have met the Nazirite code regarding family ("And he replied, 'Who are my mother and my brothers?'" Mark 3:33), it is clear that he took no special vow regarding wine and grape products (in Luke 7:34 he's accused of drunkenness by his contemporaries; in John 15:1 he refers to himself as the "true vine"; and in Mark 14:23 he uses wine as one of the central symbols of the Eucharist). Jesus seems to insist that if one wants to go further in terms of dedication, it is better to focus on what you *do* (love God and love neighbor) than what you *don't do.*

(Jesus' parable of the Good Samaritan requires the neighbor to violate two out of three laws for the Nazirite [potential contact with the dead and the use of wine; Luke 10:25–37] *in order to serve the man in the ditch.* If one is searching for extraordinary ways to witness to God's holiness, according to Jesus, this is the way to go.)

REGARDING BENEDICTION
Numbers 6:22–27

> 6:22 The LORD spoke to Moses, saying: [23] Speak to Aaron and his sons, saying, Thus you shall bless the Israelites: You shall say to them, [24] The LORD bless you and keep you; [25] the LORD make his face to shine upon you, and be gracious to you; [26] the LORD lift up his countenance upon you, and give you peace. [27] So they shall put my name on the Israelites, and I will bless them.

Several instructions have intervened to explain last-minute measures by which God's people might mark themselves in relation to God and to one another. Now the list concludes with some of the most familiar words in Numbers, citing a final way that God might mark them off as the Lord's: the priestly benediction.

Postlude or prelude. Due to the benediction's location at the end of public worship, it is often viewed as a way of "finishing up" rather than "starting out." Its location here in Numbers 6, as part of the final preparations for the journey, makes clear its basic function. As the benediction, properly viewed, equips the congregation for its sending out, so the priestly benediction, properly interpreted, is the last piece of equipment offered to every Israelite before the journey begins. Again, more important than bread or water, it is relational at its core.

I will go with you. This benediction moves forward in three movements (which thus mark it as "complete" or "whole"). Each movement begins with the same subject explicitly repeated ("the LORD") driving home its essential content and contributor. Each line concludes with two proffered gifts of the subject, which complement and complete each other, and build and cascade over one another, like a cup that overflows (in Hebrew, v. 24 has three words; v. 25 has five; v. 26 has seven). At their heart, the promised blessings have to do with presence ("bless," "make face shine," "lift up his countenance"), the gift that bears other fruits in its wake ("keep," "gracious," "peace").

Back at the beginning of this story, these travelers were promised one thing to mark them as unique. Not special horses, not superior weapons, not elaborate shields or armor. The Lord promised, "My presence will go with you" (Exod. 33:14), and *that*, it is implied, should be enough (even to bring "rest," as in Exod. 33:14; or "peace," as in Num. 6:26). When Israel is afraid, all it has to do is look to the Lord's glory at its center. To know that Israel is unique, all that others need to do is look for the fruits such presence provides ("The fruit of the Spirit is love, joy, *peace*, patience, kindness, generosity, faithfulness, gentleness, and self-control"; Gal. 5:22–23, emphasis added).

A final dress code. Perhaps it is not too big a stretch to claim that everything so far has been an attempt to spread God's glory out onto God's people—before they start to march. What has first been attempted *by action*, is now attempted *in words*: "So they [the priests] shall put my name on the Israelites" (v. 27). If this benediction works—even as they travel, even after many miles, even when they walk through dark valleys and light-squelching storms—they will be recognizable as "The LORD's, the LORD's, the LORD's." As the Lord's glory shone forth from the face of Moses (Exod. 34), so now the Lord's glory should be reflected in every face set for the march ("the LORD make his face to shine upon you"; Lev. 6:25).

10. Final Preparations
Numbers 7:1–10:10

The clock is ticking. The hour to break camp is nigh. The time for sitting in camp is almost over. The day to march has come.

PRESENTATION OF OFFERINGS
Numbers 7:1–89

7:1 On the day when Moses had finished setting up the tabernacle, and had anointed and consecrated it with all its furnishings, and had anointed and consecrated the altar with all its utensils, ² the leaders of Israel, heads of their ancestral houses, the leaders of the tribes, who were over those who were enrolled, made offerings. ³ They brought their offerings before the LORD, six covered wagons and twelve oxen, a wagon for every two of the leaders, and for each one an ox; they presented them before the tabernacle. ⁴ Then the LORD said to Moses: ⁵ Accept these from them, that they may be used in doing the service of the tent of meeting, and give them to the Levites, to each according to his service. ⁶ So Moses took the wagons and the oxen, and gave them to the Levites. ⁷ Two wagons and four oxen he gave to the Gershonites, according to their service; ⁸ and four wagons and eight oxen he gave to the Merarites, according to their service, under the direction of Ithamar son of Aaron the priest. ⁹ But to the Kohathites he gave none, because they were charged with the care of the holy things that had to be carried on the shoulders. ¹⁰ The leaders also presented offerings for the dedication of the altar at the time when it was anointed; the leaders presented their offering before the altar. ¹¹ The LORD said to Moses: They shall present their offerings, one leader each day, for the dedication of the altar.

7:89 When Moses went into the tent of meeting to speak with the LORD, he would hear the voice speaking to him from above the mercy seat that was on the ark of the covenant from between the two cherubim; thus it spoke to him.

As the time for departure draws *very* close, a peculiar procession of wagons and oxen forms in the midst of Israel's camp. Once they are in place, a twelve-day series of presentations takes place at the central tent of meeting. What is this? An advance party gathering to move out as forerunners for the people? A preparatory deposition of supplies in the central store? No. Before beginning their perilous journey through the wilderness, and as a finishing touch on the worship of the tabernacle that will travel in their midst, God's people willingly offer up some of the prize pieces in their inventory: twelve silver plates, twelve golden dishes, six covered wagons, twelve load-carrying oxen, and so on and on. What a crazy approach to survival!

And yet, again, if the primary ensign under which Israel marches is God's presence, which goes with them, and their most essential supply is the power, direction, and sustenance this relationship provides them, then what better way is there to prepare for their wilderness procession than with the preliminary parade to the sanctuary, willingly performed by a representative from every tribe?

This offering balances extravagance toward God (silver, gold, choice flour) and practicality toward one another (wagons and oxen for those who need them: the Gershonites and the Merarites; none for those who do not: the Kohathites, vv. 7–9). Each tribe's offering, though listed separately, is identical (down to the last lamb!), avoiding any squabbles over who had given more (a source of dispute as ancient as Abel and Cain; Gen. 4). Note finally the beauty of the repetition ("On the second day," v. 18; "On the third day," v. 24; "On the twelfth day," v. 78. "This was the offering of Nahshon son of Amminadab," v. 17; "of Nethanel son of Zuar," v. 23; "of Ahira son of Enan," v. 83), so superfluous to the modern-day editor (or lectionary committee!), yet so essential for this portrait of God's people at their best (the Lord too knows the danger of leaving out someone's name when giving thanks!).

It cannot be accidental, then, that the first citation of sanctuary conversation between God and Moses since the preparations began (v. 89) follows this elaborate ritual of offering up their best. As the descent of God's glory awaited the presentation of humankind's best craftsmanship (Exod. 40), so the initiation of sanctuary conversation awaits this initial offering of humankind's most essential gifts. Such offerings do *not* serve as the fee for God's speaking. Rather, this demonstration of trust (again heightened by Israel's proximity to travel) properly positions the people for hearing.

The voice that speaks from above the mercy seat and between the two cherubim is not just any voice. It is the voice of the Lord, whose presence can provoke even such extravagant giving.

What this implies for the placement of "the Offering" in public worship, we can leave to the liturgical experts (offering as response to the word, or preparation for the word). But what this implies for proper positioning of God's people vis-à-vis the Lord's speaking surely applies to us all. Clearly, we must be willing to set aside our best time and energy and objects of trust if we wish to hear the Lord's word for us today.

SETTING UP LAMPS
Numbers 8:1–4

8:1 The LORD spoke to Moses, saying: ² Speak to Aaron and say to him: When you set up the lamps, the seven lamps shall give light in front of the lampstand. ³ Aaron did so; he set up its lamps to give light in front of the lampstand, as the LORD had commanded Moses. ⁴ Now this was how the lampstand was made, out of hammered work of gold. From its base to its flowers, it was hammered work; according to the pattern that the LORD had shown Moses, so he made the lampstand.

As the people have proved obedient in their offering, now Aaron and the Levites are placed in action. God speaks and, for now, the people follow through.

The only sanctuary furnishing given special attention at this time is the preparation of the lampstand for service. More particularly, Aaron is reminded of the positioning of the lamps in connection with the lampstand, so as to provide light in front of the stand (v. 2). What is *in front* of the lampstand? The things of God: ark, table, and bread of presence. What is behind the stand? The worshiper, who has come in search of God's presence.

Before setting out, the people are in effect reminded: "As much as you might like a light to illumine the path *ahead*, or the faces of your fellow travelers *beside* you, if you light one light, shine it on *these things*. It is the vision of these things that will keep you moving forward even when the way is not clear."

Maybe we can imagine the disciple thrown into a dungeon, asking her fellow prisoners for a light. "Why?" they ask her. "To search out an escape? To better eat your meals? To ward off the attacks of fellow prisoners?" "No," she replies, "so that I might read the Scriptures." Some things *can* keep you moving forward, even when the way is not clear.

Again observe the pattern. God said (v. 1). And Aaron did (v. 3). Final preparations are still on track.

CONSECRATION OF LEVITES
Numbers 8:5–26

8:5 The LORD spoke to Moses, saying: ⁶ Take the Levites from among the Israelites and cleanse them. ⁷ Thus you shall do to them, to cleanse them: sprinkle the water of purification on them, have them shave their whole body with a razor and wash their clothes, and so cleanse themselves. ⁸ Then let them take a young bull and its grain offering of choice flour mixed with oil, and you shall take another young bull for a sin offering. ⁹ You shall bring the Levites before the tent of meeting, and assemble the whole congregation of the Israelites. ¹⁰ When you bring the Levites before the LORD, the Israelites shall lay their hands on the Levites, ¹¹ and Aaron shall present the Levites before the LORD as an elevation offering from the Israelites, that they may do the service of the LORD. ¹² The Levites shall lay their hands on the heads of the bulls, and he shall offer the one for a sin offering and the other for a burnt offering to the LORD, to make atonement for the Levites. ¹³ Then you shall have the Levites stand before Aaron and his sons, and you shall present them as an elevation offering to the LORD. ¹⁴ Thus you shall separate the Levites from among the other Israelites, and the Levites shall be mine.

In a basic way, the consecration of the Levites in Numbers 8 parallels the ordination of the priests in Leviticus 8. If there is to be worship in the tabernacle, priests must be set apart. If the tabernacle is to travel, Levites must be set apart.

However, the fact that there are differences is made clear in ways other than these chapters' headings: "ordination" for the priests, and "consecration" for the Levites. There are peculiarities in terminology: "You shall present them as an elevation offering to the LORD" (v. 13), referring to the Levites! There are variations on the rituals: the Israelites lay their hands on the Levites (v. 10), versus the priests laying their hands on the sacrificial animals. Rather than a ritual of empowerment ("ordination"), this is a matter of transference and identification, as in the Burnt Offering ("You shall lay your hand on the head of the burnt offering, and it shall be acceptable in your behalf as atonement for you"; Lev. 1:4). Before being sacrificed to the Lord's service on the firstborn's behalf, those about to "slay" them place their hands upon them, both to atone and to dedicate, to "consecrate."

All of this opens up a new dimension on our understanding of the Levites and the question of human sacrifice. Technically speaking, the Scriptures do not forbid human sacrifice. What they *do* forbid is anything so simple, expeditious, and noncostly (at least to the presenter) as literal child sacrifice. As God has "bought" the firstborn of Israel in the Passover, so they must be redeemed by others, others whose entire lives are lived out as sacrifice. "Present yourselves," the Levites might have been ordered, "as living sacrifices, holy and acceptable to God, which is your spiritual worship" (cf. Rom. 12:1).

As stated before, and dramatically enacted here, the Levites become a living reminder of the price of Israel's redemption. Even the Lord, through the dedication of the Levites, requires one life (that of the Levites) for another (the Egyptians), "life for life" (Lev. 24:18). The Lord never takes the spilling of human blood (even Egyptian), or the wasting of human life (our own?) lightly. They are precious in God's sight. Lest we forget, look at the Levites. Look at the cross.

OBSERVATION OF PASSOVER
Numbers 9:1–14

9:1 The LORD spoke to Moses in the wilderness of Sinai, in the first month of the second year after they had come out of the land of Egypt, saying: 2 Let the Israelites keep the passover at its appointed time. 3 On the fourteenth day of this month, at twilight, you shall keep it at its appointed time; according to all its statutes and all its regulations you shall keep it. 4 So Moses told the Israelites that they should keep the passover. 5 They kept the passover in the first month, on the fourteenth day of the month, at twilight, in the wilderness of Sinai. Just as the LORD had commanded Moses, so the Israelites did. 6 Now there were certain people who were unclean through touching a corpse, so that they could not keep the passover on that day. They came before Moses and Aaron on that day, 7 and said to him, "Although we are unclean through touching a corpse, why must we be kept from presenting the LORD's offering at its appointed time among the Israelites?" 8 Moses spoke to them, "Wait, so that I may hear what the LORD will command concerning you." 9 The LORD spoke to Moses, saying: 10 Speak to the Israelites, saying: Anyone of you or your descendants who is unclean through touching a corpse, or is away on a journey, shall still keep the passover to the LORD. 11 In the second month on the fourteenth day, at twilight, they shall keep it; they shall eat it with unleavened bread and bitter herbs. 12 They shall leave none of it until morning, nor break a bone of it; according to all the statute for the passover they shall keep it. 13 But anyone who is clean and is not on a journey, and yet refrains from keeping the passover, shall be cut off from the people for not presenting the LORD's offering at its appointed time; such a one shall bear the consequences for the sin. 14 Any alien residing among you who wishes to keep the passover to the LORD shall do so according to

the statute of the passover and according to its regulation; you shall have one statute for both the resident alien and the native.

As the first Passover marked the eve of Israel's transition from Pharaoh's people to the Lord's people, so this second Passover marks the eve of Israel's transition from a people in training to a people on the move. Like other enacted signs (Jesus' baptism, Jesus' transfiguration, Jesus' transformation of the Passover in the upper room), this meal is meant to equip Israel for the new exodus about to begin. The aftertaste of slaughtered lamb, unleavened bread, and bitter herbs should prove food for thought (and action) in the days and weeks ahead.

So important is this send-off supper now recognized to be that negative and positive legislation is here enacted in order to "make full" the number of people at this table.

Negative warnings. The rise and fall of Passover observance is seen throughout Israel's history as one sure test for diagnosing the nation's spiritual health. What is true for the group is also true for the individual. Here, for perhaps the first time, the sin of omission is cited as being as heinous as the sin of commission. Namely, it is as bad *not* to partake when clean, as it is *to partake* when unclean (v. 13). The threat of "cutting off" is the same threat levied against the long list of ritual violations in Leviticus 20.

Perhaps this should serve as fair warning to all those who neglect the means of grace regularly available in Christ's church, or who fail to observe them as frequently as they are allowed. Maybe the church should be as concerned with "flushing out the flock" on Communion Sunday as it has sometimes been with "fencing the Table" on the same!

Positive expansions. Here in Numbers 9, the seating at the Passover table is extended in two ways.

First, a provision is made for "alternative communion." All those who find themselves unclean or away on Passover evening are now provided an alternative celebration ("In the *second* month on the fourteenth day"; v. 11). The master of this banquet always wants more folks at this table ("so that my house may be filled"; Luke 14:23), whether this means delivering the meal to shut-ins or even something so radical as a Saturday night Eucharist. Question: Should the servants at the table be less generous than the host?

Second, provisions are also made for the outsider. Legislation elsewhere makes it clear that Passover is forbidden to the "foreigner" (such as the bound or hired servant and the uncircumcised slave; Exod. 12:43–44); yet here, with regard to "resident" aliens (cf. Exod. 12:48–49), the emphasis is more on inclusion than exclusion.

The people are about to begin a journey. This meal could bring sustenance for all. Now, the required inclusion of the Sabbath ("your male or
female slave, your livestock, or the alien resident in your towns"; Exod.
20:10) begins to encroach on Israel's most intimate festivities ("You
shall have one statute for both the resident alien and the native"; v. 14).
How should this invitation influence *our* invitations to other "secular" and
"sacred" meals?

APPEARANCE OF CLOUD AND FIRE
Numbers 9:15–23

9:15 **On the day the tabernacle was set up, the cloud covered the tabernacle, the tent of the covenant; and from evening until morning it was over the
tabernacle, having the appearance of fire. ¹⁶ It was always so: the cloud covered it by day and the appearance of fire by night. ¹⁷ Whenever the cloud
lifted from over the tent, then the Israelites would set out; and in the place
where the cloud settled down, there the Israelites would camp.**

9:23 **At the command of the LORD they would camp, and at the command
of the LORD they would set out. They kept the charge of the LORD, at the command of the LORD by Moses.**

Up to this point, ever since the descent of the cloud in Exodus 40 and the
appearance of God's glory in Leviticus 9, most of the action has been
human action, either prescribed for the future (e.g., the host of instructions) or commanded in the present (e.g., the rites of dedication, the light-
ing of the lamps). Now, as the parade is about to begin, a subtle shift of
emphasis occurs.

In painstaking detail, the movements of the cloud, which covers the tabernacle, are described. Sometimes the cloud would rise from the tabernacle
in the morning and return over the tabernacle at night. These were "traveling days" for Israel, days on which Israel, as a people, "set out" (v. 17). Other
times the cloud would remain over the tent for "a few days" (v. 20) or even
for "many days" (v. 19). Sometimes the cloud would rise in the morning and
still stay ahead as a pillar of fire at night (v. 21), and Israel would find itself
on a twenty-four-hour maneuver—all at the cue of the Lord.

Here something different is getting ready to happen, a difference that
reveals a key distinction between most of the material in Leviticus and
most of the material to follow in Numbers. It is one thing to mark off the
holy on "settled" days, when God's people are in camp, and one day flows

into another. There you mark off activity primarily through predetermined dates and schedules, as regular as the waning and waxing of the moon.

At other times, however, it is time to travel, and a much more intimate relation between God and God's people is required. When you head out, you don't know if it is for a one-day trip or two. When you pitch your tent, it is unclear whether it is for a one-night or a one-month stay. There is an intimacy between Leader and led, and among all those who travel with you "in the wilderness," that is hard to replicate once you are "in the land." There is a drama to the rising and setting of the cloud that is hard to compare to the comings and goings of priestly ritual, no matter how elaborate.

Here, no doubt, is the reason behind Israel's deep and treasured memories of this time "in the wilderness." Not only did the Lord lead Israel personally as a shepherd (Ps. 23), but also (miracle of miracles!) Israel was willing so to follow: "At the command of the LORD they would camp, and at the command of the LORD they would set out. They kept the charge of the LORD, at the command of the LORD by Moses" (v. 23).

The question for Israel and for the church is this: How do we replicate such intimate trust and obedience once we are "in the land," or at least provisionally, " in the kingdom"? Even in the midst of the ordered holiness so magnificently portrayed thus far in Leviticus and Numbers, doesn't there remain some need for a more "disordered" trust that is focused on a God who is moving?

Surely it is not accidental that one summary of Jewish law is the injunction to *walk* humbly with our God (Mic. 6:8). Surely it is not accidental that the primary command on Jesus' lips is not "observe," "do," or "remember," but "*follow*." Israel and the church are a people whose God dwells with them *and* goes before them.

MAKING TRUMPETS
Numbers 10:1–10

10:1 **The LORD spoke to Moses, saying:** [2] **Make two silver trumpets; you shall make them of hammered work; and you shall use them for summoning the congregation, and for breaking camp.** [3] **When both are blown, the whole congregation shall assemble before you at the entrance of the tent of meeting.** [4] **But if only one is blown, then the leaders, the heads of the tribes of Israel, shall assemble before you.** [5] **When you blow an alarm, the camps on the east side shall set out;** [6] **when you blow a second alarm, the camps on the south side shall set out. An alarm is to be blown whenever they are to set** out. ⁷ But when the assembly is to be gathered, you shall blow, but you shall not sound an alarm. ⁸ The sons of Aaron, the priests, shall blow the trumpets; this shall be a perpetual institution for you throughout your generations. ⁹ When you go to war in your land against the adversary who oppresses you, you shall sound an alarm with the trumpets, so that you may be remembered before the LORD your God and be saved from your enemies. ¹⁰ Also on your days of rejoicing, at your appointed festivals, and at the beginnings of your months, shall blow the trumpets over your burnt offerings and over your sacrifices of well-being; they shall serve as a reminder on your behalf before the LORD your God: I am the LORD your God.

Here, immediately before the journey, a last instrument is added to God's "holy" panoply: trumpets, marching trumpets, are to be hammered out.

What is most interesting is the way these marching instruments, almost before their construction, are converted to sedentary instruments as well. Almost immediately the players are warned to distinguish between an alarm (to get the tribes moving in march) and a blow (to assemble the tribes for consultation and festival). The trumpet thus becomes the preeminent instrument to mark both Israel's "goings out" and its "comings in" (Ps. 121).

Providentially, in many churches a similar function developed, the ringing of bells. Bells would be rung at the beginning of the service to call the people in ("time for church!") and at the end of service to send the people out ("time to serve!"). What happens to a practice or people, then, when all the signals that originally served to *get them moving*, now serve, almost exclusively, to gather them to *sit*? Crosses, according to Jesus, are meant to be carried, not hung on the wall.

Get ready! The parade is about to begin!

Part 2: In the Wilderness, the Journey of God's People

Numbers 10:1—21:9

Finally the day of march has come!

After endless hours of instruction, after countless dress rehearsals, after reading through list after list of sacrifices, skin eruptions, and family trees, we are ready to go. You can hear the creak of wagon wheels. You can hear the rumble of cattle. Above it all ring the shouts of God's people, "Arise, O Lord, let your enemies be scattered, and your foes flee before you!" (v. 35).

Like a high school graduation class squealing out of the parking lot, like a group of crack recruits on the first day of maneuvers, like a congregation recessing at the close of the perfect worship service, God's people are now on the move, and God's moving with them. "Lift high the cross!" "Onward Christian soldiers!" "The Day of Resurrection!" It doesn't get any better than this!

11. The People Start to March
Numbers 10:11–36

10:11 **In the second year, in the second month, on the twentieth day of the month, the cloud lifted from over the tabernacle of the covenant.** [12] **Then the Israelites set out by stages from the wilderness of Sinai, and the cloud settled down in the wilderness of Paran.** [13] **They set out for the first time at the command of the LORD by Moses.**

10:29 **Moses said to Hobab son of Reuel the Midianite, Moses' father-in-law, "We are setting out for the place of which the LORD said, 'I will give it to you'; come with us, and we will treat you well; for the LORD has promised good to Israel."** [30] **But he said to him, "I will not go, but I will go back to my own land and to my kindred."** [31] **He said, "Do not leave us, for you know where we should camp in the wilderness, and you will serve as eyes for us.** [32] **Moreover, if you go with us, whatever good the LORD does for us, the same we will do for you."** [33] **So they set out from the mount of the LORD three days' journey with the ark of the covenant of the LORD going before them three days' journey, to seek out a resting place for them,** [34] **the cloud of the LORD being over them by day when they set out from the camp.** [35] **Whenever the ark set out, Moses would say, "Arise, O LORD, let your enemies be scattered, and your foes flee before you."** [36] **And whenever it came to rest, he would say, "Return, O LORD of the ten thousand thousands of Israel."**

This is the day the Lord has made. Surely the key ingredient in the glory of this day is the fact that the Lord is so obviously and dramatically "in charge." The careful citation of the day ("In the second year, in the second month, on the twentieth day of the month"; v. 11) shows that this is not just any day, but a divinely appointed day (cf. "In the fifteenth year of the reign of Emperor Tiberius"; Luke 3:1). The people are moving not under their own command or even the command of Moses, but "for the first time at the command of the LORD by Moses" (v. 13). Not only has the cloud lifted and gone before them (v. 11), not only is the ark of the Lord in front and seeking out a place for them to rest (v. 33), but also the Lord God, in person, has in some sense arisen to go with them, setting loose panic in their enemies and flight in their foes (v. 35). This is one of those rare days when the Lord's hand is evident and God's way is clear.

Let us rejoice and be glad in it. Every now and then, a hymn is sung the way it's supposed to be sung, a day is lived the way it's supposed to be lived, a congregation moves out in service the way it's supposed to move out in service. This day, for Israel, is just such a day. For once, everything and everyone is in order. For once, no one is arguing about what they should do. Like that great day when God said, "Go," and Abram went, or when Jesus said, "Come, follow," and the disciples came and followed, this is a time when God's creatures do what they are created to do.

It is thus a picture of Israel and the church triumphant, like the Temple visions of Ezekiel (beginning in the fortieth chapter) or the kingdom visions of John ("After this I looked, and there was a great multitude that no one could count, from every nation, from all tribes and peoples and languages, standing before the throne and before the Lamb, robed in white, with palm branches in their hands. They cried out in a loud voice, saying, 'Salvation belongs to our God who is seated on the throne, and to the Lamb!'" Rev. 7:9–10). A little of God's glory has, for once, rubbed off on God's people. Veils, anyone (cf. Exod. 34:29–35; 2 Cor. 3:12–18)?

Who wouldn't want to be a member of a congregation like this? Not much evangelism goes on in the Pentateuch. God's people have enough trouble tending to their own. But here again, for once, the promise God made to Abram comes true ("I will bless you . . . so that you will be a blessing, . . . and in you all the families of the earth shall be blessed"; Gen. 12:2–3).

True, the nations are here represented by one father-in-law, Hobab (v. 29). True, Moses hopes to get something out of the bargain ("You will serve as eyes for us"; v. 31). But Moses knows and we know who will get the better end of this bargain ("Moreover, if you go with us, whatever good the LORD does for us, the same we will do for you"; v. 32). Yes, Hobab has to leave land and kindred (v. 30). But God's people have promised to treat him well, the Lord has promised them good, and maybe, just maybe, this "foreigner" will not only be spared destruction (see the story of the Midianites in Num. 25 and 31), but also this scout's eyes will get to see something, Someone far more glorious than a camp.

"My Lord, what a mornin'!" You almost don't want to turn the page. You're tempted to just sit tight and maybe build a booth to keep this glory in (cf. Peter's response to Christ's transfiguration in Mark 9:5). But remember, the glory of this day has to do with movement. God and God's people are on the move. This is a story of a journey!

Note. One of the problems many people have with the book of Numbers in general, and this picture of God's people "on the move" in particular, is how deeply the words and images are immersed in the world of war. This is no church picnic. This is a battalion on maneuvers!

We must surely come back to this issue later, when this army shifts from *taking casualties* (due to the Lord's discipline) to *making casualties* (with the edge of the sword). For now, let us remember that this is a story remembered and reremembered by a people whose dreams of military conquest had received a mortal blow in their defeat and captivity at the hands of a military machine known as Babylon.

Thus, although some in the synagogue, as some in the church, might begin to dream dreams of blitzkrieg and zealotry as they listen to this story of God's people on the march, doing so would involve forgetting the wider context in which this "day of glory" takes place. None of these soldiers even make it across the Jordan. The land their children later conquer will be lost to them again.

Nevertheless, even exiles know a few things. God's people cannot just sit in camp in the wilderness and expect to survive. They must be up and moving. And anyone who thinks that this large a group of folks can get up and move about, even in the wilderness, without encountering opposition, is not paying attention to life in this broken world. Even if most of the threats to this group's maneuvers prove to be "internal" rather than "external" (as will be true for this regimental brigade), some organization, some preparation, and some discipline is essential for a mission such as theirs. Unfortunately, perhaps, their best analogies for this foundational experience come from the realm of "war."

So then, be alert! Any collection of revealed writings that has the angel Gabriel, general of the Lord's heavenly armies, approach a peasant woman for enlistment in God's coup d'état ("He has brought down the powerful from their thrones"; Luke 1:52); and that views a cross outside Jerusalem as the "weapon" that finally defeats the evil inside and outside us ("If any want to become my followers, let them . . . take up their cross [not sword] and follow me"; Mark 8:34)—such Scripture is not simply offering a textbook for battalion warfare when it describes God's people disembarking from camp. That we prefer images of God's people sitting at table or moving into heavenly mansions when we dream of the kingdom only reveals that we are all too willing to forget where we are right now in the story: still in the wilderness, still on maneuvers. "*Like* a mighty army" goes the old and now much-despised hymn, "*moves* the church of God." If we no longer thrill to the sight of God's people *in motion*, maybe it's because we've been sitting and letting other people fight our "battles" for far too long.

12. The People Start to Complain
Numbers 11:1–12:16

This definitely is my favorite part in the whole story!

No sooner do the high school graduates race out of the parking lot than someone sideswipes a pole, and fists begin to fly. No sooner do the crack recruits get their tank revved up than it bogs down in the mud, and the unit wishes they were back home as civilians. No sooner does the congregation recess from worship than they get into a shoving match in the church parking lot, and the clerk of session has to intervene. After all the preparation, after all the anticipation, isn't this the way it goes? Where did all the glory go?

"Now when the people complained" (Num. 11:1). There it is, with no elaboration. The first tale of Israel's experiences "on the way!"

To feel the full impact, it is helpful to remember all that has gone before. Ever since Exodus 19:1, the Lord has been in the huddle with the Israelites at Mount Sinai. Through Moses, the Lord has taught them all that they need to know to live wise and holy lives in the world. With the Lord's own hand, God has given them water to drink and bread to eat. To forestall any disagreements, God has meticulously arranged them according to tribes, both in the camp and for the march. After delivering them from their enemies in the past, the Lord has promised to deliver them from their enemies to come (Exod. 34:11). No child was ever blessed with a more-attentive parent; no student was ever assigned a more-thorough tutor; no athlete was ever given a more-patient or more-skilled coach. All they have to do now is to follow, follow God, and the Lord will be with them always, to the end of the age (cf. Matt. 28:20).

But what is the very first thing the Israelites do when they get out of camp? Sing more praises; burn a few more offerings; welcome in another group of strangers? No! They complain—before the last wagon has even cleared the campsite! We complain—before the ushers have even finished counting the money! The world complains, though watched over by a

Creator who can distinguish even the "bald locust" from the "cricket" (Lev. 11:22)! Such is the nature of our hearts.

A drama in three acts. It is important to see that "complaining" is not just the *first* thing the people do upon leaving the camp. It's the first *three* things! It, in some way, sums up everything they are, everything they do. From the lowest to the highest; from the people, through Moses, and including the inner circle of leaders themselves—they complain "in the hearing of the LORD" (Num. 11:1). This is who we are. To paraphrase the Sunday call to confession, "We all have sinned and fallen short of your glory, . . . and there is no health in us."

ACT 1: AT TABERAH, THE PEOPLE
Numbers 11:1–3
The Story in Outline

> 11:1 **Now when the people complained in the hearing of the LORD about their misfortunes, the LORD heard it and his anger was kindled. Then the fire of the LORD burned against them, and consumed some outlying parts of the camp.** [2] **But the people cried out to Moses; and Moses prayed to the LORD, and the fire abated.** [3] **So that place was called Taberah, because the fire of the LORD burned against them.**

Numbers 11:1–3 is like a preview of coming attractions. It shows us what to expect. We can summarize the plot in five movements: (1) people complain; (2) God responds; (3) people cry out; (4) someone intercedes; and (5) the story goes on.

Yes, this is the story of our lives. Seeing it in outline helps us to understand its constitutive parts.

People complain. Again, this is what we do, and do best. Remember, this comes *after* and not *before* the gift of God's salvation, the gift of God's presence, the gift of God's instruction. All of Exodus 19 through Numbers 10 (59 chapters!) has gone before—with the Lord showing us step by step what to wear, what to eat, how to worship—and we're right back where we started (cf. a similar cycle of complaints before Sinai in Exod. 16–18, esp. 16:2 and 17:2). We are those who "murmur" in the wilderness. We are those who whine in the lap of plenty. God gives us gifts, and we call them "misfortunes" (Num. 11:1). God overwhelms us with blessings, and we experience them as burdens. Ingratitude, rebellion, and "high-handed" effrontery against the Lord (15:30) are as characteristic of this camp as the tent of meeting at its center; these traits run as deep in each of us as our DNA.

God responds. Although we have covered countless regulations for lesser sins, here no Purification or Reparation Offering will suffice. It is bad enough to dishonor your parents (Lev. 19:3). It is worse to dishonor your leaders (Num. 12:1). It is worst of all to dishonor your God (again, Num. 15:30). The Lord must act, and God does. Like the fire team that intentionally sets a "fire line" to keep the larger fire from spreading, the Holy Lord steps in with "refining" fire. And "some outlying parts of the camp" are "consumed" (11:1). Given the people's history, it's a wonder that God doesn't do more.

The people cry out. It was a cry long ago that got this story started (Exod. 2:23). This time, however, the people's oppressor is not Pharaoh, but God. Things have gone from bad to worse.

An intercessor appears. At this point an intercessor appears. Like the priest at the tabernacle, and the Great High Priest to come (Heb. 4:14), Moses carries the cries of the people to the Lord. He steps into "the breach" (Ps. 106:23) to pray and intercede and atone (for a pattern of Moses' prayer, see Exod. 34:9).

The story goes on. Here the true miracle of the story takes place. Something changes, not so much in the people as in their God. Once more the Lord is revealed at God's holiest: "The LORD, the LORD, a God merciful and gracious, slow to anger, and abounding in steadfast love and faithfulness" (Exod. 34:6). Though we do not deserve it, though we turn right around and repeat our mistakes and rebellion, the story, by God's grace, goes on.

Note. It may be helpful to pause briefly at this stage (when the outline is brief and the details do not clutter) to raise the matter of the Lord's "anger," which here kindles, burns, consumes, and abates in its most fundamental form: fire. We have already struggled with how a loving God could unleash fire against sacrificial animals (see the discussion on the Manual of Sacrifice). Now we must wrestle with the Lord unleashing fire upon God's own people.

First, it is hoped, by placing this story within its wider context, that any charge of "arbitrariness" has been dispelled. This is not a story of a fickle and petulant god who hurls bolts from heaven for no rhyme and no reason. Rather, this is the story of a parent who has rescued an orphan from a deadly environment, taught this child one-on-one all the wisdom and compassion this parent has to offer, and agreed to accompany this child wherever she may go, in order to offer food and shelter and guidance along the way. Then one day, when this child graduates from college, the parent receives no invitation. Why? Because the child "complains" that this parent is less sophisticated than some of her new friends, and she doesn't want to be "embarrassed." Read in context, it should be little surprise that this God becomes angry with this people. The miracle is how "slow" this anger is in coming.

Second and more important, like any good discipline, God's fire is never used simply to punish, but to "refine," or better, in Leviticus–Numbers, to keep God's people "moving forward." In the wilderness, Israel constantly threatens to sit down and stop marching, to take up arms and kill one another, or to turn around and head back to Egypt. What is God to do? Graciously overlook their/our faults and let us go on our way? If so, we would starve, die, or return to a bondage, which is living death. God still has gifts to give God's people. God can see, better than we can, the promise of life yet in store for us. God therefore refuses to allow our complaints and fears to waylay the parade. We properly shudder at the methods used (fire is quick and clean compared to some still ahead!), and we may see some "refining" of God's technique as we continue (a "refinement" that reaches its pinnacle on the cross!). Yet we should never forget the main thing that requires such strong medicine—our stubbornness—or that motivates its administration—God's love.

Finally, as we are now aware of Israel's ambivalent attitude to holy fire— a sign of blessing in the sanctuary, a sign of discipline in the camp—so all along we have been reminded of the danger of the journey this God and this people have undertaken. From the beginning, the Lord has been concerned that if God should go with this people for even a single moment, "I would consume" them (Exod. 33:5). This was the reason for the great care with which God has instructed Israel regarding the sanctuary: so they can *worship* without being consumed. This is now the reason that Israel will have to learn great care on its journey through the wilderness: so they can *travel* without being consumed. Israel does not continue in this relationship because it is either safe or predictable, but because the people have learned that this relationship is as precious as life itself. This is what keeps the priest tiptoeing into the Holy of Holies at great risk to himself. This is what keeps the people following the fire and the cloud at great risk to themselves. We, like they, must remember that we can be "burned" just as easily from an experience of God's discipline as by an unfettered vision of God's love. Given the fact that we are human beings, such things may well "consume" us. Yet despite the risks, which one of us would walk away from the relationship? Which one of us would give up the journey?

ACT 2: AT KIBROTH-HATTAAVAH, THE PEOPLE AND MOSES
Numbers 11:4–35
A Theme and Variations

11:4 The rabble among them had a strong craving; and the Israelites also wept again, and said, "If only we had meat to eat! [5] We remember the fish we used to eat in Egypt for nothing, the cucumbers, the melons, the leeks, the onions, and the garlic; [6] but now our strength is dried up, and there is nothing at all but this manna to look at." [7] Now the manna was like coriander seed, and its color was like the color of gum resin. [8] The people went around and gathered it, ground it in mills or beat it in mortars, then boiled it in pots and made cakes of it; and the taste of it was like the taste of cakes baked with oil.[9] When the dew fell on the camp in the night, the manna would fall with it.

11:10 Moses heard the people weeping throughout their families, all at the entrances of their tents. Then the LORD became very angry, and Moses was displeased. [11] So Moses said to the LORD, "Why have you treated your servant so badly? Why have I not found favor in your sight, that you lay the burden of all this people on me? [12] Did I conceive all this people? Did I give birth to them, that you should say to me, 'Carry them in your bosom, as a nurse carries a sucking child,' to the land that you promised on oath to their ancestors? [13] Where am I to get meat to give to all this people? For they come weeping to me and say, 'Give us meat to eat!' [14] I am not able to carry all this people alone, for they are too heavy for me. [15] If this is the way you are going to treat me, put me to death at once—if I have found favor in your sight—and do not let me see my misery." [16] So the LORD said to Moses, "Gather for me seventy of the elders of Israel, whom you know to be the elders of the people and officers over them; bring them to the tent of meeting, and have them take their place there with you. [17] I will come down and talk with you there; and I will take some of the spirit that is on you and put it on them; and they shall bear the burden of the people along with you so that you will not bear it all by yourself. [18] And say to the people: Consecrate yourselves for tomorrow, and you shall eat meat; for you have wailed in the hearing of the LORD, saying, 'If only we had meat to eat! Surely it was better for us in Egypt.' Therefore the LORD will give you meat, and you shall eat. [19] You shall eat not only one day, or two days, or five days, or ten days, or twenty days, [20] but for a whole month—until it comes out of your nostrils and becomes loathsome to you—because you have rejected the LORD who is among you, and have wailed before him, saying, 'Why did we ever leave Egypt?'" [21] But Moses said, "The people I am with number six hundred thousand on foot; and you say, 'I will give them meat, that they may eat for a whole month'! [22] Are there enough flocks and herds to slaughter for them? Are there enough fish in the sea to catch for them?" [23] The LORD said to Moses, "Is the LORD's power limited? Now you shall see whether my word will come true for you or not." ²⁴ So Moses went out and told the people the words of the LORD; and he gathered seventy elders of the people, and placed them all around the tent. ²⁵ Then the LORD came down in the cloud and spoke to him, and took some of the spirit that was on him and put it on the seventy elders; and when the spirit rested upon them, they prophesied. But they did not do so again. ²⁶ Two men remained in the camp, one named Eldad, and the other named Medad, and the spirit rested on them; they were among those registered, but they had not gone out to the tent, and so they prophesied in the camp. ²⁷ And a young man ran and told Moses, "Eldad and Medad are prophesying in the camp." ²⁸ And Joshua son of Nun, the assistant of Moses, one of his chosen men, said, "My lord Moses, stop them!" ²⁹ But Moses said to him, "Are you jealous for my sake? Would that all the LORD's people were prophets, and that the LORD would put his spirit on them!" ³⁰ And Moses and the elders of Israel returned to the camp. ³¹ Then a wind went out from the LORD, and it brought quails from the sea and let them fall beside the camp, about a day's journey on this side and a day's journey on the other side, all around the camp, about two cubits deep on the ground. ³² So the people worked all that day and night and all the next day, gathering the quails; the least anyone gathered was ten homers; and they spread them out for themselves all around the camp. ³³ But while the meat was still between their teeth, before it was consumed, the anger of the LORD was kindled against the people, and the LORD struck the people with a very great plague. ³⁴ So that place was called Kibroth-hattaavah, because there they buried the people who had the craving. ³⁵ From Kibroth-hattaavah the people journeyed to Hazeroth.

After hearing the story in outline, we are now better prepared to catch the changes rung on it next time around. While the opening and closing movements of this "complaint" remain the same, there are some interesting shifts in between.

Moses joins the complaint. It is one thing for the people to grumble "in general." It is entirely another matter when their complaints grow "specific." Although the first complaint involved a general murmuring concerning "misfortunes," the outcry now moves to a strong and specific craving: "We want meat!" Not only are they not busy with their grain offerings (Lev. 2). Not only have they grown weary with the Lord's bread, or manna (Num. 11:6). Now they want to go back to the fish they ate "for nothing" in Egypt (v. 5; talk about selective memory!), as well as "the cucumbers, the melons, the leeks, the onions, and the garlic" (v. 5; a specific complaint indeed!).

You can almost see this parade grinding to a halt. From "Hup, two, three, four," to "Cucumbers, melons, and leeks!" Before long, the whole lot has stopped marching, and they're sitting at their tent entrances and weeping (v. 10). Israel's "Grand Beginning" now seems like a lifetime ago.

Clearly this proves too much for Moses. Rather than interceding for others, he now petitions for himself, though in a backhanded fashion indeed. More accurately, Moses laments, Moses cries out, Moses complains.

"Why, LORD, have you treated me, your servant, so badly? Why have you burdened me with this people? Did I conceive them, birth them, nurse them?" The obvious answer is "No" (cf. Deut. 32:18; Isa. 40:11; Hos. 11:3–4). "I'm not able to carry this people alone!" Having just implied that the Lord carries this people, Moses now assumes this role himself. "For they are too heavy for me." Of course! "If this is the way you're going to treat me, go ahead and put me out of my misery. Shoot!"

It is important to see here that Moses, like the people, has failed. Called to be a mediator, he has stepped out of the breach. Carried along on eagle's wings by God, he acts as if he has been the eagle. Given life, he chooses death rather than more life like this as a leader. Though understandable (these people *are* burdensome), though explainable ("He's only human"), Moses has nevertheless failed—though at least he's still talking (cf. the Psalms of Lament, e.g., Ps. 13), and though, in some deeply mysterious way, his very suffering may be serving as intercession (cf. the laments of Jeremiah, e.g., Jer. 15:15–18; 20:7–18).

However, if everything points toward failure on the *human side* of this relationship, everything on God's side points elsewhere. Indeed, here at this point (where the people's complaint becomes more specific, and Moses' complaint most pathetic), God moves to help—first Moses, God's servant, through providing a remedy for his solitary leadership (the gift of the seventy); and then, the people (with a "blessing" that ends as "curse," the quails).

While leaders—prophets, priests, and kings—are precious gifts to God's people, and while anyone who has read Leviticus must well wonder how God's people could ever get by without them (Who would place the sacrifices? Who would approach the altar? Who would receive a word from the Lord?), when push comes to shove, what is essential is not the character of the Lord's leaders but the character of the Lord. The One who has carried the people thus far on their journey is the One, and the only one, who can be trusted to carry them home.

Blessings and curses. Although God's "response" and God's "relief" in the first complaint story were quite simple (fire broke out, fire abated; 11:1–3), more specific complaints require more specific resolutions. Graciously, God will not simply leave us alone in our rebellion. God acts, dealing first with Moses (through a change in polity), then with the people (through the power of "answered prayer").

"So the LORD *said to Moses, 'Gather for me seventy of the elders of Israel'"* (v. 16). As revealed in the Scriptures, God is engaged in a constant battle against the solitary nature of our lives: whether as individuals ("It is not good that the man should be alone"; Gen. 2:18), as deliverers ("Afterward Moses *and Aaron* went to Pharaoh and said, 'Thus says the LORD . . .'"; Exod. 5:1), or as spiritual leaders ("I will take some of the spirit that is on you and put it on them; and they shall bear the burden of the people along with you so that you will not bear it all by yourself"; Num. 11:17).

This pattern continues in the New Testament: with Christ and the disciples ("I will not leave you orphaned"; John 14:18), with the leaders in the Jerusalem church ("They were all together in one place"; Acts 2:1), and the members of Christ's body in general ("You are the body of Christ and individually members of it"; 1 Cor. 12:27). God is interested in leadership for the long haul. This requires a spreading out of both the gifts and the burdens.

The only problem comes when we begin to view this persistent and overflowing "blessing" as a "curse": "Joshua son of Nun, the assistant of Moses, one of his chosen men, said, 'My lord Moses, stop them!'" (v. 28). This is unfortunately not a problem peculiar to the Israelite camp: "John said to him, 'Teacher, we saw someone casting out demons in your name, and we tried to stop him, because he was not following us,'" (Mark 9:38). Would that all God's people were as generous, as Christ-like, as God-like as is Moses, the "failure," at this point: "But Moses said to him, 'Are you jealous for my sake? Would that all the LORD's people were prophets, and that the LORD would put his spirit on them!'" (v. 29). This is a dream that would later become God's own: "Then afterward I will pour out my spirit on all flesh; your sons and your daughters shall prophesy, your old men shall dream dreams, and your young men shall see visions" (Joel 2:28).

"Then a wind went out from the LORD, *and it brought quails from the sea"* (v. 31). "Better watch what you pray for," says the wise elder. "You may get just what you ask for." Sometimes God judges us by giving us just what we want, and more (cf. the "gift" of a king in 1 Sam. 8–15). This picture of God's people up to their waists in quail (two cubits equals about three feet!) for a whole month (not one day; not two, five, or twenty days; but . . . ; Num. 11:19) has to be one of the best pictures of crime-specific judgment in all literature (cf. the various "Midas" folktales about greed). This is judgment through surfeit, slow death through overabundance. Beside this very modern-sounding fate, the quick plague with which this episode ends (v. 33) might almost come as relief.

So, to the question "Is the LORD's power limited?" (v. 23), this second complaint cycle answers "No." Not only is the Lord able to feed these 600,000 in the wilderness, but God also does so in such a way that more than just full stomachs and reassured leaders result. We have here a marvelous picture of the "gracious" discipline of God, by means of which the story keeps moving forward, *and* God's people learn lessons along the way. The people learn that there are dangers in "plenty" as well as "want." Moses learns that by "giving up" or "sharing," he may "receive." Just as Jesus teaches lessons about hunger and sharing as he responds to the crowd's plight and the disciples' doubts in the Feeding of the Five Thousand (Mark 6), so the Lord uses this occasion (in Num. 11) to deepen the people's trust regarding God's ability to provide. The specifics of God's discipline in this story succeed in humbling everybody, especially those who presume to know what amounts to "curse" and what amounts to "blessing" with regard to God's providential care toward us all.

One step forward, two steps back? Perhaps. But at least, as the closing verses point out, these people are still moving: "From Kibroth-hattaavah the people journeyed to Hazeroth" (v. 35). Unfortunately, with each new step and each lesson learned, the dangers and the need for discipline increase.

ACT 3: AT HAZEROTH, MIRIAM AND AARON
Numbers 12:1–16
Complaints in the Inner Circle

12:1 While they were at Hazeroth, Miriam and Aaron spoke against Moses because of the Cushite woman whom he had married (for he had indeed married a Cushite woman); ² and they said, "Has the LORD spoken only through Moses? Has he not spoken through us also?" And the LORD heard it. ³ Now the man Moses was very humble, more so than anyone else on the face of the earth. ⁴ Suddenly the LORD said to Moses, Aaron, and Miriam, "Come out, you three, to the tent of meeting." So the three of them came out. ⁵ Then the LORD came down in a pillar of cloud, and stood at the entrance of the tent, and called Aaron and Miriam; and they both came forward. ⁶ And he said, "Hear my words: When there are prophets among you, I the LORD make myself known to them in visions; I speak to them in dreams. ⁷ Not so with my servant Moses; he is entrusted with all my house. ⁸ With him I speak face to face—clearly, not in riddles; and he beholds the form of the LORD. Why then were you not afraid to speak against my servant Moses?" ⁹ And the anger of the LORD was kindled against them, and he departed. ¹⁰ When the cloud went away from over the tent, Miriam had become leprous, as white as snow. And Aaron turned towards Miriam and saw that she was leprous. [11] Then Aaron said to Moses, "Oh, my lord, do not punish us for a sin that we have so foolishly committed. [12] Do not let her be like one stillborn, whose flesh is half consumed when it comes out of its mother's womb." [13] And Moses cried to the Lord, "O God, please heal her." [14] But the Lord said to Moses, "If her father had but spit in her face, would she not bear her shame for seven days? Let her be shut out of the camp for seven days, and after that she may be brought in again." [15] So Miriam was shut out of the camp for seven days; and the people did not set out on the march until Miriam had been brought in again. [16] After that the people set out from Hazeroth, and camped in the wilderness of Paran.

What had first been a complaint by the people, then a complaint by the people and Moses, now becomes a personal complaint against Moses lodged by the members of his inner cabinet: Miriam and Aaron, Moses' sister and brother, his fellow leaders.

Their complaint begins with an attack on Moses on account of his wife (probably Zipporah, a Midianite with links to Cush; cf. Hab. 3:7), then moves to a more substantive charge regarding authority ("Has the Lord spoken only through Moses? Has he not spoken through us also?" v. 2). (Ironically, the narrative has just dealt with God's inclusion of another Midianite, Hobab [Num. 10:29–32] and with Moses' defense of shared leadership [11:29].) Moses opens not his mouth against his accusers (cf. Isa. 53:7), but the Lord does, through a personal arbitration at the tent of meeting. Undoubtedly, the Lord's words are only salt in the wound, pointing out the superiority of words to visions (Moses is always viewed as far more than a "seer"), the comprehensive nature of Moses' authority ("He is entrusted with all my house"; Num. 12:7), and the face-to-face (or "mouth-to-mouth" in the Hebrew) nature of their relationship (v. 8). The Lord then "departs" (v. 9).

However, the Lord is not yet through. The "insider" now becomes the "outsider"—Miriam is made leprous, as white as snow (cf. Lev. 13). Aaron cries out, Moses intercedes, and the Lord pronounces a judgment with a limited term ("Let her be shut out of the camp for seven days"; Num. 12:14). The story continues.

A few comments.

From failure to star pupil. What a difference a chapter makes! Moses goes from chief complainant to a figure of Christlike proportions: receiving accusations without comment (cf. Christ at his trial, in Mark 15:5), and praying for his enemies (cf. Matt. 5:44; though Moses' prayer does seem a tad "perfunctory"). "Now the man Moses was very humble, more so than anyone else on the face of the earth" (v. 3). This is exceptional language of praise, quite rare in the Scriptures, at least with a Homo sapiens as its referent (cf. David, "a man after his [God's] own heart," in 1 Sam. 13:14; and Mary, "Greetings, favored one," in Luke 1:28). Moses reminds us what glorious creatures we can be when we are aligned with God's purposes and led by God's Spirit.

Rules are made to be broken. It is curious that rules the Lord has so recently made seem so quickly overturned. Miriam is pronounced "leprous" but is allowed to return after only seven days. Even "eruptions" no deeper than the skin require two seven-day waiting periods (Lev. 13:4–6). Whether this is a demonstration of Moses' power as an intercessor (though Moses appeals for no waiting period at all; v. 13) or God's power to redefine the rules (as with Christ's "You have heard that it was said, . . . but I say," in Matt. 5) is unclear. What is clear is that as soon as a lesson is learned, God is ready to move on.

No thanks to us. What is most clear in this cycle of complaints is that the parade is moving forward—from Taberah to Kibroth-hattaavah to Hazeroth to deeper into the wilderness of Paran—with no help from God's people. About the best that can be said at this stage is that at least Israel's rebellion has remained at the level of talk. That will change soon enough. In the meantime, this first cycle of complaints leaves us with some interesting church names for those honest enough to confess their past history and ongoing identity. Rather than "First," or "Saint Peter's," or "Saint Paul's," how about these: "Roasting Church" (Num. 11:3); "Craving Church" (11:34); "Leprous Church" (12:10). Onward and upward!

Note. We cannot leave this play in three acts without one closing comment. In the space of three brief chapters, we have covered the entire range of God's relationship with God's people: from the "Sunday Morning Parade," through the "Monday Morning Complaint," to the "Tuesday–Friday Response." It's all in there. Whatever the day may be, wherever our trip may lead, we right now are somewhere in this pattern of God's relationship with God's people.

What is most extraordinary about this story is how it refuses to gloss over either the glorious potential or the inglorious realities of our stories with God. The church can be a magnificent portrait of God's grace in motion, with the ark out three days ahead of God's people as Christ is three days and one resurrection in front of us (10:33). But the first action of the church—Lord, have mercy—is what? "When the people complained" (11:1). Not "if," but "when." The rest of the story, then, and most of our lives, is the negotiated response that follows, as we who always deserve annihilation receive instead a tailor-made discipline that keeps us learning, fearing, and trusting on the way: needing God's presence, but risking being consumed; needing to share responsibilities, but fighting against hierarchies; needing food, but needing trust of God even more. Indeed, the words of this story surely become food for our souls.

That a people could describe themselves this honestly ("now when the people complained"), reveal the character of their God this clearly (truly a God who travels with us "for richer, for poorer; in joys and in sorrows; in sickness and in health"), capture the complexity of their relationship this simply (where "blessing" becomes "curse," and "curse" becomes "blessing")—all this is, undoubtedly, the main miracle of Numbers 10–12. Surely they have begun a journey that includes us all.

13. The People Attempt an Invasion
Numbers 13:1–14:45

God is a God of second chances. No sooner have the outlying parts of the camp stopped smoldering, the quails been cleared, and Miriam's leprosy healed, than God gives the people a chance to redeem themselves. It is indeed the ultimate chance for redemption: immediate entry into the Promised Land.

But before this long-anticipated event can take place, there will be a couple of delays: one, a demonstration of God's generous accommodation to our fears and uncertainties; the other, the result of our capitulation to the same. This story follows the basic outline of the preceding complaint stories, with a preemptive blessing at the beginning and a misconceived attempt to repent at the end.

ACT 1: A FORETASTE OF THE FUTURE
Numbers 13:1–24

13:1 The LORD said to Moses, ² "Send men to spy out the land of Canaan, which I am giving to the Israelites; from each of their ancestral tribes you shall send a man, every one a leader among them." ³ So Moses sent them from the wilderness of Paran, according to the command of the LORD, all of them leading men among the Israelites.

13:16 These were the names of the men whom Moses sent to spy out the land. And Moses changed the name of Hoshea son of Nun to Joshua. ¹⁷ Moses sent them to spy out the land of Canaan, and said to them, "Go up there into the Negeb, and go up into the hill country, ¹⁸ and see what the land is like, and whether the people who live in it are strong or weak, whether they are few or many, ¹⁹ and whether the land they live in is good or bad, and whether the towns that they live in are unwalled or fortified, ²⁰ and whether the land is rich or poor, and whether there are trees in it or not. Be bold, and bring some of the fruit of the land." Now it was the season of the first ripe grapes. [21] So they went up and spied out the land from the wilderness of Zin to Rehob, near Lebo-hamath. [22] They went up into the Negeb, and came to Hebron; and Ahiman, Sheshai, and Talmai, the Anakites, were there. (Hebron was built seven years before Zoan in Egypt.) [23] And they came to the Wadi Eshcol, and cut down from there a branch with a single cluster of grapes, and they carried it on a pole between two of them. They also brought some pomegranates and figs. [24] That place was called the Wadi Eshcol, because of the cluster that the Israelites cut down from there.

Though they have only traveled a short time from orientation camp at Mount Sinai, God's people are already close enough to their destination to send out an advance party for reconnoitering. Leaders from each of the twelve tribes are chosen, their names are duly recorded, and with little fanfare, they are sent to spy out the land, bring back a report, and even fetch "some of the fruit of the land" (v. 20). The time is ripe. "Now it was the season of the first ripe grapes" (v. 20).

What is most interesting about this expedition is its conception in the command of God: "The LORD said to Moses, 'Send . . .'" (v. 1). Why in the world does *God* need a search party? The whole earth belongs to God (Exod. 19:5), including the Negeb, the hill country, the grapes, and the peoples therein. Surely God knows the wilderness of Zin and the wilderness of Rehob as well as God knows the wilderness of Sinai. Why the delay? What's the purpose? Isn't the quickest way always the best?

Could it be that this initial "delay" demonstrates how *God* is learning, as the *people* are learning, as their newly "mobile" relationship progresses?

God knows the greatest threat to this mission is not the people and the walled cities of this land of milk and honey, no matter how well "fortified" (Num. 13:19). No, the greatest threat to the forward motion of this story is the fear ever welling up in the hearts of these travelers. God's people were and still are far more proficient at sitting and wailing, than at marching and praising. We quickly grow nostalgic for the past, even a past of slavery, whenever "the future" is uncertain, even that future as far out as our next cup of water, or our next bite of bread. As this people gets ready to face their greatest test of the future (their entry into a new land of promise), the Lord only knows that they will need some help, a lot of help, and the more tangible the better. So God offers them a "foretaste of the future," in word (the report) and in sacrament (the fruit), so that they might "be bold," as were these leaders, when the time to "cross over" arrives.

God knows us better than we know ourselves. If you have ever had a present you wanted to give someone but for whatever reason were "delayed," you must know a little of what God continued to feel all through Numbers. The land that God has prepared for these people is waiting. Its fields and its fruits are already in blossom. All they need to do is cross over, under the Lord's banner and with the Lord's strength and protection, and their days of wandering and worrying will be over.

But God wants *everyone* to make this journey, both the strong *and* the weak. God knows that the success of this mission will have less to do with mastering arms and armaments than with overcoming fears. Therefore the Lord slows down the journey and delays the full arrival of God's kingdom, allowing time for the advance party to go out and return.

Surely any child in the camp who asks her parents why they are sitting and waiting while the spies go out and return might be given this reply: "The Lord is not slow about his promise, as some think of slowness, but is patient with us, not wanting any to perish, but all to come to *repentance*" (cf. 2 Pet. 3:9), or a new way of seeing. God graciously accommodates *God's* time to *our* time, so that the journey *and* the relationship might succeed.

The word spoken and made visible. As we shall see, the main extra and preemptive gift God wants to give God's people is a "good report," an encouraging account of what the future holds in store for this people, if only they can keep moving. God has already described this place for them (Exod. 3:8), but God knows they will trust it better from some of their own lips (we are not different!), so the Lord sends them out.

But, again knowing us better than we know ourselves, God is aware that words alone are difficult to trust. While some few can believe without seeing, most would prefer to see and even taste (cf. John 20:24–29). No one who has read the New Testament, where Christ is the Vine who offers up the fruit of the kingdom through his death on the cross, can help but see sacramental language bubbling over as the spies return from the Wadi "Eschol" (meaning "cluster") with a single cluster of grapes borne on a pole between two people (Num. 13:23). God provides not only forewords and foresights, but foretastes as well.

An invitation to scouting. One might also wonder why we not only suffer this delay, but also have it extended in the narrative with the listing of each and every spy. We may be getting used to this in Numbers and adept at skimming over the names, yet this listing practice demands explanation.

Surely some of this is foreshadowing: those of us who know the story and thus read this census as we read the census in chapter 1 are painfully aware that most of the names on this list will all too soon disappear.

But the naming of them all, and especially the renaming of one ("Hoshea" becoming "Joshua," v. 16), makes one wonder if a wider invitation is here being given. It's not just that a later "pioneer and perfecter of our faith" (Heb. 12:2) will also be sent out ahead of us with the Hebrew name of "Joshua" changed to "Jesus" (in Greek and Latin). It's more that, as the roll is called, we are asked to wonder how we would have replied to this invitation and what sort of report we would bring back. Is it too big a stretch to see both church and synagogue as "communities of the future," people who have in some sense been sent ahead by God to live and eat and drink the life of the coming kingdom so that we can help others trust its advent? From this vantage point, we come out of the first act of this Numbers drama with both a deepened appreciation for the kingdom's "delay" and our responsibility to serve as "harbingers" of its arrival.

ACT 2: THANKS, BUT NO THANKS
Numbers 13:25–14:4

13:25 At the end of forty days they returned from spying out the land. [26] And they came to Moses and Aaron and to all the congregation of the Israelites in the wilderness of Paran, at Kadesh; they brought back word to them and to all the congregation, and showed them the fruit of the land. [27] And they told him, "We came to the land to which you sent us; it flows with milk and honey, and this is its fruit. [28] Yet the people who live in the land are strong, and the towns are fortified and very large; and besides, we saw the descendants of Anak there. [29] The Amalekites live in the land of the Negeb; the Hittites, the Jebusites, and the Amorites live in the hill country; and the Canaanites live by the sea, and along the Jordan." [30] But Caleb quieted the people before Moses, and said, "Let us go up at once and occupy it, for we are well able to overcome it." [31] Then the men who had gone up with him said, "We are not able to go up against this people, for they are stronger than we." [32] So they brought to the Israelites an unfavorable report of the land that they had spied out, saying, "The land that we have gone through as spies is a land that devours its inhabitants; and all the people that we saw in it are of great size. [33] There we saw the Nephilim (the Anakites come from the Nephilim); and to ourselves we seemed like grasshoppers, and so we seemed to them."

14:1 Then all the congregation raised a loud cry, and the people wept that night. [2] And all the Israelites complained against Moses and Aaron; the whole congregation said to them, "Would that we had died in the land of Egypt! Or would that we had died in this wilderness! [3] Why is the LORD bringing us into this land to fall by the sword? Our wives and our little ones will become booty; would it not be better for us to go back to Egypt?" [4] So they said to one another, "Let us choose a captain, and go back to Egypt."

At first, it looks as though we may have turned a corner in this wilderness story. Not only do the spies go out without protest; they also return having accomplished their mission, including grapes, pomegranates, and figs. They've done all they were asked, and more.

Even their report starts out well enough, though they show some confusion as to who has sent them ("you" the congregation, versus "You," God; v. 27). They confirm that this land ahead is indeed a land that "flows with milk and honey" (v. 27, the first time these words to Moses show up in the peoples' mouths; Exod. 3:8). They even hold out its produce: "and this is its fruit" (Num. 13:27).

But then, one word: "yet" (v. 28). A pause. Can you feel it? The entire forward momentum of this story is suddenly placed in jeopardy. What God has meant for "good" is about to be used for "ill." Like a "casual" comment toward the end of a counseling session, or a quick "by the way" before signing a contract, the whole expedition now begins to unravel. The spies lift their eyes from the *fruit* of this land toward the *people* of this land, and suddenly a future filled with promise becomes overwhelmed with threat. The people of this land grow and grow until they are the size of the prehistoric Nephilim (Gen. 6:4), while the Israelites have been reduced to grasshoppers (Num. 13:33). The land of milk and honey becomes a land that "devours its inhabitants" (v. 32). Though Caleb tries to quiet them (v. 30), the first-person-plural pronouns proliferate ("*We* are not able," v. 31; "They are stronger than *we*," v. 31; "To ourselves *we* seemed like grasshoppers, and so *we* seemed to them," v. 33) and the third-person-singular with respect to God disappears entirely. Having reduced the entire enterprise to a purely human level, their report becomes highly "unfavorable" (v. 32), and we're back up to our old tricks: lifting up our voices in lamentation, dreaming of the good old days in Egypt, and proposing a counterexpedition to the south (v. 4)!

This is "gossip" on a grand scale; a war of words and worldviews. If we didn't know it before, we know it now: there has never been a more untrue piece of wisdom than "Sticks and stones may break my bones, but words will never hurt me." False. Not only can words "hurt"; they can also "destroy": body and spirit, individuals and groups, the fragile fabric of relationships and the ever-precious will to move forward.

Those who were sent out to encourage and embolden come back and spread contagion through the camp. All *we*, who have "heard and seen, tasted and touched" (cf. 1 John 1:1), should stand forewarned. As these words of Jesus are appropriate for the spies in Numbers, so they are potentially appropriate for all who would serve as witnesses: "If any of you put a stumbling block before one of these little ones who believe in me, it would be better for you if a great millstone were fastened around your neck and you were drowned in the depth of the sea" (Matt. 18:6).

ACT 3: A PROPHET STANDS (OR FALLS) IN THE BREACH
Numbers 14:5–19

14:5 Then Moses and Aaron fell on their faces before all the assembly of the congregation of the Israelites. 6 And Joshua son of Nun and Caleb son of Jephunneh, who were among those who had spied out the land, tore their clothes 7 and said to all the congregation of the Israelites, "The land that we went through as spies is an exceedingly good land. 8 If the LORD is pleased with us, he will bring us into this land and give it to us, a land that flows with milk and honey. 9 Only, do not rebel against the LORD; and do not fear the people of the land, for they are no more than bread for us; their protection is removed from them, and the LORD is with us; do not fear them." 10 But the whole congregation threatened to stone them. Then the glory of the LORD appeared at the tent of meeting to all the Israelites. 11 And the LORD said to Moses, "How long will this people despise me? And how long will they refuse to believe in me, in spite of all the signs that I have done among them? 12 I will strike them with pestilence and disinherit them, and I will make of you a nation greater and mightier than they." 13 But Moses said to the LORD, "Then the Egyptians will hear of it, for in your might you brought up this people from among them, 14 and they will tell the inhabitants of this land. They have heard that you, O LORD, are in the midst of this people; for you, O LORD, are seen face to face, and your cloud stands over them and you go in front of them, in a pillar of cloud by day and in a pillar of fire by night. 15 Now if you kill this people all at one time, then the nations who have heard about you will say, 16 'It is because the LORD was not able to bring this people into the land he swore to give them that he has slaughtered them in the wilderness.' 17 And now, therefore, let the power of the LORD be great in the way that you promised when you spoke, saying, 18 'The LORD is slow to anger, and abounding in steadfast love, forgiving iniquity and transgression, but by no means clearing the guilty, visiting the iniquity of the parents upon the children to the third and the fourth generation.' 19 Forgive the iniquity of this people according to the greatness of your steadfast love, just as you have pardoned this people, from Egypt even until now."

Moses and Aaron now do all they can do: they fall on their faces. They've been down this road before; they know what comes next: God's response. Given the extent and the depth of the people's rebellion, they know that this will be a big one (note the escalation, from talking about Egypt, 11:5; to electing new leaders: "Let *us* choose a captain," 14:4).

God does indeed step in, with no patience left, threatening to finish off this entire experiment with Israel ("striking" them and "disinheriting" them; v. 12) in order to make room for a new nation "greater and mightier than they" (v. 12). This is the end act, the final solution. This march is well-nigh over.

God's appearance, however, is now bracketed by two interventions: the first, by Joshua and Caleb, directed at the people; and the second, by Moses alone, directed toward God.

A plea with the people. While Moses and Aaron are reduced to lying prostrate (v. 5), Joshua and Caleb step forward a second time, rip their clothes (v. 6), and try to mend the tear that is rapidly widening between God and God's people. God's Spirit has indeed spread out into the camp (Num. 11), as demonstrated by the straightforward potency of this sermonic duet.

Joshua and Caleb repeat the fact that the land is good, "exceedingly good" (v. 7). They reintroduce the Lord into the equation ("the LORD," v. 8; "the LORD," v. 9; "the LORD," v. 9), the key ingredient that has been missing ("the LORD" appears not once in Numbers 13:25–33!). They make clear that the real danger is *not* the inhabitants of the land, no matter how big they are, but rebellion *against the Lord*, who is right next door ("Only, do not rebel against the LORD"; v. 9). As the *scope* of the Lord's providential care increases, so the *threat* of the people in the land decreases. The Lord who provides this people daily bread will now offer up the people of this land as "bread for us" (v. 9). Reversing the angel's usual sermon, "Fear not; the Lord is with you" (cf. Luke 1:28, 30), Joshua and Caleb conclude, "The LORD is with us; do not fear" (Num. 14:9).

It is an excellent and powerful sermon, but its results are all too familiar (for preachers, ordained and lay). Not only does it not help; it makes matters worse. "But the whole congregation threatened to stone them" (v. 10). From talking and dreaming, we've moved to action and violence.

Even so, in this first intervention, by Joshua and Caleb, we are all invited to serve as bearers of the word. Furthermore, we are reminded not to judge our faithfulness by results. Then and now, people will listen but not understand; will hear but not obey. Worse, they may even threaten to stone you (v. 10) or throw you off a cliff (Luke 4:29).

A plea with God. In contrast to the people's dull ears, the Lord's ears prove surprisingly receptive. Moses pulls out all the stops and delivers one of the most audacious petitions in all of Scripture.

He begins by reminding God that others are watching. Though the Israelites are out in the wilderness, they're not off the world's stage. The Egyptians have seen them go; the inhabitants of the land have heard they are on the way. As Joshua and Caleb have tried to lift the peoples' eyes, so Moses attempts to lift the Lord's eyes: "This story is not just about your blessing of one nation, but your plan to bless the world. Others will talk.

"Second, it's not just a matter of Israel's success or failure vis-à-vis the nations that's at stake here. The Egyptians and the inhabitants of this land both know that you, the LORD, go with us. Thus if *we* fail, in some sense *you* fail. It's not only a question of ability, of them saying, 'The LORD was not able' [v. 16], but also a question of honor, your honor, O LORD." Moses has now lifted God's vision above the nations and above Israel itself. It's a dangerous ploy. Reminding God of God's honor can lead to judgment ("It is not for your sake, O house of Israel, that I am about to act, but for the sake of my holy name"; Ezek. 36:22) as well as mercy ("For my name's sake I defer my anger, for the sake of my praise I restrain it for you, so that I may not cut you off"; Isa. 48:9).

Perhaps realizing the critical nature of the juncture at which he now stands (with the same power for good and ill as the "yet" in 13:28), Moses pulls out his trump card, the last hopeful word in his arsenal. Back, way back in similar critical negotiations, God had granted Moses a special glimpse of God's character (Exod. 34). It was one of the most intimate moments between God and any human being, perhaps even better than seeing the Lord "face-to-face" (Exod. 33:20). Moses now pulls out this note, puts it on the table, and places the whole rest of this story on the line: "Let your power be great in that way that its greatness is clearest and holiest, in the power of costly forgiveness" (Num. 14:18 paraphrased).

If your teeth are not on edge now, you are not paying attention. God's glory is shimmering right now at the heart of a camp in total rebellion. The only thing that stands between this people and utter destruction are words, the words of two (Joshua and Caleb), and then one (Moses). This last person concludes his plea by quoting the Lord's own words and then issuing a final, singular request of God: "Forgive" (v. 19).

The intercessor's task is fearsome. By God's grace, the intercessor's task is also necessary. If anyone would doubt the power of prayer (for God and for us), or if anyone thinks prayer is boring or a place for polite talk only, have them read Moses' intercession. In this space between Moses' prayer and the Lord's response, we might join with the psalmist, on Moses' behalf, and ask with wonder: "What are human beings that you are mindful of them?" (Ps. 8:4). What are we creatures of dust that you would listen to us?

ACT 4: GOD'S GRACIOUS DISCIPLINE CONTINUES
Numbers 14:20–38

14:20 Then the LORD said, "I do forgive, just as you have asked; ^{21} nevertheless—as I live, and as all the earth shall be filled with the glory of the LORD— ^{22} none of the people who have seen my glory and the signs that I did in Egypt and in the wilderness, and yet have tested me these ten times and have not obeyed my voice, ^{23} shall see the land that I swore to give to their ancestors; none of those who despised me shall see it. ^{24} But my servant Caleb, because he has a different spirit and has followed me wholeheartedly, I will bring into the land into which he went, and his descendants shall possess it. ^{25} Now, since the Amalekites and the Canaanites live in the valleys, turn tomorrow and set out for the wilderness by the way to the Red Sea." ^{26} And the LORD spoke to Moses and to Aaron, saying: ^{27} How long shall this wicked congregation complain against me? I have heard the complaints of the Israelites, which they complain against me. ^{28} Say to them, "As I live," says the LORD, "I will do to you the very things I heard you say: ^{29} your dead bodies shall fall in this very wilderness; and of all your number, included in the census, from twenty years old and upward, who have complained against me, ^{30} not one of you shall come into the land in which I swore to settle you, except Caleb son of Jephunneh and Joshua son of Nun. ^{31} But your little ones, who you said would become booty, I will bring in, and they shall know the land that you have despised. ^{32} But as for you, your dead bodies shall fall in this wilderness. ^{33} And your children shall be shepherds in the wilderness for forty years, and shall suffer for your faithlessness, until the last of your dead bodies lies in the wilderness. ^{34} According to the number of the days in which you spied out the land, forty days, for every day a year, you shall bear your iniquity, forty years, and you shall know my displeasure." ^{35} I the LORD have spoken; surely I will do thus to all this wicked congregation gathered together against me: in this wilderness they shall come to a full end, and there they shall die. ^{36} And the men whom Moses sent to spy out the land, who returned and made all the congregation complain against him by bringing a bad report about the land— ^{37} the men who brought an unfavorable report about the land died by a plague before the LORD. ^{38} But Joshua son of Nun and Caleb son of Jephunneh alone remained alive, of those men who went to spy out the land.

As words brought on this crisis, now words begin its resolution.

First, gospel words: "I do forgive, just as you have asked" (v. 20). It is hard to know which is more breathtaking: the free nature of the gift (with no sacrifice or offering required!), or the "footnoting" of Moses' participation ("as you have asked"). Regardless, in the space of one verse, the world has changed. Those who were as good as dead are brought back to life.

"Nevertheless" (v. 21), discipline must follow. In this case, though, the iniquity will be visited only upon this first generation (in contrast to the third and the fourth; v. 18). God is "by no means clearing the guilty" (v. 18). As discussed before (in the first complaint cycle), *if* these people are going to learn, if *we* are going to keep moving forward with God in God's way, outright rebellion must have consequences. Although we Christians should remain forever grateful that all ultimate consequences have been borne by someone else (who intercedes in a way even more fearsome and costly than Moses'), God's gracious discipline is as much a part of our experience of growth in "holiness" or "sanctification" as it was for Israel. What patterns of God's discipline can here be discerned?

God's discipline is never arbitrary. Every parent knows that the key to effective discipline is matching the discipline with the crime. If a child can see no correlation between what she has done and the consequences, the behavior may be stopped but little learning will occur.

As we have already seen and will see again, there is a marvelous and terrible match between Israel's behavior and God's discipline. As the spies spent forty days on this mission, the people will spend forty years in their wandering (v. 34): this is no random event. The very fate that these people hid behind (that their "little ones" should fall on the way; v. 3) now becomes their own ("I will do to you the very things I heard you say"; v. 28)—teaching us that our words do matter, for good (Moses) and for ill (people). Though this whole generation is now forbidden to cross over ("They shall come to a full end"; v. 35), the demise of ten of the spies is immediate ("The men who brought an unfavorable report about the land died by a plague before the LORD"; v. 37)—reminding us that "to whom much has been given, much will be required" (Luke 12:48).

There is only one thing worse than living in a world where God exercises discipline. That is living in a world without God, where all events are random. With God's discipline, the Lord makes certain that we know from whence and because of what it occurs.

God's discipline is never vindictive. Every good parent also knows not to discipline in anger. Wait. Think. Devise a discipline that not only matches the crime, but that might also lead to growth.

There is an irony at the heart of this "delay." Although its first motivation is the necessary "visiting of iniquity," its secondary fruit may prove blessing. In later times, Israel looked back on the whole of its wanderings as the best of times. Why? Because of the intimacy of the relationship that was experienced here, and the depth of the trust that was born here. Just as with Adam and Eve's expulsion from the garden, there is some hint of a "Fortunate Fall" in this delay. Though this "fall" will cost the first generation dearly, it also makes possible the rest of the stories in Numbers, through which following generations of God's people will learn even more about God's discipline and God's grace. God caused the first delay in sending the spies so that all might be ready. Could it be that in some way God caused this second delay with those remaining, so that at the end of forty years, at least some will be ready?

God's discipline can "by no means" be set aside. According to our story, Caleb (and Joshua?), in contrast to the rest of the people, has "a different spirit" and has followed the Lord "wholeheartedly" (v. 24). Thus Joshua and Caleb, again in contrast with the rest of those sent to spy out the land, are remembered as having brought a "favorable" versus an "unfavorable" report to God's people (vv. 36–37). In the end, then, on the basis of their words and their actions, they find themselves separated out from the judgment that is necessary and unavoidable for the rest (v. 38). But what happens if there is only *one* such person who proves wholeheartedly obedient in deeds and in word? And what if that person willingly steps forward to receive the judgment that is due the rest? And what if, because of this, this one "alone" ends up dead rather than alive (again, v. 38)? Well, clearly, that is another story for another time. But it is one toward which this story at least whispers. No, God's discipline can "by no means" be set aside. At least for now.

ACT 5: A FALSE SHOW OF PIETY
Numbers 14:39–45

14:39 **When Moses told these words to all the Israelites, the people mourned greatly. ⁴⁰ They rose early in the morning and went up to the heights of the hill country, saying, "Here we are. We will go up to the place that the Lord has promised, for we have sinned." ⁴¹ But Moses said, "Why do you continue to transgress the command of the Lord? That will not succeed. ⁴² Do not go up, for the Lord is not with you; do not let yourselves be struck down before your enemies. ⁴³ For the Amalekites and the Canaanites will confront you there, and you shall fall by the sword; because you have turned back from following the Lord, the Lord will not be with you." ⁴⁴ But they presumed to go up to the heights of the hill country, even though the ark of the covenant of the Lord, and Moses, had not left the camp. ⁴⁵ Then the Amalekites and the Canaanites who lived in that hill country came down and defeated them, pursuing them as far as Hormah.**

This episode is not quite over yet.

In a final twist, the people "get religion" and decide to do better. After mourning "greatly" (v. 39), they get up "early in the morning" (a virtuous sign; v. 40) and head out for the very hill country they have just now despised. "Here we are," they say (using the words of God's faithful servants down through the ages; cf. Isaiah in Isa. 6:8; Mary in Luke 1:38). "We will go up to the place that the LORD has promised, for we have sinned" (v. 40).

This is repentance at its best, a literal turning around. They were headed one way (to Egypt); now they're headed the other way (to the Promised Land). Won't this make the Lord happy? Won't this make Moses proud? No, on both counts. We must ask "Why?"

Word cues. The people are still fixated on the first-person plural: "*We* will go up" (v. 40). From the word "go," it's clear to Moses (and the reader) that these people have not learned a thing.

Plot cues. As Moses points out, though this would have been a laudable action one chapter ago, it now overlooks what has just transpired. The Lord has forbidden these people to go up to the hill country (v. 25) and they now propose to do so. Nothing good can come from this.

Ark cues. At the very beginning of this parade, it was clear who was in charge. Every movement of this people is supposed to be choreographed by God. It's clear to Moses, and should be clear to the people that, on this day, the ark has "not left the camp" (v. 44). Neither, then, should they; or else they should fear, for the Lord's *not* with them.

This final act thus becomes a marvelous illustration of human presumption ("But they presumed to go up to the heights of the hill country"; v. 44; cf. 10:35). Actions that would have been obedient at an earlier time prove to be disobedient now. Faithfulness is often more a matter of proper timing than proper (and improper) actions. Words that would have served as a perfect confession earlier ("for we have sinned"; v. 40) ring quite hollow now: words and actions must coincide. Most of all, this story is not so much about where these people are going as who is going with them ("Because you have turned back from following the LORD [even though they've turned toward the Promised Land], the LORD will not be with you"; v. 43). God's people are always discerned by their Companion, not by their coordinates.

Being a part of this holy journey is not easy. One must be always watching and waiting and listening. But this much is sure. Anytime human beings "presume" to "make a name for ourselves" (Gen. 11:4), or offer fire by themselves (Lev. 10:1), or "go up to the place that the LORD has promised" on their own (Num. 14:40), you can be quite sure how things will end up: "Then the Amalekites and the Canaanites who lived in that country came down and defeated them, pursuing them as far as Hormah" (v. 45).

Attempted Invasion #1 is now over. It's time to move on.

14. Further Instructions #2
Numbers 15:1–41

15:1 The Lord spoke to Moses, saying: [2] Speak to the Israelites and say to them: When you come into the land you are to inhabit, which I am giving you, [3] and you make an offering by fire to the Lord from the herd or from the flock—whether a burnt offering or a sacrifice, to fulfill a vow or as a freewill offering or at your appointed festivals—to make a pleasing odor for the Lord, [4] then whoever presents such an offering to the Lord shall present also a grain offering, one-tenth of an ephah of choice flour, mixed with one-fourth of a hin of oil.

15:27 An individual who sins unintentionally shall present a female goat a year old for a sin offering. [28] And the priest shall make atonement before the Lord for the one who commits an error, when it is unintentional, to make atonement for the person, who then shall be forgiven. [29] For both the native among the Israelites and the alien residing among them—you shall have the same law for anyone who acts in error. [30] But whoever acts high-handedly, whether a native or an alien, affronts the Lord, and shall be cut off from among the people. [31] Because of having despised the word of the Lord and broken his commandment, such a person shall be utterly cut off and bear the guilt. [32] When the Israelites were in the wilderness, they found a man gathering sticks on the sabbath day. [33] Those who found him gathering sticks brought him to Moses, Aaron, and to the whole congregation. [34] They put him in custody, because it was not clear what should be done to him. [35] Then the Lord said to Moses, "The man shall be put to death; all the congregation shall stone him outside the camp." [36] The whole congregation brought him outside the camp and stoned him to death, just as the Lord had commanded Moses. [37] The Lord said to Moses: [38] Speak to the Israelites, and tell them to make fringes on the corners of their garments throughout their generations and to put a blue cord on the fringe at each corner. [39] You have the fringe so that, when you see it, you will remember all the commandments of the Lord and do them, and not follow the lust of your own heart and your own eyes. [40] So you shall remember and do all my commandments,

and you shall be holy to your God. [41] I am the Lord your God, who brought
you out of the land of Egypt, to be your God: I am the Lord your God.

Suddenly and without warning, we find ourselves back in the classroom.
Having received the word that they now have forty years of wandering still
ahead of them, and having been forced to accept the without-parole nature
of this sentence by their quick defeat at the hands of the Amalekites and the
Canaanites, the Israelites decide to use this time constructively with some
"continuing ed" in holy living. Like a battalion on maneuvers when the
rain sets in, God's people park their wagons, pitch their tents, and return to
the role of students, which they learned so well back at Mount Sinai.

Moses begins his lessons with a return to "Holiness 101: The Types of
Sacrifices." We're right back to where we started in Leviticus 1, but this
time with a twist. Given the judgment and mercy that they have just experienced, there is the apparent desire on *their* part and willingness on *God's*
part to push these instructions deeper and wider, to interweave them more
closely into the warp and woof of their lives in the land yet to come.

To follow thee more nearly, day by day. There is nothing in Numbers
15 that has not already been covered in some sense: offerings in general
(Lev. 1–7); inclusion of resident aliens in festival worship (Num. 9:14);
offering of firstfruits (Lev. 23:9–14); "unintentional" versus "intentional"
sins (Lev. 5:14–6:7); condemnation of fires on the Sabbath, of which gathering sticks must be the prelude (Exod. 35:3); and proper weaves for garments (Lev. 19:19).

What the Lord makes possible in Numbers 15 is an extension of all these
instructions—out and down and around. Previously, only a few "special"
offerings were accompanied by grain and drink offerings (First Fruits and
Weeks, in Lev. 23; and Nazirite, in Num. 6); now flour and wine are added
to them "all" ("each and every one"; Num. 15:12). Previously, it was made
clear that the resident alien could participate in certain "high holy days"
(e.g., Passover, in 9:14); now the resident alien is welcomed into "daily"
worship ("There shall be for both you and the resident alien a single statute,
a perpetual statute throughout your generations"; 15:15). Previously, only
the firstfruits "of the fields" required special notice (Lev. 23); now the firstfruits "of the kitchen" (and by application, of the lab and factory and study!)
require special recognition and thanks ("From your first batch of dough
you shall present a loaf as a donation"; Num. 15:20). Previously, the difficult distinction between "unintentional" versus "intentional" was applied to
only a few, scattered violations (Lev. 5–6); now this "interior" component of

behavior is spread out onto all areas of potential violation ("if you unintentionally fail to observe all these commandments"; Num. 15:22; "but whoever acts high-handedly [in any area of these instructions], whether a native or an alien, affronts the LORD, and shall be cut off from among the people"; v. 30). Previously, a person had to "kindle a fire" on the Sabbath in order to be "put to death" (Exod. 35:2); now (not only on the books but in practice!) simply gathering sticks with the avowed "intention" of making such Sabbath smoke is sufficient for the stones to fly (Num. 15:36). Previously, just making sure your garments contained only one "kind" of material was sufficient for being "well-dressed" as an Israelite (Lev. 19:19); now a blue cord must be woven into the fringe at every corner of the garment, so that every time they brush your wrist or flash in your peripheral vision, "you will remember all the commandments of the LORD and do them, and not follow the lust of your own heart and your own eyes" (Num. 15:39).

As Israel had tried to do better in their presumptive attempt to take the hills by storm (Num. 14), now they are provided constructive ways to demonstrate "the breadth and length and height and depth" (Eph. 3:18) of their obedient gratitude to God for continuing them on this journey. The whole chapter reminds one of a much-later chapter where a similar group of travelers pause for special instructions from their Master: "You have heard that it was said, . . . but I say to you . . ." (Matt. 5:21–48). As God's holiness and judgment as well as God's patience and mercy become clearer and clearer to God's people, those areas of their lives and others' lives open to "sanctification" and growth in holiness expand ever outward.

Missing the forest for the trees. The only problem with this entire growth toward holiness in Numbers 15 is its refusal to accept the key lesson of what has just happened. Practically all the Israelites have just proved themselves guilty of the worst sin of all: "high-handed" and persistent refusal to follow the Lord's command, not just regarding details of the camp, but also for the entire direction of the march. This was not just "picking up sticks" or "cutting corners," but outright rebellion, deserving of utter and complete annihilation at the hands of the Lord ("I will strike them with pestilence and disinherit them, and I will make of you a nation greater and mightier than they"; Num. 14:12).

And yet, when the Lord and Moses go into consultation regarding this offense, what is the result? Yes, the unfaithful spies die by a plague, their army suffers defeat at the hands of the Amalekites and Canaanites, and none of the adults (except for Caleb and Joshua) will be allowed to cross over to the other side; but the whole camp is not "stoned" immediately by the Lord! Indeed, Moses appeals to the Lord to make God's power great in the manner that goes to the very core of God's holiness: forgiveness (14:19). One cannot help but wonder when the Lord's instruction and the people's obedience will shine forth with this same holy power of forgiveness.

Some progress is made here as the areas for the people's thanksgiving are expanded, the boundaries of the worshiping congregation are widened, and the appreciation for the interior as well as the exterior dimensions of obedience is deepened. But one cannot help but think that the "pleasing odor" with which this chapter begins (15:14) is somehow offset by the clatter of stones near its end (v. 36). What would have happened (particularly given the vexing and complex topic of "Sabbath observance"!) if this teacher had come out with the verdict of a later Teacher in similar circumstances: "Let anyone among you who is without sin be the first to throw a stone at her" (John 8:7).

The thread of gospel woven in. Despite the harshness of this chapter's only narrative, there is much encouragement for those who can read between the lines.

First, there is the reminder that this journey is not just about destinations, but especially about relationship. Exiled from the Promised Land, we might expect God's people just to sit on their hands. No, this is an opportunity for waiting in a new way. Giving thanks not just to get something, but also because that is who we are created to be.

Second, these instructions continue to be ones that are "in reach." In the words of Deuteronomy, these commandments are not "too hard for you" or "too far away," but "very near to you" (Deut. 30:11, 14), as near as one's flour and wine, or the tassels on one's sleeves.

Third, and most important, at first glance, this whole exercise seems wasted. Why? Because these are instructions meant for a settled people living settled lives (with access to flour and wine and ovens in which to bake bread; Num. 15:20)—lives, on this earth, that none of the adults in this class shall taste ("In this wilderness they shall come to a full end, and there they shall die"; 14:35).

But if this is the Lord teaching these things through Moses, then somebody, someday must be going to cross over! God's people are thus invited to start practicing the life of a kingdom that none of them can reach by their efforts alone. Like the blue thread of their garments, there's a "forward tilt" to both the instructions and the narratives of this book ("a perpetual statute throughout your generations"; 15:15), because and only because there's a "forward tilt" to its Lord: "I am the LORD your God, who brought you out of the land of Egypt, to be your God: I am the LORD your God" (v. 41).

15. The People Rebel, Threats from Within
Numbers 16:1–17:13

16:1 Now Korah son of Izhar son of Kohath son of Levi, along with Dathan and Abiram sons of Eliab, and On son of Peleth—descendants of Reuben—took ² two hundred fifty Israelite men, leaders of the congregation, chosen from the assembly, well-known men, and they confronted Moses. ³ They assembled against Moses and against Aaron, and said to them, "You have gone too far! All the congregation are holy, every one of them, and the Lord is among them. So why then do you exalt yourselves above the assembly of the Lord?" ⁴ When Moses heard it, he fell on his face. ⁵ Then he said to Korah and all his company, "In the morning the Lord will make known who is his, and who is holy, and who will be allowed to approach him; the one whom he will choose he will allow to approach him. ⁶ Do this: take censers, Korah and all your company, ⁷ and tomorrow put fire in them, and lay incense on them before the Lord; and the man whom the Lord chooses shall be the holy one. You Levites have gone too far!" ⁸ Then Moses said to Korah, "Hear now, you Levites! ⁹ Is it too little for you that the God of Israel has separated you from the congregation of Israel, to allow you to approach him in order to perform the duties of the Lord's tabernacle, and to stand before the congregation and serve them? ¹⁰ He has allowed you to approach him, and all your brother Levites with you; yet you seek the priesthood as well! ¹¹ Therefore you and all your company have gathered together against the Lord. What is Aaron that you rail against him?" ¹² Moses sent for Dathan and Abiram sons of Eliab; but they said, "We will not come! ¹³ Is it too little that you have brought us up out of a land flowing with milk and honey to kill us in the wilderness, that you must also lord it over us? ¹⁴ It is clear you have not brought us into a land flowing with milk and honey, or given us an inheritance of fields and vineyards. Would you put out the eyes of these men? We will not come!" ¹⁵ Moses was very angry and said to the Lord, "Pay no attention to their offering. I have not taken one donkey from them, and I have not harmed any one of them." ¹⁶ And Moses said to Korah, "As for you and all your company, be present tomorrow before the Lord, you and they and Aaron; ¹⁷ and let each one of you take his censer, and put incense on it, and each one of you present his censer before the LORD, two hundred fifty censers; you also, and Aaron, each his censer." [18] So each man took his censer, and they put fire in the censers and laid incense on them, and they stood at the entrance of the tent of meeting with Moses and Aaron. [19] Then Korah assembled the whole congregation against them at the entrance of the tent of meeting. And the glory of the LORD appeared to the whole congregation. [20] Then the LORD spoke to Moses and to Aaron, saying: [21] Separate yourselves from this congregation, so that I may consume them in a moment. [22] They fell on their faces, and said, "O God, the God of the spirits of all flesh, shall one person sin and you become angry with the whole congregation?" [23] And the LORD spoke to Moses, saying: [24] Say to the congregation: Get away from the dwellings of Korah, Dathan, and Abiram. [25] So Moses got up and went to Dathan and Abiram; the elders of Israel followed him. [26] He said to the congregation, "Turn away from the tents of these wicked men, and touch nothing of theirs, or you will be swept away for all their sins." [27] So they got away from the dwellings of Korah, Dathan, and Abiram; and Dathan and Abiram came out and stood at the entrance of their tents, together with their wives, their children, and their little ones. [28] And Moses said, "This is how you shall know that the LORD has sent me to do all these works; it has not been of my own accord: [29] If these people die a natural death, or if a natural fate comes on them, then the LORD has not sent me. [30] But if the LORD creates something new, and the ground opens its mouth and swallows them up, with all that belongs to them, and they go down alive into Sheol, then you shall know that these men have despised the LORD." [31] As soon as he finished speaking all these words, the ground under them was split apart. [32] The earth opened its mouth and swallowed them up, along with their households—everyone who belonged to Korah and all their goods. [33] So they with all that belonged to them went down alive into Sheol; the earth closed over them, and they perished from the midst of the assembly. [34] All Israel around them fled at their outcry, for they said, "The earth will swallow us too!" [35] And fire came out from the LORD and consumed the two hundred fifty men offering the incense.

16:41 On the next day, however, the whole congregation of the Israelites rebelled against Moses and against Aaron, saying, "You have killed the people of the LORD." [42] And when the congregation had assembled against them, Moses and Aaron turned toward the tent of meeting; the cloud had covered it and the glory of the LORD appeared. [43] Then Moses and Aaron came to the front of the tent of meeting, [44] and the LORD spoke to Moses, saying, [45] "Get away from this congregation, so that I may consume them in a moment." And they fell on their faces. [46] Moses said to Aaron, "Take your censer, put fire on it from the altar and lay incense on it, and carry it quickly to the congregation and make atonement for them. For wrath has gone out from the LORD; the plague has begun." [47] So Aaron took it as Moses had ordered, and ran into the middle of the assembly, where the plague had already begun among the people. He put on the incense, and made atonement for the people. [48] He stood between the dead and the living; and the plague was stopped. [49] Those who died by the plague were fourteen thousand seven hundred, besides those who died in the affair of Korah. [50] When the plague was stopped, Aaron returned to Moses at the entrance of the tent of meeting.

17:1 The LORD spoke to Moses, saying: [2] Speak to the Israelites, and get twelve staffs from them, one for each ancestral house, from all the leaders of their ancestral houses. Write each man's name on his staff, [3] and write Aaron's name on the staff of Levi. For there shall be one staff for the head of each ancestral house. [4] Place them in the tent of meeting before the covenant, where I meet with you. [5] And the staff of the man whom I choose shall sprout; thus I will put a stop to the complaints of the Israelites that they continually make against you. [6] Moses spoke to the Israelites; and all their leaders gave him staffs, one for each leader, according to their ancestral houses, twelve staffs; and the staff of Aaron was among theirs. [7] So Moses placed the staffs before the LORD in the tent of the covenant. [8] When Moses went into the tent of the covenant on the next day, the staff of Aaron for the house of Levi had sprouted. It put forth buds, produced blossoms, and bore ripe almonds. [9] Then Moses brought out all the staffs from before the LORD to all the Israelites; and they looked, and each man took his staff. [10] And the LORD said to Moses, "Put back the staff of Aaron before the covenant, to be kept as a warning to rebels, so that you may make an end of their complaints against me, or else they will die." [11] Moses did so; just as the LORD commanded him, so he did. [12] The Israelites said to Moses, "We are perishing; we are lost, all of us are lost! [13] Everyone who approaches the tabernacle of the LORD will die. Are we all to perish?"

One of two things happen when a group of people find themselves in a "borderline" situation, where the present is full of threat and the future is clouded with uncertainty: the group pulls together, or the group flies apart. Now to the mix add the diagnosis that none of the adults will complete this journey, and the stakes ratchet up even higher. Like survivors stranded following a shipwreck, or a group of patients with terminal diagnoses, or a congregation whose future prospects are dim, this is either a time to rally, or rebel—against everything and anything that holds one back, or might be to blame for one's plight.

At first, following the spies' report and their forty-year sentence, things looked on the up-and-up. With the exception of mercy and forgiveness (see last section), the people seemed to sincerely want to do better, deepening their response to God's call for obedience and opening the life of the camp to even the aliens in their midst. All over camp, perhaps, you could see the flash of blue tassels, reminding these travelers to use the Lord's commandments as their road map toward the future, not the lusts of their own hearts and their own eyes (Num. 15:39).

Then without warning, all hell breaks loose (quite literally!), among and then beneath them. What provoked this cataclysm? An army of marauding Amalekites? A swarm of stinging scorpions? Some group of malevolent pagans come to hijack the buildings and programs of a congregation just struggling to get by? No, it begins quite harmlessly: "Now Korah son of Izhar son of Kohath son of Levi, along with Dathan and Abiram sons of Eliab, and On son of Peleth—descendents of Reuben—took two hundred fifty Israelite men, leaders of the congregation, chosen from the assembly, well-known men, and they confronted Moses" (16:1–2). Like a "spontaneous" gathering in the kitchen of the fellowship hall or an "informal" discussion following evening Bible study, it all starts harmlessly enough—with the best of the best, the salt of the earth, the saints of the church.

A threefold rebellion. A straightforward reading of this story is not easy. It starts and stops; moves in one direction, then another; focuses on some characters extensively (Korah) and seems to forget others entirely (On). Scholars trace this to a complex history of transmission and the melding of several stories. Regardless, its very messiness and complexity add to the sense of a camp, almost a world, sliding into chaos. Just as God had ordered the primeval waters, so God had ordered the lives of this people. But this will turn out to be one of those days when the Lord speaks, and the earth begins to melt (Ps. 46:6).

One way of viewing this rebellion is as a three-pronged attack.

First, it begins with Korah, a Levite, gifted in rhetoric, yet bitter in heart. Though granted the privilege of helping with the transport of the things of the sanctuary (as were all Levites; Num. 3), and given the extra responsibility of handling the holiest pieces of this process (reserved for the Kohathites; Num. 4), this was not enough. Korah lusted after the privileges and responsibilities of the priests, if not of Aaron and Moses themselves. Hiding behind a noble argument of "the priesthood of all believers" ("All the congregation are holy, every one of them, and the LORD is among them"; 16:3; all "true" statements, reminding us that even the devil can quote Scripture; cf. Matt. 4), he accuses Moses of "exalting" himself above the people (a charge that runs against the reluctant nature of Moses' calling, in Exod. 3, and the meek way Moses encountered the last such protest from Aaron and Miriam, in Num. 12:3). Moses has "gone too far" (Did the added instructions of Num. 15 push Korah over the edge?), and Korah wants to make sure he goes no farther. This is a head-on assault on Moses' office as "priest," a person with special access to the holy, and thus on Aaron and the other priests as well.

Second, along with Korah, there are Dathan and Abiram, descendants of Reuben. With genealogies traceable to Jacob's firstborn (versus the Levites, third-born), there is no doubt that these two were none too pleased with the leadership roles assigned to them: fifth in line, behind three tribes and the Levites (10:18). From the day of Jacob's blessing, they had been given larger dreams, especially with regard to rank ("Reuben, you are my firstborn, my might and the first fruits of my vigor, excelling in rank and excelling in power"; Gen. 49:3). Their confrontation then is one of power ("that you must also lord it over us"; Num. 16:13); their methods are more crude and basic than Korah's ("Show us the milk and honey!" cf. v. 14). In an amazing rewrite of history, they think back to their "milk and honey" days *in Egypt* (v. 13), making it clear they would prefer *Pharaoh's* leadership to *Moses'*. Theirs then is a frontal assault on Moses' "kingly" responsibilities toward this people, Moses' prerogatives as ruler. Combined with the arguments of Korah, it's enough to bring 250 others along for the ride.

Third, and in some ways most discouragingly, all the people join this revolt. Initially, they simply decide to take sides with the rebels, standing with Korah at the entrance to the tent of meeting (v. 19). But later (amazingly enough after Moses has saved their lives by warning them away from proximity to the rebels!), they rise against Moses and Aaron, accusing them of what? (A hint: it's not very subtle.) Murdering the best of the best: "You have killed the people of the LORD" (v. 41). This is the most basic attack on Moses yet, taking those who know the story back to taunts he suffered during his preprophetic days in Egypt ("Do you mean to kill me as you killed the Egyptian?" Exod. 2:14), and effectively rejecting his claim to be the Lord's "prophet"—burning bush, parting seas, fire in the sanctuary or not!

Though woven together in ways that work against any too-neat analysis, this much is clear. Beginning with one, growing to three (or four, counting On), further to 250, then out and inclusive of "the whole congregation" (v. 19), this rebellion is a revolt in its purest sense, spurning Moses' role as priest, king, and prophet, and thus Moses' claim to any divinely appointed "office" at all.

Regardless of this narrative's origins (some trace it to ongoing battles between priests and Levites down through the centuries), and despite the many uses to which it has been put (in defense of just about any adapted hierarchy or antihierarchy one might imagine), this uprising is finally and clearly cast as a very personal revolt against a highly personal person,

Moses. This is the person whom the Lord has used to get them thus far on their journey, and now they "presume" to change things around. What is clear is that the Lord is no more "with them" in this endeavor than God was "with them" on their assault on the hill country two chapters back (Num. 14:43). The fact that the Lord is indeed "among them," and will insist on keeping them "holy" (as Korah has argued; 16:3), will become apparent all too soon.

A threefold response. The deadly correlation between people's sin and the Lord's discipline is made clear, too clear in God's response to this assault.

Korah wanted to get close to God's fire; 250 do get close to God's fire, literally: they are "consumed" (v. 35). Dathan and Abiram are upset that Moses lords it "over them"; well, now everybody will stand "over them," as they are swallowed alive down beneath the earth (v. 32). The people are concerned that Moses is the cause of the killing; so the Lord commences to kill by that form so frequent in Exodus through Numbers: the plague (v. 46).

For chapter after chapter, verse after verse, the Lord has been arranging the details of this camp: "you to the north, you to the south; you first in line, you second." After a series of spreading complaints (Num. 11–12) and a refusal to move forward (Num. 13–14), the camp now explodes into full-scale revolt. The Lord responds, and the Lord responds quickly, forcefully, this time even including members of the next generation: "together with their wives, their children, and their little ones" (16:27; cf. v. 32). (If this image of the "little ones" standing at the entrance of their tents doesn't haunt you, you have a heart of stone; compare Sisera's mother standing by the window in Judg. 5:28.)

It is never terribly productive to compile a ranking of human sins, what's the worst, what's next to the worst, and so forth. However, after going through instruction after instruction, and abomination after abomination, this much is clear. Nothing provokes the Lord quite as quickly as fights among God's people. Other things may require examination, adjudication, and deliberation, but if God's people start arguing about who's "the greatest," and "Why can't I do what she does?"—watch out! Before you know it, the Lord (Mark 9:33) or one of the Lord's apostles (1 Cor. 1:10–17) will surely and swiftly butt in.

From bad to worse. It's a difficult task to trace any progress, at least any "human" progress in the Scriptures. Surely it's next to impossible in Numbers. It's one thing to be ungrateful and to complain about the size and shape of the gifts God has given you. It's another thing to be fearful and unwilling or unable to muster the courage to move when the day to march arrives. It's another thing entirely to actively seek the overthrow of the good order God's hand has provided, just because we do not care for the particular role we've been assigned in this parade.

At its heart, Korah and the others involved in this rebellion are rejecting God's ability to choose. While they are focused on the small scale (why has God chosen *Moses* to do this, and *me* to do that?), they have now either forgotten or rejected God's choosing on the larger scale (why has God chosen *Israel* as the means of blessing and not some *other nation?*). It's as if a rescuer has chosen six people to ride out of a war zone in a car before the bombs fall, and he looks up, and the car is sitting there, and the bombers are approaching. Why? Because the six who have been chosen are fighting over who gets to sit by the windows!

More needs to be said at this point, but before we move on, this much should be clear. If we are going to find hope and forward movement in the stories of the wilderness, we must look somewhere other than "the people," the group that reminds us most damningly of exactly who *we* are. Before any of us dare to be "offended" by Aaron's, Moses', or God's actions in this story, we must first be "repulsed" by our own!

Signs of hope in the midst of chaos. This story, unlike the story of the flood long, long ago, has no ark riding out the waves of the storm, assuring us that this situation will someday get better if only we can wait. But there are at least three planks of an ark bobbing on these waters, if we have the eyes to see.

First, there is the sign with which God's part in this story concludes. Remarkably, it is quite similar to the sign with which the story of the flood concludes. There, a dove comes back with a freshly picked olive leaf in its beak (Gen. 8:11), assuring God's people that life on this earth will go on, once the waters beneath their boat fully subside. In Numbers 17, the staff of Aaron puts forth buds, produces blossoms, and bears ripe almonds (v. 8), assuring God's people that God's gracious choosing of leaders for this journey will go on, once the rumblings all through and under this camp in the wilderness fully subside. As corpses, ashes, and fissures in the earth are negative signs of God's determination to choose those best suited for God's purpose at each stage of God's journey, so also this staff, tucked away in the sanctuary (v. 10), serves as a positive sign that this saving selection will continue into the future. Rebels, beware.

Second, though at extreme cost, some fissure finally opens in the hearts of God's people, and they wail not just about their current situation, but also the relationship with which this all began: "We are perishing; we are lost, all of us are lost! Everyone who approaches the tabernacle of the

LORD will die. Are we all to perish?" Suddenly, we are back to the situation with which Leviticus began ("Woe to us, for we are a people of unclean lips, living in the midst of nations with unclean lips, with whom the Lord God has come to dwell"; cf. Isa. 6:5), a situation full of promise for new trust, new gratitude, and new service (as our study of Leviticus makes clear). Though it has required much trauma, for them and for God, "circumcised hearts" are fruits more precious than almonds, as the rest of this story makes clear.

Third, while "the people" offer us little to hope in until this final outpouring, there are other more redemptive signs as the story unfolds. That God can bring good things out of bad is made evident first in the "censers of the sinners," which become "holy" at the cost of the lives of those that bore them (Num. 16:38). In some mysterious way, this copper for the altar assures us that even the deaths of rebels, if part of God's story, will never be "in vain." God can use the worst of our actions to accomplish "holy" purposes, as any disciples of the cross surely know.

More important, the witness of Moses and Aaron demonstrate that the very situations that show some people at their worst, with the Spirit's help, can cause other people to shine. It must be admitted that Moses does not here pray for his enemies, Korah and his cohorts (we can only go one step at a time?). And one must wonder if they would have acted differently if they knew the rest of this story (as well as God does?). Yet Moses and Aaron do once more "intervene" on behalf of these people who have spurned them, first with words of intercession (v. 22) and warning (v. 23); and then with actions, dangerous actions, which place their very lives on the line ("So Aaron took it [his censer] as Moses had ordered, and ran into the middle of the assembly, where the plague had already begun among the people"; v. 47). We here approach something quite "holy" indeed. It's one thing to "fall on your face" continually in response to people's rebellion all around you (I will always picture the Moses of Numbers as a man with a broken and bleeding nose!). It's another thing to make "atonement" for those who have persecuted you, by standing "between the dead and the living," so that the plague stops at your toes (vv. 47–48). To paraphrase: "Good shepherds are those who lay their lives on the line for the sheep" (cf. John 10:11). Ironically, the very rebellion of God's people provides the opportunity for the wisdom of God's selection to shine. Again, the stories of Numbers point us toward the cross.

Attacks from without or within. Perhaps what is most instructive in this story from the camp is what is most obvious, the most appropriate target for our fear.

God's people, then and now, especially when off the road and resting in camp, spend a great deal of time scanning the horizon and posting the guards to ward off any attacks that may come their way from outside. Maybe the anticipated enemies are wolves and lions. Maybe they are Amalekites and Canaanites. Maybe "secular humanists" or "fundamentalists"; "new agers" or "materialists." So God's people spend a lot of time and energy circling the wagons, building walls and fortresses, separating themselves and putting on exterior armor to keep the forces of evil out.

Surprise, surprise, then, when the attack comes. For it explodes not from the horizon, but from the very heart of the camp. What is most heartbreaking in the book of Numbers is the fact that God spends far more time and energy quelling the fights among God's own people than fending off the raids of outsiders. Whatever decisions we make about polity, ordination, and those whom we discern God has chosen as leaders, this most basic point of Numbers 16–17 is a warning we must keep ever in mind.

16. Further Instructions #3
Numbers 18:1–19:22

Now, once more, it's time to regroup. Boundaries have been crossed, relationships shattered. Somehow they must be restored. The smells of fire and death still hang over their tents, the grave of Korah and crowd runs like a ravine through their midst, and the bronze covering the altar and the almonds on Aaron's rod have yet to lose their sheen. Momentarily, at least, Israel is alert and attentive. Indeed, the last words heard in the camp cry out from the very bowels of God's people: "Are we all to perish?"

Never wont to miss a "teachable moment," the Lord grants Moses and Aaron some further instructions meant to address this specific and pressing concern. "No," the answer comes back, "you will not all perish—if you maintain proper relations with the priests and Levites, and follow proper procedures with the dead."

PROPER RELATIONS WITH THE PRIESTS AND LEVITES
Numbers 18:1–32

18:1 The LORD said to Aaron: You and your sons and your ancestral house with you shall bear responsibility for offenses connected with the sanctuary, while you and your sons alone shall bear responsibility for offenses connected with the priesthood. ² So bring with you also your brothers of the tribe of Levi, your ancestral tribe, in order that they may be joined to you, and serve you while you and your sons with you are in front of the tent of the covenant. ³ They shall perform duties for you and for the whole tent. But they must not approach either the utensils of the sanctuary or the altar, otherwise both they and you will die. ⁴ They are attached to you in order to perform the duties of the tent of meeting, for all the service of the tent; no outsider shall approach you. ⁵ You yourselves shall perform the duties of the sanctuary and the duties of the altar, so that wrath may never again come upon the Israelites. ⁶ It is I who now take your brother Levites from among

the Israelites; they are now yours as a gift, dedicated to the Lᴏʀᴅ, to perform
the service of the tent of meeting. [7] But you and your sons with you shall diligently perform your priestly duties in all that concerns the altar and the area
behind the curtain. I give your priesthood as a gift; any outsider who
approaches shall be put to death.

In Numbers 16–17 all the lines of demarcation and mutual responsibility
among the priests, the Levites, and the people were crossed over and broken. Now God steps in once more, bringing order out of chaos, life out of
death, through a careful arrangement of God's people around the altar
and throughout their lives.

The priests and the Levites are first reminded that their perpetual privilege and duty is to stand, like Aaron, "between the dead and the living"
(16:48). Specifically, they are to form two concentric circles around
God's presence: the priests on the front line, with the Levites one ring
out "in reserve" (18:2–3). The Levites are thus given to the priests as gifts
(v. 6), and both priests and Levites serve the people as gifts, by regularly
and faithfully approaching the altar on their behalf. The people's outcry is
thus answered: "No, not everyone who approaches the tabernacle of the
Lord will die. Just those unauthorized so to risk their life and limb: the
outsider, the nonpriest" (cf. v. 7).

In return for this gift of service, priest and Levite then will be given a
portion of the people's offerings: the priests, selected portions of the sacrifices, or their "redemptive" value (vv. 8–20); the Levites, their tithes of
the land (Lev. 27:30–32), from which they in turn will give back "a tithe,"
or 10 percent (Num. 18:25–32). As laborers deserve their food (Matt.
10:10), and preachers of the gospel their living (1 Cor. 9:14), so the priests
and Levites deserve a cut of the people's offerings. This, rather than land,
is their share (Num. 18:20). This, and this alone, sealed with the salt of the
covenant (v. 19), is their "portion forever" (Ps. 73:26).

As a seamstress slowly pulls back together the ragged edges of a tear in
fabric, running threads back and forth across the gap until the sides of the
cloth meet and the shirt or pants are made whole, so the Lord weaves the
lives of God's servants back together with tangible threads of mutual
responsibility and service. It is a precarious arrangement: with the priests
and the Levites ever in danger of "being consumed" on the one hand (due
to the holiness of the Lord), and having nothing "to consume" on the
other (due to the stinginess of God's people). It is a system always open to
abuse: the priests and Levites seek to leverage their proximity to God for
profit, and the people seek to curry favor with priest and Levite under the

guise of generosity toward God. Nevertheless, the genius of the system is how the worship of the Lord is the impetus for benefits on both sides: the people can now approach the sanctuary without dying (thanks to the service of the priests), and the priests can serve the Lord without starving (thanks to the ongoing praise of the people).

A delicate web of mutual obligations is now cast over the cracks and fissures caused by the recent rebellion, and the fear cast over the camp begins to subside. Like the Twelve Jesus sent out with instructions (encumbered with the gospel for others, yet dependent on others for their food; Matt. 10:10), the Lord is once more equipping God's people for the journey, a journey none of them can make alone.

PROPER PROCEDURES WITH THE DEAD
Numbers 19:1–22

19:1 The Lord spoke to Moses and Aaron, saying: [2] This is a statute of the law that the Lord has commanded: Tell the Israelites to bring you a red heifer without defect, in which there is no blemish and on which no yoke has been laid. [3] You shall give it to the priest Eleazar, and it shall be taken outside the camp and slaughtered in his presence. [4] The priest Eleazar shall take some of its blood with his finger and sprinkle it seven times towards the front of the tent of meeting. [5] Then the heifer shall be burned in his sight; its skin, its flesh, and its blood, with its dung, shall be burned. [6] The priest shall take cedarwood, hyssop, and crimson material, and throw them into the fire in which the heifer is burning. [7] Then the priest shall wash his clothes and bathe his body in water, and afterwards he may come into the camp; but the priest shall remain unclean until evening. [8] The one who burns the heifer shall wash his clothes in water and bathe his body in water; he shall remain unclean until evening. [9] Then someone who is clean shall gather up the ashes of the heifer, and deposit them outside the camp in a clean place; and they shall be kept for the congregation of the Israelites for the water for cleansing. It is a purification offering. [10] The one who gathers the ashes of the heifer shall wash his clothes and be unclean until evening. This shall be a perpetual statute for the Israelites and for the alien residing among them.

While the people's fears regarding their own deaths are thus eased, the deaths of others still hang heavy on the camp. In earlier instructions, specific guidelines had been given for priests and Nazirites regarding proximity to the dead, carefully explicating who can go to whose funerals without incurring ritual defilement (Lev. 21; Num. 6). But now, all the people—priests,

Levites, and Nazirites included—find themselves in a camp with 14,700 corpses (Num. 16:49), plus the ashes of the 250 (16:35), and Korah and crowd underfoot (16:31–33)! How will any of them ever approach the Lord in this state, without making further additions to the casualties?

Ever eager to build bridges, but ever vigilant against people approaching the deaths of others "casually," the Lord proposes a new sacrifice to add to the manual already provided. A cow, not just any cow, but a red heifer with no blemish or defect, is to be burned outside the camp, completely, a "holocaust" to the Lord (see Lev. 1). Its ashes then can be mixed with water and then sprinkled forth via the moisture-friendly leaves of hyssop (Num. 19:18), to make the people and objects it touches "clean." This death thus serves to "atone" for the people's contact with these other deaths; worship can continue, and the journey can resume.

Some more specific observations.

Red, red, red. This must be a red cow. It is burned with crimson material (cf. Lev. 14:6). Its blood must be burned with the cow. Red, red, red. Surely the key to this symbolism is the color of blood. As they have contacted the blood of the dead, so they must offer up the blood of the living in order to be restored. Blood is always precious in God's eyes, even the blood of rebels. Before the march can resume, before worship and walking can resume, respect must be paid.

Washed with water (and with blood). Israel first came to life through its washing in the waters of the Red Sea. Thus ritual washings were early on established as a symbolic means of purification and a tangible way to remember just whose these people were. Now with the addition of ashes (residual blood) another washing is also remembered—back at Sinai, when they were born as God's covenantal people (Exod. 24). Thus this sprinkling becomes symbolic of restoration not just following contact with the dead, but also whenever some break has cut off a person or people from God: "Purge me with hyssop, and I shall be clean" (Ps. 51:7); "One of the soldiers pierced his side with a spear, and at once blood and water came out" (John 19:34).

The perfect sacrifice. As the rebellions of God's people deepen, and the casualties on this journey mount, prior means of purification and reconciliation no longer seem adequate. The Lord could just leave us on our own to come up with more extravagant demonstrations of remorse and thankfulness, but that is not God's way. Rather, the Lord is ever at work, trying to devise some new and costly demonstration that might somehow make us whole. It must be a rare creature, like a red cow. It must be without blemish or defect (Dare we imagine?) "without" and "within." It cannot be a creature that has served any other purpose than this for which it has been dedicated ("on which no yoke has been laid"; Num. 19:2). Everything—skin and flesh, blood and dung—must be offered up in this sacrifice, accompanied by the crimson thread of God's loving purpose running through it (vv. 5–6). Though this death must take place outside the camp, by means of water its effects shall be brought inside the camp and made available to each and every one who has need.

It then should not surprise us that some Jews are yet seeking this perfect red heifer as a sign of the Messiah's arrival. It should not surprise us either that Christians believe that in Jesus Christ, this sacrifice has already come: "For if the blood of goats and bulls, with the sprinkling of the ashes of a heifer, sanctifies those who have been defiled so that their flesh is purified, how much more will the blood of Christ, who through the eternal Spirit offered himself without blemish to God, purify our conscience from dead works to worship the living God!" (Heb. 9:13–14).

This camp is moving from death to life, thanks be to God!

17. Further Rebellions, Defeats, Victories
Numbers 20:1–21:35

Finally, the people are moving again!

After their "grumbling" approach to the Promised Land from the south, the Israelites had been thrown back into the wilderness of Paran "as far as Hormah" (near Arad; Num. 14:45), following their ill-fated and presumptive attempt to take the land "on their own" (Num. 14). Since then, they have been engaged in extensive tutorials (Num. 15; 18–19), with a brief and unfortunate "break" for full-scale rebellion (Num. 16–17). Now they strike their tents, yoke their oxen, and resume the journey northward into the wilderness of Zin, retracing the earlier route taken by the spies (13:21).

It is true that causes for optimism are few and far between. The stages of their journey thus far read like the pages of a police blotter: Taberah ("Burning," 11:3); Kibroth-hattaavah ("Graves of Craving," 11:34); Hazeroth (site of Aaron's and Miriam's revolt, Num. 12); and the wilderness of Paran (the place at which they received the spies' report, the place toward which the Amalekites and the Canaanites pursued them, and the camp within which Korah and crowd were swallowed up; Num. 13–19). This is not the kind of travelogue one is eager to share with one's neighbors. From their glorious dreams of holiness in camp at Mount Sinai, this people has been reduced to procedures for cleanup following the latest pile of corpses (Num. 19).

However, as will soon become clearer, these people follow a God of second chances (and third, tenth, and 70 x 7 chances!). Maybe their outcry at the end of their latest brawl ("We are perishing; we are lost, all of us are lost!" 17:12), will lead to a genuine "foxhole" conversion. At least they seem to be listening to Moses' and Aaron's latest sermons. They now carry the ashes of the red heifer in their pockets. Miriam's death, once they're in motion (20:1; the first recorded death so far not directly related to some immediate rebellion or intrigue), is not only sobering, but also a hint that the death of the first generation may be beginning, and the flourishing of the second generation drawing nigh.

REBELLION AT MERIBAH
Numbers 20:1–13

20:1 **The Israelites, the whole congregation, came into the wilderness of Zin in the first month, and the people stayed in Kadesh. Miriam died there, and was buried there.** [2] **Now there was no water for the congregation; so they gathered together against Moses and against Aaron.** [3] **The people quarreled with Moses and said, "Would that we had died when our kindred died before the LORD!** [4] **Why have you brought the assembly of the LORD into this wilderness for us and our livestock to die here?** [5] **Why have you brought us up out of Egypt, to bring us to this wretched place? It is no place for grain, or figs, or vines, or pomegranates; and there is no water to drink."** [6] **Then Moses and Aaron went away from the assembly to the entrance of the tent of meeting; they fell on their faces, and the glory of the LORD appeared to them.** [7] **The LORD spoke to Moses, saying:** [8] **Take the staff, and assemble the congregation, you and your brother Aaron, and command the rock before their eyes to yield its water. Thus you shall bring water out of the rock for them; thus you shall provide drink for the congregation and their livestock.** [9] **So Moses took the staff from before the LORD, as he had commanded him.** [10] **Moses and Aaron gathered the assembly together before the rock, and he said to them, "Listen, you rebels, shall we bring water for you out of this rock?"** [11] **Then Moses lifted up his hand and struck the rock twice with his staff; water came out abundantly, and the congregation and their livestock drank.** [12] **But the LORD said to Moses and Aaron, "Because you did not trust in me, to show my holiness before the eyes of the Israelites, therefore you shall not bring this assembly into the land that I have given them."** [13] **These are the waters of Meribah, where the people of Israel quarreled with the LORD, and by which he showed his holiness.**

First day out, God's people run into a problem: no water.

This is not an incidental problem (they are in the desert), but neither is it an unfamiliar one (on their initial journey from Egypt to Sinai, they had encountered the bitter waters of Marah [Exod. 15], and the lack of water at Rephidim [Exod. 17], with the twelve springs of Elim in between [15:27]). Surely they must know that as the Lord has watched over them in the past, the Lord will watch over them now. "Suffering produces endurance, and endurance produces character, and character produces hope, and hope does not disappoint us," right? (Rom. 5:3–5).

"So they gathered together" (Num. 20:2)—to seek the Lord's help through prayer? to organize a scouting party for nearby springs? to ask Moses and Aaron to intervene for them once more as they had done so effectively in the past? No. "So they gathered together *against* Moses and *against* Aaron." Here we go again.

Same ole, same ole? At first glance, this simply seems to be another in a long series of complaint stories. They've updated the mercy killing they desire for themselves: from a death in Egypt (14:2) to a death with Korah and crowd ("before the Lord," 16:35) a few chapters back. They've shifted their grocery list: from the cucumbers, melons, and leeks of Egypt (11:5) to the figs, pomegranates, vines, and grain of the Promised Land (13:23; 20:5). But once again, they take aim directly at Moses and Aaron with their "quarrel" at Meribah ("Why have *you* brought the assembly of the Lord . . . ?" 20:4; "Why have *you* brought us up . . . ?" v. 5), which, as we have just learned (the rebellion in Num. 16–17), is tantamount to taking aim at God (who elected these leaders). Get ready. You know the pattern. Fire is on the way!

Only it's not. Moses and Aaron, true to form, go to the tent of meeting and fall on their faces, obviously ready to either duck or intercede against the response about to come. But the Lord speaks up not with judgment, but remedy: "Take the staff, and assemble the congregation, you and your brother Aaron, and command the rock before their eyes to yield its water" (v. 8). Be alert, Moses and Aaron. Watch your step. The Lord seems to have returned to patterns more familiar at the beginning of this journey (cf. Exod. 15–17), where the people are provoked to cry out for legitimate needs (food and water), and the Lord hastens to reply. Though it's hard to detect any shift in God's people, there may be a slight shift in the strategies of their God. Despite the clamor of this people, and despite the history of their whining, will Moses and Aaron catch this shift in strategy, or not?

And then there were two. With the exit of Miriam, this episode begins with two-thirds of the original triumvirate: Moses, Aaron, and Miriam. Though these three have had fallings out with one another (Num. 12), they have so far never joined any of the outright rebellions against their God. Miriam submitted to the discipline required of her (12:15), and Aaron even put his life on the line (16:47). Intentionally or unintention- ally, on God's part, it seems that the time for testing has come: "The LORD spoke to Moses, saying, Take the staff, and assemble the congregation, you and your brother Aaron, and command the rock before their eyes to yield its water" (vv. 7–8).

At first, everything seems to be on track. Moses takes the staff from before the Lord (most likely Aaron's staff from Num. 17). First command completed, check #1. Moses and Aaron ("you and your brother," check #2) gather the people together ("assemble the people," check #3) before the rock ("before their eyes," check #4; God wants them to *see* this), and Moses begins to speak ("and command the rock . . . to yield its water," check #5). Everything seems be going according to plan, but remember, serving God is an awe-full and power-full task. It's like messing with explosives. Easy as you go.

Then, first hint, Moses speaks not to the rock, but the people (Psst! Moses! Face *that* way!). "Listen," he says (Moses, they're supposed to "watch," remember?). He calls the people "You rebels" (entirely understandable, but a flourish God has not requested). "Shall *we* bring water for you out of this rock?" (those pesky but crucial pronouns; we propose, "Shall *the* LORD bring water for you out of this rock?"). Then Moses lifts up his hand (this isn't in the script!) and strikes the rock (versus "command the rock"), not just once, but twice with his staff. "Water came out abundantly, and the congregation and their livestock drank" (v. 11). All's well that ends well? Not quite.

Though the signals aren't completely clear, and though the basic command was followed, something fundamental has gone wrong, as we learn by the next verse: "Because you did not trust in me [the same fault of the people in the spy story; 14:11], to show my holiness before the eyes of the Israelites [Moses' key function from Sinai till now], therefore you [Moses *and* Aaron] shall not bring this assembly into the land that I have given them [now placing them under the same sentence as the crowd; 14:28–35]." In a flash, despite everything that has gone before, the last two-thirds of the initial triumvirate goes down in flames. What went wrong?

You shall be holy, for I the LORD your God am holy. Here we tread on holy ground. Few issues in the Pentateuch have provoked more consternation and more dissertations than this "sin" of Moses. Clearly, Moses stands out by the ambiguity of his sin (in contrast to that of the people). Clearly, Moses stands out in the justification for his sin (if anybody has an excuse to be more "frayed" than "afraid," it was he). Clearly, Moses stands out in that this verdict does not sit well with later expositors (in Deut. 4:21–22, God is angry with Moses "because of you [the people]"). But, just as clearly, Moses stands out in the fact that his sentence is delivered so personally, and is recorded so faithfully before this story is over (Deut. 34). What is going on? Let us try at least three things.

First, it is ironic that Moses fails to hang with this story at that very "curve" in God's character that he had professed so passionately: the Lord's inclination toward mercy, the Lord's focus on forgiveness ("And now, therefore, let the power of the LORD be great in the way that you promised when you spoke, saying, 'The LORD is slow to anger, and abounding in steadfast love, forgiving iniquity and transgression, but by no means clearing the guilty";' Num. 14:18). As the twist in the pattern made clear, God had decided to respond to this outcry with water, not fire, but Moses (his eye on his "neighbors" more than his "God") couldn't shift gears quickly enough. Understandably, all Moses could see were these people, these "rebels," who had caused him such suffering. What he missed, however, was what was going on in the heart of God, and thus the specifics of what he was commanded to do. Like Jonah in the Old Testament, and Saul in the New, even the best of God's servants have trouble following the movements of God's mercy. That's where the Lord's holiness shines brightest, and God's ways diverge most clearly from our own ("For I am God and no mortal, the Holy One in your midst, and I will not come in wrath"; Hos. 11: 9).

Second, it has to be said: What's bad news for Moses is good news for us. Why? If one of the leaders (in contrast to subordinates and future leaders like Joshua and Caleb?) had managed to make it over the Jordan by his or her merit alone, then the challenge to be holy as the Lord is holy would simply come to us at face value. But even Moses fails, and even Moses is remembered more for his "attitude" toward God ("whom the Lord knew face to face"; Deut. 34:10) than for his "aptitude for holiness." All of our lives and actions are meant to reflect the holiness of the Lord in our midst, and yet this remains a bar too high for any of us to attain.

Finally, it now becomes even clearer why later interpreters discern a third person at this scene at Meribah. Yes, there's the Lord, and there's Moses with the staff, but what or who is that rock he's hitting? ("For they drank from the spiritual rock that followed them, and the rock was Christ"; 1 Cor. 10:4.) Moses' very failure leaves God's people waiting for another prophet who will be able to hang with the merciful "curves" of God's character, even if the "rebels" seek to crucify him, and beat him with a staff until "living" water comes forth, and he, like Moses, dies. Maybe the most amazing thing about this Rock to come is that he can make "rocks" out of people like Peter and Moses, like you and like me. Yes, "these are the waters of Meribah, where the people of Israel quarreled with the LORD," then and now, "and by which he showed his holiness" (Num. 20:13) to all who had eyes and hearts to "see."

EDOM'S REFUSAL
Numbers 20:14–21

> 20:14 Moses sent messengers from Kadesh to the king of Edom, "Thus says your brother Israel: You know all the adversity that has befallen us: [15] how our ancestors went down to Egypt, and we lived in Egypt a long time; and the Egyptians oppressed us and our ancestors; [16] and when we cried to the LORD, he heard our voice, and sent an angel and brought us out of Egypt; and here we are in Kadesh, a town on the edge of your territory. [17] Now let us pass through your land. We will not pass through field or vineyard, or drink water from any well; we will go along the King's Highway, not turning aside to the right hand or to the left until we have passed through your territory." [18] But Edom said to him, "You shall not pass through, or we will come out with the sword against you." [19] The Israelites said to him, "We will stay on the highway; and if we drink of your water, we and our livestock, then we will pay for it. It is only a small matter; just let us pass through on foot." [20] But he said, "You shall not pass through." And Edom came out against them with a large force, heavily armed. [21] Thus Edom refused to give Israel passage through their territory; so Israel turned away from them.

The pace of Israel's travels now begins to pick up. For the first time, they venture beyond any portion of the wilderness that either they or the spies had previously covered. They begin here a wide swing to the east, hoping first to travel northward through the smaller kingdoms of Edom and Moab, then cross over the Jordan from east to west. Straight through the middle of this territory runs a travel path known as the King's Highway. All they need or request is safe passage.

For the first episode in a long time, God's people run into an obstacle other than their own rebellion and fractiousness: the nation of Edom. They have received no signals from the Lord that they are on the wrong path. The ark this time is with them (in contrast to their only other wilderness encounter so far; Num. 14). What will they do?

For a story that will later be awash in enemies' blood, it is amazing how peacefully it all begins. Moses sends messengers from Kadesh to the king of Edom, telling him their story and assuring him of their friendly intentions. They are refused passage and threatened ("or we will come out with the sword against you"; 20:18). They come back again, assuming the refusal to be a matter of "hidden costs" and promising to pay. It is just a "small matter," they assure the king; "just let us pass through on foot" (v. 19). But for a second time, they are refused, and Edom comes out against them "with a large force, heavily armed" (v. 20). So Israel turns away from them and sidles further east.

Maybe it's just in contrast with what's to follow, but there's something quite surprising about this shift. The Lord of hosts is with them and has promised them victory over all their foes (Exod. 23:28 and 34:11). Besides, the Edomites are kinfolk (Father Esau and Father Jacob being brothers), which makes this refusal all the more galling. Caleb had assured them that, with the Lord, they could slay giants, but they had not listened (Num. 13:30; 14:7–9). Here was a chance to set things right. "Arise, O Lord, let your enemies be scattered, and your foes flee before you" (10:35).

Yet, because there was another route, because God's people were in some sense "reluctant warriors," and because, most of all, this threat was not coming at them in a fashion that demanded defense of the Lord's honor (no taunts on the part of the Edomites, no complaint on the part of God's people), the path of least resistance is allowed. They are a traveling people; all they need is passage; through the Lord's provision, they stand ready to pay for any transit costs they may incur ("We will stay on the highway; and if we drink of your water, we and our livestock, then we will pay for it. It is only a small matter; just let us pass through on foot"; 20:19).

Later in this story, one might wish that similar restraint would be exercised. As Jesus said to his disciples, if you encounter resistance in one village, just wipe their dust off your feet and go to another (Mark 6:11). If Christ's church sees itself as a similar "pilgrim people," and if the Lord has blessed it with sufficient resources to pay the "transit costs" on the way to the kingdom, then surely Christians might be expected to exercise similar restraint as they encounter similar barriers on their journey, correct?

But other times the resistance is more direct and aggressive, and other solutions need be applied.

THE DEATH OF AARON
Numbers 20:22–29

20:22 **They set out from Kadesh, and the Israelites, the whole congregation, came to Mount Hor.** [23] **Then the Lord said to Moses and Aaron at Mount Hor, on the border of the land of Edom,** [24] **"Let Aaron be gathered to his people. For he shall not enter the land that I have given to the Israelites, because you rebelled against my command at the waters of Meribah.** [25] **Take Aaron** and his son Eleazar, and bring them up Mount Hor; ²⁶ strip Aaron of his vestments, and put them on his son Eleazar. But Aaron shall be gathered to his people, and shall die there." ²⁷ Moses did as the LORD had commanded; they went up Mount Hor in the sight of the whole congregation. ²⁸ Moses stripped Aaron of his vestments, and put them on his son Eleazar; and Aaron died there on the top of the mountain. Moses and Eleazar came down from the mountain. ²⁹ When all the congregation saw that Aaron had died, all the house of Israel mourned for Aaron thirty days.

The people make it from Kadesh to Mount Hor. They are making progress, but time is passing. And with the passing of time, so continues the passing of the first generation. At Mount Hor, the three original leaders are whittled down to one: it is now Aaron's time to die.

Note first the assertion that our lives and our deaths are in the hands of God ("You turn us back to dust, and say, 'Turn back, you mortals'" [Ps. 90:3]; "In your book were written all the days that were formed for me, when none of them as yet existed" [139:16]; "So teach us to count our days that we may gain a wise heart" [90:12]). Though death may be experienced as our enemy, it is never an enemy outside the boundaries of God's providential control: "Then the LORD said to Moses and Aaron at Mount Hor, . . . 'Let Aaron be gathered to his people.' . . . and Aaron died there on the top of the mountain" (Num. 20: 23–24, 28).

Observe also the care with which the Lord oversees this process: knowing the time, picking out the place, requiring time on the part of God's people. Aaron's life had not been perfect, but he had reflected his share of God's glory ("Precious in the sight of the LORD is the death of his faithful ones" [Ps. 116:15]; "Are not two sparrows sold for a penny? Yet not one of them will fall to the ground apart from your Father" [Matt. 10:29]). The Lord does indeed watch over both our comings in and our goings out (Ps. 121:8), and God's people rightly mark the passing over of this servant with thirty days of mourning (no slight task when encamped in the wilderness!).

Finally recognize the Lord's keen desire to pass on gifts and authority: "Strip Aaron of his vestments, and put them on his son Eleazar" (Num. 20:26). Though God's judgment rumbles within this ("because you rebelled against my command at the waters of Meribah"; v. 24), God's grace also shines ("Moses and Eleazar came down from the mountain"; v. 29). This story is moving on, despite the death of Aaron. And like Elijah passing the mantle to Elisha, and Jesus breathing the Spirit on the disciples, none of the gifts God has given will be lost.

VICTORY OVER ARAD AND KINGS SIHON AND OG
Numbers 21:1–3, 10–35

21:21 Then Israel sent messengers to King Sihon of the Amorites, saying, [22] "Let me pass through your land; we will not turn aside into field or vineyard; we will not drink the water of any well; we will go by the King's Highway until we have passed through your territory." [23] But Sihon would not allow Israel to pass through his territory. Sihon gathered all his people together, and went out against Israel to the wilderness; he came to Jahaz, and fought against Israel. [24] Israel put him to the sword, and took possession of his land from the Arnon to the Jabbok, as far as to the Ammonites; for the boundary of the Ammonites was strong. [25] Israel took all these towns, and Israel settled in all the towns of the Amorites, in Heshbon, and in all its villages. [26] For Heshbon was the city of King Sihon of the Amorites, who had fought against the former king of Moab and captured all his land as far as the Arnon.

21:33 Then they turned and went up the road to Bashan; and King Og of Bashan came out against them, he and all his people, to battle at Edrei. [34] But the LORD said to Moses, "Do not be afraid of him; for I have given him into your hand, with all his people, and all his land. You shall do to him as you did to King Sihon of the Amorites, who ruled in Heshbon." [35] So they killed him, his sons, and all his people, until there was no survivor left; and they took possession of his land.

With the beginning of chapter 21, a new chapter in the story of Israel's wanderings begins. Up to this point, all the threats to God's people's forward progress have been internal (feuds, fights, despair) or, if external (as with Edom in Num. 20), fairly easily avoided. Indeed, the key reason for Israel's circuitous wanderings, which take up ten verses at the heart of Numbers 21 (vv. 10–20), is its desire, at least while on the east bank of the river Jordan, to "pass through" this territory without a fight. But here, at this point in the journey, the resistance to this priestly nation's transit in the world stiffens, and its swords are for the first time unsheathed—not against rebels and malcontents in its own ranks, but against a series of three enemies without. They are in order: the king of Arad ("the Canaanite," 2:1), and the kings of the Amorites and of Bashan, King Sihon and King Og.

Rather than treating all three of these encounters separately, they will be dealt with together, first in terms of similarities, then in terms of differences.

Similarities. Sometimes the most obvious points are the most essential points. Such is the case here. All three of these stories concern peoples who come out in direct opposition to Israel's forward motion: the king of

Arad ("fought against Israel and took some of them captive"; 21:1), King Sihon ("went out against Israel"; 21:23), and King Og ("came out against them, he and all his people"; 21:33). This is no small detail. Before God's people unsheathe their swords, they need to encounter not just resistance or persecution or opposition, but direct attack on the next stage of their journey. These are stories of human beings setting themselves in direct opposition to God's people's way in the world, and thus stand in immediate opposition to God's continuing purpose. No matter who they are at this point, and no matter how understandable their stance, from a human point of view, they must be told, "Get behind me, Satan!" (Mark 8: 33). These are not so much stories of the preservation of God's people as the inevitability of God's purposes. God makes a way where there is no way, as long as the way is truly the Lord's. These are not offensive actions on the part of God or God's people, but surgical strikes made necessary by offensive actions on the part of others.

Second is something we can see only in the larger sweep of the narrative: all these stories end in victory. Up to this point, since the Red Sea, all of Israel's stories have been ones of casualties within the camp and one huge defeat at the hands of persons outside the camp (Num. 14). Now the tide seems to be shifting, and the scorecard turned upside down. Surely it is not accidental that this shift marks not only the peoples' proximity to the Promised Land, but also the progressive disappearance of the first rebellious generation. Though progress on the part of God's people is always a slippery concept in Scripture, Israel's protests are here severely muted. When confronted with flesh-and-blood opponents, armed and ready to fight (or already successful regarding captives), God's people make vows, draw their swords, and hearken to God's word to "fear not" (21:34). This surely seems like a different generation from those who "raised a loud cry" and wept (14:1) when confronted only with *reports* of enemies up ahead. A tide is changing, and that tide will continue on up and past the end of Numbers.

Differences. The key difference in these accounts has to do with the nature of Israel's response to each of these oppositions in turn. With the king of Arad, Israel makes a vow ("If you will indeed give this people into our hands, then we will utterly destroy their towns"; 21:2) and follows through ("and they utterly destroyed them and their towns" [21:3], which leads to the naming of the place, Hormah, a pun on the Hebrew word *ḥerem*, for ban or "devoted to destruction"). With King Sihon, Israel puts him to the sword, takes possession of his land, and settles in his cities (21:24–26, 31), though the poem inserted into the middle of the story describes a more utterly devouring fire (21:27–30). With King Og, they "killed him, his sons, and all his people, until there was no survivor left; and they took possession of his land" (21:35). Why the differences? Are they significant?

For the purpose of this ongoing story, probably not. An obstacle to Israel's forward progress has been removed, and the journey may continue. But for the purpose of these stories' later interpretation, these details are important indeed.

What we encounter here are the first examples of Israel's debate concerning *ḥerem* or "holy war." Though this is a topic too broad for this study, and though a full treatment would have to deal with passages far beyond these chapters, at least one comment must be in order.

One reason there may be a distinction between the utter destruction and lack of possession in the first encounter, and the more muted destruction in the second and third (in terms of possible survivors in the second case, and the sparing of the cities in both), may have to do with some ambiguity regarding the location of the king of Arad versus that of Sihon and Og. Arad is identified as a "Canaanite" while both Sihon and Og are on the King's Highway, west of the river Jordan. Thus while the destruction of the king of Arad is a foreshadowing of the coming *conquest*, Sihon and Og represent temporary settlements for the purpose of *transit* (at least up until the point in the story when we find out that some of the Israelites would prefer to stay here; Num. 32). This key distinction should remind us of the distinctions regarding types of sacrifice with which this story began (some sacrifices where the worshipers and priests partake in portions of the offering, and others where they do not).

Again, at first glance, a burnt, whole offering seems the most barbaric of the offerings, and a total waste of precious life and blood. However, the key to its power, in an essential sense, rested in the fact that it accrued no direct benefit to the worshiper: it all went up in smoke. While our first reaction to mass destruction is and surely should be abhorrence, it is worth wondering how many territorial, social, and ecclesiastical assaults might be forestalled if, from the beginning, one knew there would be no booty to follow, no peoples, cities, and land to possess. Human beings who know the greed and covetousness always lurking in the human heart are always inclined to dig beneath the principles and platforms with which a war is justified, for the booty and bounty underneath. For all its heinousness, *ḥerem* at least forestalls any attack driven for gain. Here these stories foreshadow a looming conflict that will come to fruition in Numbers 31 and will haunt Israel's story and the church's ever after.

THE FIERY SERPENTS
Numbers 21:4–9

> 21:4 **From Mount Hor they set out by the way to the Red Sea, to go around the land of Edom; but the people became impatient on the way.** [5] **The people spoke against God and against Moses, "Why have you brought us up out of Egypt to die in the wilderness? For there is no food and no water, and we detest this miserable food."** [6] **Then the LORD sent poisonous serpents among the people, and they bit the people, so that many Israelites died.** [7] **The people came to Moses and said, "We have sinned by speaking against the LORD and against you; pray to the LORD to take away the serpents from us." So Moses prayed for the people.** [8] **And the LORD said to Moses, "Make a poisonous serpent, and set it on a pole; and everyone who is bitten shall look at it and live."** [9] **So Moses made a serpent of bronze, and put it upon a pole; and whenever a serpent bit someone, that person would look at the serpent of bronze and live.**

Into the midst of these stories of battles avoided and engaged, another story appears. While connected to the others by its theme of detour ("to go around the land of Edom"; 21:4), its basic themes and patterns take us all the way back to the first day of Israel's journey from the camp at Mount Sinai. Here, like there, the people complain, God responds with judgment, the people cry out, Moses intercedes, and the people are spared. Almost on cue, to offset the apparent progress in obedience the people have made regarding battles with outside forces, Israel now threatens once more to implode from within. They complain against God and against Moses concerning the lack of water and food, and the surfeit of manna (cf. 11:4–34). Even God's judgment is closer than the English may indicate (the adjective translated "poisonous" can also mean "fiery," as in the NRSV note for v. 6; cf. the "fire" in 11:1). It's the same ole story and the same ole people. Will anything, or anyone, ever change? The answer may well be first "No," then "Yes."

No, nothing and no one changes. Notice the lack of overall progress God's people have made on this journey. Though there may be some truth to the emerging contrast between the first and second generation, a contrast that will be most clear after the second census, in Numbers 26 (see Olson, *Numbers*), it is also true that God's people never arrive at perfection in the Scriptures. As controversy breaks out even after Pentecost over the sheltered possessions of Ananias and Sapphira in Acts 5, so disputes arise even after the census over the newly acquired booty of the warriors in Numbers 31 (see later discussion). It is simply a pattern of God's story with God's people that when things are going well, "Watch out," things are about to fall apart; and when things have fallen apart, "Get ready," something good is on the way. Israel's encounter with the king of Arad is so perfect in its account of obstacles encountered and overcome that the reader should expect a counternarrative to follow. And follow it does, providing bookends for Israel's journey, from Day One to almost the end.

Yes, something and someone can change. Nevertheless, having identified similarities between this story and Israel's opening story of complaint in Numbers 11, it is now time to recognize a few small, yet key distinctions.

The initial cause for complaint. One key that marks this story as toward the end of the journey versus the beginning is the rationale for Israel's complaint given in 21:4. "But the people became impatient on the way." Although Israel immediately backs up this general "impatience" with the same specific outcome (death) and the same proximate causes for dissent (water and food) they have had all along, this story no longer sounds like simply the tale of a people who once were wanderers but are so no longer. Though the reason for this detour is obvious (the king of Edom who has come out against them "with a large force, heavily armed"; 20:20), and though they are very near to the place where they first learned a heavy lesson on the fruits of impatience (their first attempt to take the Promised Land by storm in Num. 14), they nevertheless are growing weary with this journey, and with the God and the human leader at their head. The movement from fear for survival to impatience on the way may at first glance seem a negligible shift, but it opens this story to a whole new dimension of applicability for a people yet on the journey. How many rebellions of the church are due to "impatience on the way," and how many are the resources of Scripture meant to counter these! "I waited patiently for the LORD" (Ps. 40:1). "But if we hope for what we do not see, we wait for it with patience" (Rom. 8:25). "Let us run with perseverance ['patience' in some translations] the race that is set before us" (Heb. 12:1).

The means of grace. One reason why this text has proved to be a favorite of the rabbis and the preachers (this passage alone counts for three of the seven appearances of Leviticus–Numbers in the Revised Common Lectionary) is the means through which the Lord responds to Moses' intercession. Rather than simply eradicating the serpents (see comment to follow) or have Moses wave a hand or a rod for healing, God commands Moses to make a fiery serpent, set it on a pole, so that "everyone who is bitten shall look at it and live" (Num. 21:8). For the rabbis this has caused concern regarding overtones of both idolatry and magic ("Take care and watch yourselves closely, so that you do not act corruptly by making an idol for yourselves, in the form of any figure, . . . the likeness of anything that creeps on the ground" [Deut. 4:15–16, 18]; and in 2 Kgs. 18:4 King Hezekiah shatters Nehushtan, the bronze serpent). For the preachers, this has provided an immediate link to Christ's setting up on the cross (as quoted by Jesus to Nicodemus in John 3:14–15, "And just as Moses lifted up the serpent in the wilderness, so must the Son of Man be lifted up, that whoever believes in him may have eternal life"). The important interpretive point made here (though it must be said it is not in the text itself!) is that the healing taking place comes from *the God* who commands this solution, for all those who turn toward this solution in trust (cf. the apocryphal Wisdom of Solomon 16:7, "For the one who turned toward it was saved, not by the thing that was beheld, but by you, the Savior of all"). It thus serves as a type for all visible signs of invisible graces, including the sometimes seemingly idolatrous and magical sacraments of baptism and communion.

The scope of the solution. A final cue that perhaps marks this as a story for people still on the way is the fact that God's solution does not rid this people of fiery snakes that bite, but simply provides a cure for those who would keep going. Unlike most of the other grumbling stories that precede this, where the complaining and judgment are resolved in the response, this is a solution yet in effect for all those whose impatience causes them to be "snakebitten." This too makes this a story not just for this generation in the wilderness, but also for all who follow. Even those who look to the cross of Christ may be bitten and grow ill on the way. But God does provide means for keeping going, in the synagogue and the sanctuary and through other ordinary and extraordinary means of grace.

Part 3: At Camp in Moab, Preparation for Conquest

Numbers 22:1–36:13

18. Enemies Attack, Threats from Without
Numbers 22:1–24:25

God's people are now just a stone's throw from the Promised Land. After all the preparations, trials, and testing, they are situated in the valley of Moab across from Jericho, with only the Jordan River in between. Surely, having missed this opportunity forty years previous, their thoughts are preoccupied with the conquest dead ahead: Who is marching behind whom? Who will blow the trumpets? Who will wield the sword? Are there really giants and supernatural creatures hiding in the hills across the way?

Little do they know, however, that the biggest battle of the first five books of the Bible (excluding the victory at the Red Sea) is staring them dead in the face—closer than Jericho, indeed as close as the hills above their heads. While their journey has been continually jeopardized by threats *within*, and while the chapters preceding and following this story provide practice skirmishes regarding threats *without*, the Mother of All Battles now looms in these hills so peaceful in appearance ("Is that smoke, or just fog on that peak toward Bamoth-baal?" see Num. 22:41); yet all they, their leaders, and Moses do (for the next three chapters!) is "camp" (22:1). We enter now one of Scripture's grandest stories of the providential care and protection of our God. "O the depth of the riches and wisdom and knowledge of God! How unsearchable are his judgments and how inscrutable his ways!" (Rom. 11:33).

Israel unawares. First, observe how God's major battles often take God's people by surprise. One of the major themes in the Balaam story is Israel's total lack of *involvement* and even lack of *knowledge* of the battle raging in the hills above the plains of Moab. Surely if one of the Israelites was reciting Psalm 23 before retiring for the night, she did not fully appreciate the context: "Even though I walk through the darkest valley, I fear no evil; for you are with me; your rod and your staff—they comfort me" (v. 4). Surely if another of the Israelites began his morning prayer with Psalm 121, he did not recognize how the hills above the valley of

Moab were filled with threat as well as promise: "I lift up my eyes to the hills—from where will my help come? My help comes from the LORD, who made heaven and earth" (vv. 1–2, though this more ominous reading may well capture the original meaning of these verses). Surely if some of the troops, in the midst of drills, found themselves singing Psalm 124, they could not know that as this song had been true *in the past* (at the Red Sea) and would be true *in the future* (during the conquest), so it was true *even right now* when they were caught unaware: "If it had not been the LORD who was on our side—let Israel now say—if it had not been the Lord who was on our side, when our enemies attacked us, then they would have swallowed us up alive" (vv. 1–3).

Surely Moses, or someone in the camp, became cognizant of this battle at some point soon afterward, or else how have we received the gift of this story (like Jesus' prayer in the Garden of Gethsemane—so similar in theme and substance—while the disciples were sleeping)? However, from the point of view of the narrative, God's people are most notable by their absence. God's saving story has a way of sneaking up on us, of becoming clear only after the fact, of arriving in our ears as good news of a victory already accomplished without our raising a finger.

Unexpected Savior. As the real Savior of this story is hidden (the Lord God), so the flesh-and-blood savior of this story is the very last person such a holy story should attract. Not Moses or Aaron, who have been charged with leading this people through the wilderness. Not Joshua or Caleb, who have proved faithful in the past and will prove faithful in the future. Not even some unexpected lad or lass, older woman or feebler man within the camp, who is unexpectedly given the vision and the courage to get God's people through (such as David in the Old Testament, or Mary in the New). No, out of the east comes Balaam, a pagan hired-gun seer, who nevertheless calls the Lord by name and pronounces upon Israel the grandest blessing in the Pentateuch. Hold on to your hats. Like stories of Cyruses and Samaritans and unexpected saviors elsewhere in Scripture, this is a story that bursts the bounds of the kinds of people and nations with whom we would like the Lord to be familiar. This is a radical story not only in the bounds of God's blessing, but also due to the boundaries of God's saving work.

Comedy versus tragedy. Yet third, and for this very reason, we must not overlook the fact that this story is told as a comedy. Yes, a comedy. Not in the sense that there is no pain and suffering in the world. The Bible is full to overflowing with pain and suffering. Even this story makes clear that we live in a world where lions lick the blood of their prey, and foes endure broken bones and the piercing of arrows (Num. 23:24; 24:8).

No, in the most basic sense, the story of the Bible is *comedy* rather than *tragedy* simply because pain and suffering do not win in the end. In this story, they don't even come close. And so like the somewhat similar and surprising books of Jonah and Esther (which some have read quite seriously as "melodrama" or "farce"), the story of Balak and Balaam versus Israel, or King Balak versus King Yahweh (with Balaam along as aide) ends up with blessing rather than curse, and preservation rather than destruction.

Indeed, the sad fact is that the only people in all the world who might miss the essential tone of this narrative are we churchgoers. Since we are so well trained in taking matters of faith seriously, we forget that the overall movement of the Scriptures is toward comedy. Thus in this story, full of powerful people who play the fool, an ass who speaks, and outsiders who are more faithful than insiders, we, God's people, must laugh—or prove ungrateful for the hilariously surprising stories which have won us life.

And now let the play begin.

BALAK SUMMONS BALAAM TO CURSE ISRAEL
Numbers 22:1–6

22:1 **The Israelites set out, and camped in the plains of Moab across the Jordan from Jericho.** [2] **Now Balak son of Zippor saw all that Israel had done to the Amorites.** [3] **Moab was in great dread of the people, because they were so numerous; Moab was overcome with fear of the people of Israel.** [4] **And Moab said to the elders of Midian, "This horde will now lick up all that is around us, as an ox licks up the grass of the field." Now Balak son of Zippor was king of Moab at that time.** [5] **He sent messengers to Balaam son of Beor at Pethor, which is on the Euphrates, in the land of Amaw, to summon him, saying, "A people has come out of Egypt; they have spread over the face of the earth, and they have settled next to me.** [6] **Come now, curse this people for me, since they are stronger than I; perhaps I shall be able to defeat them and drive them from the land; for I know that whomever you bless is blessed, and whomever you curse is cursed."**

It goes without saying that it's been a long time since anyone, much less a king, was afraid of Israel! For most of its history, God's people Israel, like God's people the church and God's Messiah the Christ, will serve better as the butt of the jokes of those in power ("Watch out! Shady Grove Presbyterian is mobilizing!") than the stuff of their nightmares ("The Pharisees went out and immediately conspired with the Herodians against him, how to destroy him"; Mark 3:6). But every now and then, evidence of blessing becomes apparent even to the most worldly-wise, like Balak. Israel is drawing near to the Promised Land. Like the almost imperceptible shifts in the waterline at the seashore, the tide is beginning to turn. Stories of battles already won begin to multiply (Num. 22:2). The old threat of victory through procreation (v. 3) rears its ugly head (cf. "But the Israelites were fruitful and prolific; they multiplied and grew exceedingly strong, so that the land was filled with them"; Exod. 1:7). The blessing of offspring as numerous as the stars in the heavens or the sands on the shore begins to shine through the cracks and the valleys of Moab, and this time it's somebody else's turn to be sore afraid (Num. 22:3).

So what does a king do when his people are under dire threat? He summons his horses and his chariots! But what if they are not enough? He appeals to his own advisers and prays to his own gods! But what if they are not sufficiently wise or powerful? He calls together his best emissaries and loads them with the best stuff in his treasury and sends them far to the northeast, toward a cradle of civilization, and the residence of the most respected seer of his generation (so well known that there may be archaeological evidence of his influence in the ancient Near East; see Dozeman, *Numbers*, 177–78): Balaam son of Beor at Pethor.

A king under threat. Watch out in Scripture, and in the world, when you encounter a king under threat. From Pharaoh in the Old Testament, to Herod and Pilate and Caesar in the New, when God's people begin to threaten the powers that be, bad things are apt to happen. All God's people want, or should want, is permission to pass through; we are travelers and sojourners on this earth. But when we win a few small victories in this world (as Israel just has with the Amorites; Num. 22:2), and when our numbers begin to grow (cf. Exod. 1:9, "Look, the Israelite people are more numerous and more powerful than we"), and when, most important, these outward signs are seen as evidence of inward blessing (as numbers and latent power are in Exodus, and a single birth and visiting powers are in Matthew), *watch out!* As fear can cause a small creature or people to run (Num. 13:33, "There we saw the Nephilim, . . . and to ourselves we seemed like grasshoppers, and so we seemed to them"); so fear can cause a slightly larger creature or people to attack (22:4, "This horde will now lick up all that is around us, as an ox licks up the grass of the field"). It's flight or fight, and in the case of Balak, son of Zippor, King of Moab, the choice is clear.

The king's magicians. The first thing a threatened king does, if he's wise, is gather his advisers: the joint chiefs of staff, leaders of the scientific community, the wisest of the wise. At the beginning of Exodus, this is what Pharaoh did when threatened by a staff-wielding shepherd named

Moses. At the beginning of Matthew, this is what Herod did when he received word that a star had risen and a child been born. But what do you do if you're just a medium-sized potentate, lacking the budget for a full-time council of advisers? Well, you hire a temporary, a consultant; yet in this case, it has to be the very best. So enters Balaam "son of Beor at Pethor, which is on the Euphrates, in the land of Amaw" (v. 5), the first, biblical "wise man from the East."

Blessings and curses. The key to understanding the magnitude of the engagement now at hand is to pick up on the strategy of Balak's attack. This is no program of infanticide, as with Pharaoh and Herod, as obscene and wicked as that may be. No, this is something far worse. It has to do with "principalities and powers." It entails destruction of man, woman, and beast not only in the present, but also for the future. It's akin to robbing someone of one's birthright; worse than the slaughter of one's firstborn; similar in magnitude to germ warfare or nuclear holocaust. King Balak wants to take away Israel's only true treasure (its blessing by God) and replace it with its polar opposite (a curse): "Come now, curse this people for me, since they are stronger than I; perhaps I shall be able to defeat them and drive them from the land; for I know that whomever you bless is blessed, and whomever you curse is cursed" (v. 6). Balak, in a way he surely does not fully comprehend, is fighting fire with fire.

"Do not fear those who kill the body but cannot kill the soul," Jesus says; "rather fear him who can destroy both soul and body in hell" (Matt. 10:28). From its inception, Israel's sole reason for existing has been to be blessed in order to bless others (Gen. 12). Take that away, and the Israelites may win some battles, but they've lost the war. Make no mistake. This is the Mother of All Battles, the War to End All Wars.

And so, it becomes all the more incredible that this is a war that will take place with Israel, unawares. If they were aware of the plot against them, surely they would have been engaged in all-night prayer, extra sacrifices, and beefed-up security on the perimeters. Certainly it's tempting to speculate what Moses was up to during this time of great testing: adjudicating types of thread in one person's garments, ruling on an alleged blemish in another's sacrificial lamb, writing the first drafts of the books to hand on to us. We don't know. The Bible doesn't say. All it says is that Israel "set out, and camped in the plains of Moab" (Num. 22:1). This is a war that King Yahweh will fight on behalf of God's people, using the most surprising of instruments, all without Israel lifting a finger, much less an arm or leg or army.

From the very beginning, however, there are signs of trouble, at least from *Balak's* point of view.

FIRST REFUSAL
Numbers 22:7–14

22:7 **So the elders of Moab and the elders of Midian departed with the fees for divination in their hand; and they came to Balaam, and gave him Balak's message.** [8] **He said to them, "Stay here tonight, and I will bring back word to you, just as the LORD speaks to me"; so the officials of Moab stayed with Balaam.** [9] **God came to Balaam and said, "Who are these men with you?"** [10] **Balaam said to God, "King Balak son of Zippor of Moab, has sent me this message:** [11] **'A people has come out of Egypt and has spread over the face of the earth; now come, curse them for me; perhaps I shall be able to fight against them and drive them out.'"** [12] **God said to Balaam, "You shall not go with them; you shall not curse the people, for they are blessed."** [13] **So Balaam rose in the morning, and said to the officials of Balak, "Go to your own land, for the LORD has refused to let me go with you."** [14] **So the officials of Moab rose and went to Balak, and said, "Balaam refuses to come with us."**

You would think that a combined delegation of Moabites and Midianites, laden with fees for divination, would get most anybody's attention and allegiance, but Balaam's not just anybody's lackey, and somebody else is part of this visitation! First, Balaam makes the delegation cool their heels (v. 8). Balaam is following his own time clock, not theirs. Second, Balaam's word, when it comes, will not be his word, but somebody else's (v. 8). Balaam is less of a speaker and more of a messenger. Third, another delegation, far more impressive than Balak's, comes calling that night ("God came to Balaam and said, 'Who are these men with you?'" v. 9—as if God didn't know!). Unknown to Balak and his messengers, there's another King in this drama, and this King's come to visit: "You shall not go with them; you shall not curse the people, for they are blessed" (v. 12). It's an open-and-shut case. "So Balaam rose in the morning, and said to the officials of Balak, "Go to your own land, for the LORD has refused to let me go with you" (v. 13). Without another word, they are sent packing. Opening round: Yahweh, 1; Balak, 0. It's the Pharaoh story all over again. And Balak's just as stubborn.

A note on names. It is crucial to recognize that the names for the main actor in this story vary from verse to verse. God may be called "God" in one verse (*Elohim*, 22:9), and the "Most High" (*Elyon*, 24:16) or the "Almighty" (*Shaddai*, 24:16) elsewhere (see Olson, *Numbers*, 141). In these shifts some would see evidence of the story's transmission by various storytellers down through the centuries. Others would discern in this a wide-ranging testimony to God's power and spheres and methods of revelation.

But here in the opening move of this story, on the most intimate level, Balaam also refers to God as "the LORD": "I will bring back word to you, just as the LORD speaks to me" (22:8).

The Hebrew here is "Yahweh," and this is the personal form of God's name, revealed to Moses back in the wilderness of Sinai through a voice out of a burning bush (Exod. 3). This marks the beginning of an intimately personal and saving relationship between God and Moses, which has brought God's people to the point of this encampment here in Moab.

Yet here this name appears, without fanfare, on the lips of a pagan seer from the east, who is not part of this saved and saving family. He has not seen God's power revealed by the Red Sea, or heard the Lord's voice thunder from the mountain or the tent of meeting. He is not a son of Abraham or Isaac or Jacob, nor of Sarah or Rebekah or Rachel. He is not circumcised in the flesh, but he may well be circumcised in the heart, as his ability to wait, listen, and respond with flexibility and faithfulness makes clear. Balaam thus becomes a forerunner (like Melchizedek, Gen. 14) of all those strange figures in the Scriptures (from those other wise men through Philip and Cornelius and the Gentiles), who should not be clued into the story and yet are. This is indeed a surprising story, not only of God's power, but also of the scope of God's revelation, to which we shall return later.

REGROUP, RELOAD, RETURN
Numbers 22:15–21

22:15 **Once again Balak sent officials, more numerous and more distinguished than these.** [16] **They came to Balaam and said to him, "Thus says Balak son of Zippor: 'Do not let anything hinder you from coming to me;** [17] **for I will surely do you great honor, and whatever you say to me I will do; come, curse this people for me.'"** [18] **But Balaam replied to the servants of Balak, "Although Balak were to give me his house full of silver and gold, I could not go beyond the command of the LORD my God, to do less or more.** [19] **You remain here, as the others did, so that I may learn what more the LORD may say to me."** [20] **That night God came to Balaam and said to him, "If the men have come to summon you, get up and go with them; but do only what I tell you to do."** [21] **So Balaam got up in the morning, saddled his donkey, and went with the officials of Moab.**

Persistence is a trait not limited to Israel, especially when you have a king who's afraid, and so Balak hardens his heart, repositions his delegation (v. 15) and his treasury (by implication, v. 18), and sends them back with a speech far more regal and desperate than the first: "Do not let anything hinder you from coming to me; for I will surely do you great honor, and whatever you say to me I will do; come, curse this people for me" (vv. 16–17). Again, Balaam makes this delegation wait ("You remain here," v. 19). Again, another King comes to call, this time telling Balaam to go with them (v. 20).

This time Balaam gives Balak, through his messengers, a speech as remarkable as any servant's speech in Scripture (v. 18). This prophet/seer is not one who can be bought. He is finally subservient to only one King. Yahweh, 2; Balak, 0. The story should be over, but due to Balak's stubbornness, it's not.

Some lessons thus far on the way. First, Balaam, from the start, stands out as a model of the faithful servant of the Lord. He worships God, not mammon. He acknowledges only one King in this world. He speaks only as he has been spoken to. This is surely the model for any faithful disciple, preacher/prophet, or church! Second (here's the joke), he's a pagan from the east. How does he know the God of Israel? How has he learned to pattern his speech and actions so closely to the will of the Lord? Why does Balaam (a figure whose credentials are elsewhere held up to severe disrepute) here appear as a servant less reluctant than Moses, more obedient than Jonah, and worlds more faithful than either Israel or the church? In some basic and fundamental way, perhaps the story is reminding us: It's not about Balaam, but about God, who made heaven, who made earth, who can make even the stones to shout. Third, while it may appear that God changes strategies (at one point telling Balaam to stay, at another telling him to go), the Lord God of Israel does not switch blessings. Though neither Balak nor Balaam may know it, a shift in God's blessing is not something human beings can maneuver or wait out. God's blessings are always, in some deeply fundamental way, irrevocable—whether kings, seers, or even God's people know it or not. This is the fundamental truth of which this victory of blessing over curse in the valley of Moab is but a sign.

AN INTERLUDE: THE STORY OF BALAAM'S ASS
Numbers 22:22–35

> 22:22 **God's anger was kindled because he was going, and the angel of the Lord took his stand in the road as his adversary. Now he was riding on the donkey, and his two servants were with him.** [23] **The donkey saw the angel of the Lord standing in the road, with a drawn sword in his hand; so the don-**

key turned off the road, and went into the field; and Balaam struck the donkey, to turn it back onto the road. [24] Then the angel of the Lord stood in a narrow path between the vineyards, with a wall on either side. [25] When the donkey saw the angel of the Lord, it scraped against the wall, and scraped Balaam's foot against the wall; so he struck it again. [26] Then the angel of the Lord went ahead, and stood in a narrow place, where there was no way to turn either to the right or to the left. [27] When the donkey saw the angel of the Lord, it lay down under Balaam; and Balaam's anger was kindled, and he struck the donkey with his staff. [28] Then the Lord opened the mouth of the donkey, and it said to Balaam, "What have I done to you, that you have struck me these three times?" [29] Balaam said to the donkey, "Because you have made a fool of me! I wish I had a sword in my hand! I would kill you right now!" [30] But the donkey said to Balaam, "Am I not your donkey, which you have ridden all your life to this day? Have I been in the habit of treating you this way?" And he said, "No." [31] Then the Lord opened the eyes of Balaam, and he saw the angel of the Lord standing in the road, with his drawn sword in his hand; and he bowed down, falling on his face. [32] The angel of the Lord said to him, "Why have you struck your donkey these three times? I have come out as an adversary, because your way is perverse before me. [33] The donkey saw me, and turned away from me these three times. If it had not turned away from me, surely just now I would have killed you and let it live." [34] Then Balaam said to the angel of the Lord, "I have sinned, for I did not know that you were standing in the road to oppose me. Now therefore, if it is displeasing to you, I will return home." [35] The angel of the Lord said to Balaam, "Go with the men; but speak only what I tell you to speak." So Balaam went on with the officials of Balak.

You, the readers, have probably all heard the jokes. The ones that lead off with, "If God can speak through an ass, maybe he can speak through . . ." The jokes that feature Protestant clergy, Catholic priests, and Balaam's ass appear in various church situations or dilemmas. Some take note of this equine's gender (female) and lack of domesticity (in Hebrew, this animal is less likely a domesticated donkey and more likely an ass of wilderness environs, hence a "wild ass" or "she ass" or both!) to stir the pot of female versus male issues, in the church and out. Even as serious a commentator as John Calvin cannot help but pun when confronted with Numbers 22 as a teaching moment: "But, since he [Balaam] had been so unteachable, he is treated according to his desert, when, after having made some proficiency in the school of the ass, he [Balaam] begins to listen to God" (*Commentaries*, 3:196).

"Hah, hah," shout God's people, or better, "Hee, Haw!" roar all God's creatures, and such laughter is undoubtedly in order upon reading such a story, part of whose function is surely comic relief. As the Mother of All Battles is nearing; as kings and their advisers consult and maneuver; as sacrifices are about to be made, visions seen, and blessings and curses pronounced—the Scriptures pause for this little comedy on the way. Can it truly be accidental that even in the English language, the word "ass" has a double meaning? (1) "Any of several hoofed mammals of the genus Equus." (2) "A vain, self-important, silly, or aggressively stupid person" (*American Heritage Dictionary*, 110). From heaven's point of view, all the happenings on earth are but the wanderings of restless creatures. The wisest of those creatures (infrequently populated by the likes of kings and seers!) are they who look out on all of this and join the Lord in God's laughter at all human pretense: "He who sits in the heavens laughs; the LORD has them in derision. . . . Now therefore, O kings, be wise; be warned, O rulers of the earth. Serve the LORD with fear, with trembling kiss his feet. . . . Happy are all who take refuge in him" (Ps. 2:4, 10–12).

But just as surely, it is wrong to cast the God of Scriptures, and certainly the God made known in Jesus Christ, primarily as a God who laughs "at" us rather than "with" us. Having gotten the little jokes in Numbers 22 out of the way, let us go back and see if we can find some of the bigger jokes lurking underneath.

From God's point of view. One of the most remarkable themes that emerges in the overall wilderness narrative is the marvel of God's timing. God's job, as with any good parent, is not just to get one's child from point *A* to point *B*, but to make sure that this child learns each lesson appropriate to each stage of the journey all along the way. This, in a basic way, is the key to understanding the why of the wilderness wanderings and the why of the whole earthly sojourn of which we are a part. And so, in a little way, it becomes a part of this interlude regarding Balaam on the way.

At Balaam's first encounter with the Lord, he was told to stay put (v. 12). At his second encounter, the orders are reversed (v. 20). Now, inexplicably and seemingly out of the blue, God's mind has changed and "God's anger was kindled because he was going" (v. 22). This shift in God's thinking has led to the spilling of much commentary ink, especially in Reformed circles, under the rubric of the "unchangeableness" of God. Such questions have it all wrong.

From the beginning of this journey, God, in order to remain a good parent, has necessarily been shifting and adapting: taking a southern route through the desert, rather than straight northeast along the Mediterranean coast; providing a second set of tablets when the first got smashed following the incident of the golden calf; revising the itinerary by an entire generation after the bad report of the spies back in Numbers 13. God's purpose has been constant from the beginning: to lead God's people from a life of slavery in Egypt toward a life of freedom in the Promised Land. This is a promise that will not be broken, but rather fulfilled. However, all along the way God's strategies have had to shift because of the shiftless people with whom God is stuck—modifying and adapting, sending one messenger then another, telling Israel to move forward and then backward, depending on the circumstances (exterior and interior) at that time. God is a good parent, a wise teacher, and a faithful partner and as such must constantly adapt divine methods for God's children and pupils, ourselves. Consistency, it turns out, is not only the hobgoblin of little minds but, we might argue, of little gods! This interlude is part and parcel of the larger narrative that it now "interrupts"!

From the point of view of Balaam. One of the major problems with seers is their blindness! Having received a word for one day, we want to keep it for the next. Having been granted a vision for one particular part of the journey, we want to apply it for the whole. From the beginning, the key to Balaam's character has been his willingness to wait and to listen, to see what the Lord rather than he himself intends: "Stay here tonight," he says to the first visitors (v. 8); "I could not go beyond the command of the LORD my God, to do less or more," he says to the second (v. 18). But, once on his ass, Balaam's "listen-ability," "see-ability," and "sense-ability" diminish. As we shall see, when Balaam is listening, he is able to see farther into the future than many if not most of Israel's own prophets and dreamers and seers; yet here on his ass, he proves unable to see an angel of the Lord with a sword unsheathed, three times, dead in his path. In Balaam, God has chosen a surprising instrument through which to make God's blessing clear. To get this strange instrument to the right place at the right time, God must perform at least two miracles: God must open the mouth of an ass so she can speak (v. 28); and God must open the eyes of the seer so that he can see (v. 31). It is left to the reader to decide which of these is the greater miracle.

From the point of view of the ass. Here, at the heart of this passage's humor, we attempt to go even deeper toward the biggest joke of them all.

God chooses what is foolish to shame the wise. There's a big joke inherent in the New Testament's characterization of God's people as sheep—if you've ever been around sheep! Likewise, there's a big joke inherent in having the most faithful creature in the whole wilderness narrative, and thus the model for all faithful seers and servants, be an ass—if you've ever been around asses! True, the image of a faithful donkey, always obedient to her master's command and desirous of his welfare, provides a great picture of what faithful service and discipleship should be all about, for church and for synagogue. But to make a compliant donkey and a seeing steed out of a she-ass must be the Lord's doing and, joking aside, a living example of what God is up against with us. Ishmael, a living sign of Abram and Sarai's lack of trust in God's promise, is characterized as a "wild ass of a man" in Genesis 16:12. Israel, in later days of faithlessness and willfulness, is characterized as a wild ass in heat in Jeremiah 2:24. When God thus uses a she-ass to teach a lesson to Balaam about wisdom, and when Jesus uses a donkey to show forth his messiahship as he rides into Jerusalem, we are reminded not only what God can accomplish, but why: "God chose what is foolish in the world to shame the wise; God chose what is weak in the world to shame the strong; God chose what is low and despised in the world, things that are not, to reduce to nothing things that are, so that no one might boast in the presence of God" (1 Cor. 1:27–29). Now we're talking about both church and synagogue, and about us.

The thin line between foolishness and violence. The structure of this story follows the patterns of many jokes. The ass sees the angel at first and turns off the road. The ass sees the angel a second time and scrapes Balaam's foot against the wall. We go from bad to worse. Then the third time (something's got to give!), the ass sees the angel, has nowhere to turn, and thus lies down under Balaam in the middle of the road. Again, you can imagine this story staged or filmed, with a laugh track underneath.

Except, first, for the violence involved. The faithful ass is struck once, then twice, then a third time with a rod by her master. Like the hangman's noose and threat of holocaust in Esther, and the cross and cruel floggings in the Gospels, there is an edge to this farce that should not go unnoticed. A supposedly wise Homo sapiens is beating a supposedly stupid equine even as the latter is trying to save the former's life. Something else is going on here.

Second, listen to the cause of Balaam's rage when his ass's mouth is opened and she asks simply, yet directly, "What have I done to you, that you have struck me these three times?" (Num. 22:28). "Because you have made a fool of me!" Balaam replies, adding: "I wish I had a sword in my hand! I would kill you right now!" (v. 29). Watch out when wise men, pharaohs, or kings are made fools of! Don't be surprised by how quickly swords can appear! From the halls of junior high school to the battlefields and throne rooms and church courts of this world, don't make a fool of someone and expect to get off lightly, especially if you are an ass!

Third, it can't go unnoticed that the sword Balaam wishes was "in [his] hand" has repeatedly been at his throat. The very violence he contemplates toward his ass is the violence from which he has been saved. "The donkey saw me, and turned away from me these three times," the angel informs Balaam. "If it had not turned away from me, surely just now I would have killed you [as you would have killed her] and let it [her] live" (v. 33). This ass is turning, scraping, and lying down not just to save her hide, but his. This is suffering not for one's own sins, but for the sins and threatened violence of others. While this beast had her mouth opened for her (versus the lambs and sheep that open not their mouths; Isa. 53:7), she answers not in kind, but simply and directly, "Am I not your donkey, which you have ridden all your life to this day? Have I been in the habit of treating you this way?" (v. 30) "All we like [Balaam, Israel, and] sheep have gone astray; we have all turned to our own way, and the LORD has laid on him [others] the iniquity" that should be our own (Isa. 53:6). As the wise Balaam beat his faithful beast, so the sage leaders and crowd later flogged the Messiah, and sophisticates today (ordained and lay) disparage the church. We human beings don't like to be made fools of. Whoever does so, for whatever reasons, will pay.

By her bruises we are healed. The real joke of this story is not just that Balaam's ass saves him in a physical sense, but also that the ass's faithfulness and suffering save him in a deeper sense. Balaam is indeed turned around by this experience, driven to his knees, and placed in need of forgiveness: "I have sinned, for I did not know that you were standing in the road to oppose me. Now therefore, if it is displeasing to you, I will return home" (Num. 22:34). This Moab Road story thus anticipates a later Damascus Road experience that has become the type for all biblical conversion stories. Balaam may later wander off the way, yet for now he is back on path, thanks to the costly ministry of his ass. This little story, this little joke, thus becomes an interruption that may be as revelatory as the larger narrative of which it is a part.

The Lord God is intent on preserving the blessing that God has bestowed upon Israel. To do so, God lifts up Balaam from the east as an instrument of this blessing. However, Balaam is no simple puppet. Indeed, he is a willful fool, an aggressively stupid person, like the rest of us human beings. Yet God has a way of raising up surprising means of grace in our lives, fellow creatures who can work even through our violence, waywardness, and willfulness to bring us back toward home. Again, though Balaam may later wander off the path, for now at least, he is a person on the way— thanks to the ass who saved his life, and the God who can use all sorts of surprises (including the church!) to save the world. No, this is not just a story for "Hah, hah" or "Hee, haw," but in a light and ironic sense (which may be the only way we, as violent fools all, can take it) for "Hallelujah."

THE MAIN ACT

Prologue
Numbers 22:36–40

> 22:36 **When Balak heard that Balaam had come, he went out to meet him at Ir-moab, on the boundary formed by the Arnon, at the farthest point of the boundary.** [37] **Balak said to Balaam, "Did I not send to summon you? Why did you not come to me? Am I not able to honor you?"** [38] **Balaam said to Balak, "I have come to you now, but do I have power to say just anything? The word God puts in my mouth, that is what I must say."** [39] **Then Balaam went with Balak, and they came to Kiriath-huzoth.** [40] **Balak sacrificed oxen and sheep, and sent them to Balaam and to the officials who were with him.**

After successfully traversing the territory between the land of Amaw and Moab, thanks to his ass; and having successfully traversed the far more difficult territory between his own ability to see and God's ability to help him see, again thanks to his long-suffering ass; Balaam now is ready to see Israel—not just from the world's perspective (strong versus weak), but from God's perspective (blessed versus cursed). To demonstrate his readiness for this crucial assignment, and surely also as a test and explanation for what is to follow, we have our first face-to-face encounter between Balaam and Balak, king of Moab.

Balak's impatience and anger confirm our suspicions of his poor vision. He is a person who can see on the *horizontal* plane only, where kings are high up ("Did I not send to summon you?"), seers are lower down ("Why did you not come to me?"), and gold and silver are means for raising and lowering people or gaining them honor ("Am I not able to honor [give *kābôd*] you?"). The truth we know, even before the story really begins, is that true honor or glory [*kābôd*] belong only to God, and are only God's to bestow. True wisdom entails seeing in both the *horizontal* and the *vertical* dimensions, a task that requires more listening than speaking, more being shown than seeing. Balaam says to Balak, "I have come to you now [but not without a lot of directing and redirecting], but do I have the power to say just anything [the foolishness of which has just been made painfully clear to me]? The word God puts in my mouth [as God will later place words on the tongues of prophets such as Isaiah, Jeremiah, and Ezekiel], that [and no other] is what I must say [I can do none else]."

Balaam's prologue speech thus serves as a primer on discernment for anyone who would try to see where God's blessing or curse might or might not be at work. As we shall see, while things on the horizontal plane (like beauty and number and size) may be outward signs of more inward truths, that is not always the case. The true seer must also be able, by God's grace, to see on the *vertical* plane, where powers such as promise and real glory are at work. On to act 1.

Act 1
Numbers 22:41–23:12

22:41 **On the next day Balak took Balaam and brought him up to Bamoth-baal; and from there he could see part of the people of Israel.**
23:1 **Then Balaam said to Balak, "Build me seven altars here, and prepare seven bulls and seven rams for me."** [2] **Balak did as Balaam had said; and Balak and Balaam offered a bull and a ram on each altar.** [3] **Then Balaam said to Balak, "Stay here beside your burnt offerings while I go aside. Perhaps the LORD will come to meet me. Whatever he shows me I will tell you." And he went to a bare height.** [4] **Then God met Balaam; and Balaam said to him, "I have arranged the seven altars, and have offered a bull and a ram on each altar."** [5] **The LORD put a word in Balaam's mouth, and said, "Return to Balak, and this is what you must say."** [6] **So he returned to Balak, who was standing beside his burnt offerings with all the officials of Moab.** [7] **Then Balaam uttered his oracle, saying:**

    "Balak has brought me from Aram,
        the king of Moab from the eastern mountains:
    'Come, curse Jacob for me;
        Come, denounce Israel!'
[8] **How can I curse whom God has not cursed?**
        How can I denounce those whom the LORD has not denounced?
[9] **For from the top of the crags I see him,**
        from the hills I behold him;
    Here is a people living alone,
        and not reckoning itself among the nations!
[10] **Who can count the dust of Jacob,**
        or number the dust-cloud of Israel?
    Let me die the death of the upright,
        and let my end be like his!"
[11] **Then Balak said to Balaam, "What have you done to me? I brought you to curse my enemies, but now you have done nothing but bless them."** [12] **He answered, "Must I not take care to say what the LORD puts into my mouth?"**

Now begins a strange, comic, and yet inspired minuet of life and death in the hills above Moab, with the surprising couple of Balak and Balaam and that unseen, yet all-important partner, God. Each round of this dance will follow a certain order: traversal to a certain vantage point (as if true seeing were just a matter of perspective!), offering up sacrifices (as a way of clearing the channels between earth and heaven), Balaam's drawing aside to meet with God (first by going "aside," then "over there," then without moving at all), God's meeting with Balaam (finally simply through God's spirit coming upon him), Balaam's pronouncement of an oracle (of increasing length and breadth and depth, with a fourth thrown in gratis), and Balak's reactions (which, like Balaam's in the preceding story, become increasingly angry and increasingly severe). This is a dance not of music, but of words—words that will bear the weight of blessing and of curse, not just in the days and weeks ahead, but for generations and generations to come. And, all the while, Israel sleeps!

Balaam now opens his mouth and sings a song that would be music to Moses' ears, but is a nightmare come true for Balak. First, he sets in contrast King Balak, who has brought him from the east, and King Yahweh, who alone has the power to curse or denounce (v. 7). If the Lord has not cursed or denounced Israel, Balaam declares, then neither can he (v. 8). This battle is over before it's even started; Israel's enemies had best get out of the way. Next, Balaam makes clear that this is indeed a nation like no other nation; a nation set apart and thus holy, consecrated by God (v. 9). This is truly a peculiar people, resident aliens, marked by "the loneliness of election" (Mays, *Leviticus–Numbers*, 124), not counting itself as just one nation among others (note the ambiguity of Israel's "aloneness," which can denote the isolation of the leper [Lev. 13:46]; the burden of the prophet [Jer. 15:17]; or the security of God's people [Deut. 33:28]). It is a people "in whose existence the government of God is hidden" (Mays, 124) and from whom shall one day come a person in whom this same government will become clearer. They are indeed passing through this valley and through this world, and those who bless them will be blessed, and those who curse them will be cursed (Gen. 12). Therefore, finally, by God's promise, they are and will be like the dust of this earth, spreading and swirling where it will. Those who are wise, like Balaam, will long to be part of this parade (Num. 23:10). Those who are fools, like Balak, will find Israel to be a stumbling block in their path, revealing their true faith and loyalty, and marking them as in opposition to the growth of God's kingdom in the world. Like another child to follow, this child, Israel, "is destined for the falling and the rising of many . . . , a sign that will be opposed so that the inner thoughts of many will be revealed" (Luke 2:34–35).

Act 2
Numbers 23:13–26

23:13 **So Balak said to him, "Come with me to another place from which you may see them; you shall see only part of them, and shall not see them all; then curse them for me from there."** [14] **So he took him to the field of Zophim, to the top of Pisgah. He built seven altars, and offered a bull and a ram on each altar.** [15] **Balaam said to Balak, "Stand here beside your burnt offerings, while I meet the L**ORD** over there.** [16] **The L**ORD** met Balaam, put a word into his mouth, and said, "Return to Balak, and this is what you shall say."** [17] **When he came to him, he was standing beside his burnt offerings with the officials of Moab. Balak said to him, "What has the L**ORD** said?"** [18] **Then Balaam uttered his oracle, saying:**

> **"Rise, Balak, and hear;**
>> **listen to me, O son of Zippor:**
> [19] **God is not a human being, that he should lie,**
>> **or a mortal, that he should change his mind.**
> **Has he promised, and will he not do it?**
>> **Has he spoken, and will he not fulfill it?**
> [20] **See, I received a command to bless;**
>> **he has blessed, and I cannot revoke it.**
> [21] **He has not beheld misfortune in Jacob;**
>> **nor has he seen trouble in Israel.**
> **The L**ORD** their God is with them,**
>> **acclaimed as a king among them.**
> [22] **God, who brings them out of Egypt,**
>> **is like the horns of a wild ox for them.**
> [23] **Surely there is no enchantment against Jacob,**
>> **no divination against Israel;**
> **now it shall be said of Jacob and Israel,**
>> **'See what God has done!'**
> [24] **Look, a people rising up like a lioness,**
>> **and rousing itself like a lion!**
> **It does not lie down until it has eaten the prey**
>> **and drunk the blood of the slain."**
> [25] **Then Balak said to Balaam, "Do not curse them at all, and do not**
>> **bless them at all."** [26] **But Balaam answered Balak, "Did I not**
>> **tell you, 'Whatever the L**ORD** says, that is what I must do'?"**

With the second oracle, the pace of this dance quickens, and the dependability and bite of this blessing deepens. First, Balaam sees clearly that God is God, and not a human being (v. 19). While God may change God's mind about specifics of timing (as Balaam has learned only too well!), God does not change God's mind about promises made and blessings spoken. Not only should human beings be able to stand on the promises of God, but blessings of God, once spoken, also cannot be retrieved, negated, or overturned (v. 20). Once more, this is a done deal, a finished battle. "Surely there is no enchantment against Jacob [declares the world's most famous enchanter], no divination against Israel [Balak had better just call it quits]; now it shall be said of Jacob and Israel, 'See [speaks the seer] what God [not Balaam, Balak, or Israel] has done [past perfect, complete]!'" (v. 23).

Furthermore, this irrevocable blessing is evident within Israel in at least two ways: (1) While Israel has seen its share of testing and heartbreaking defeats, God has not seen either misfortune in Jacob (with a capital *M*) or trouble in Israel (with a capital *T*) because God has not allowed it (v. 21). The very Misfortune and Trouble Balak desires for this people has been overruled from above. (2) The surest sign that this is a people whose God goes with them is the fact that occasionally, imperfectly, and fitfully, they acclaim this God as "king among them" (v. 21). God's throne is in the midst of their camp. Their leaders are prophet and priest, but no human king (that comes later in the story, and with very mixed results). "The Lord is King!" is one of their favorite camp songs (cf. Pss. 93; 96; 97; 99; etc.). Even now, as King Balak conspires, King Yahweh is worshiped, enthroned on the praises of Israel.

Finally, and worst of all for Balak's sake, the blessing of Israel by God is about to take on a new edge (v. 24). While Israel appears to be sleeping and resting in the valley of Moab, the eyes of the seer see her rising up and rousing herself "like a lion." While Balak's fear of Israel had mostly to do with numbers (they were so numerous, Num. 22:3) and the destruction their brute size might cause ("this horde will now lick up all that is around us, as an ox licks up the grass of the field," Num. 22:4), Balaam now sees a people, by God's power, far more lethal (v. 24). Better stay in those hills, Balak, or find some place higher! God's blessing of this people carries a bite.

Act 3
Numbers 23:27–24:14

> 23:27 **So Balak said to Balaam, "Come now, I will take you to another place; perhaps it will please God that you may curse them for me from there."**

²⁸ So Balak took Balaam to the top of Peor, which overlooks the wasteland. ²⁹ Balaam said to Balak, "Build me seven altars here, and prepare seven bulls and seven rams for me." ³⁰ So Balak did as Balaam had said, and offered a bull and a ram on each altar.

24:1 Now Balaam saw that it pleased the LORD to bless Israel, so he did not go, as at other times, to look for omens, but set his face toward the wilderness. ² Balaam looked up and saw Israel camping tribe by tribe. Then the spirit of God came upon him, ³ and he uttered his oracle, saying:

> "The oracle of Balaam son of Beor,
>> the oracle of the man whose eye is clear,
> ⁴ the oracle of one who hears the words of God,
>> who sees the vision of the Almighty,
>> who falls down, but with eyes uncovered:
> ⁵ how fair are your tents, O Jacob,
>> your encampments, O Israel!
> ⁶ Like palm groves that stretch far away,
>> like gardens beside a river,
> like aloes that the LORD has planted,
>> like cedar trees beside the waters.
> ⁷ Water shall flow from his buckets,
>> and his seed shall have abundant water,
> his king shall be higher than Agag,
>> and his kingdom shall be exalted.
> ⁸ God who brings him out of Egypt,
>> is like the horns of a wild ox for him;
> he shall devour the nations that are his foes
>> and break their bones.
> He shall strike with his arrows.
> ⁹ He crouched, he lay down like a lion,
>> and like a lioness; who will rouse him up?
> Blessed is everyone who blesses you,
>> and cursed is everyone who curses you."

¹⁰ Then Balak's anger was kindled against Balaam, and he struck his hands together. Balak said to Balaam, "I summoned you to curse my enemies, but instead you have blessed them these three times. ¹¹ Now be off with you! Go home! I said, 'I will reward you richly,' but the LORD has denied you any reward." ¹² And Balaam said to Balak, "Did I not tell your messengers whom you sent to me, ¹³ 'If Balak should give me his house full of silver and gold, I would not be able to go beyond the word of the LORD, to do either good or bad of my own will; what the LORD says, that is what I will say'? ¹⁴ So now, I am going to my people; let me advise you what this people will do to your people in days to come."

The dance now rushes toward its finale, with Balaam's consultations with God becoming briefer, Balaam's oracles blessing Israel longer, and Balak's shock, disappointment, and rage boiling over. Things are not going as Balak planned them. In fact, the very opposite is the case. First he reprimands Balaam for going against orders (23:11). Next he orders Balaam to neither bless nor curse (23:25). Finally, he claps his hands (a final royal gesture) and orders him to go home (24:11). But by now, the damage is done, and a bonus blessing is to follow.

With oracle #3, Balaam bursts into a new kind of song, simply in praise of the beauty that accompanies God's blessing. "How fair are your tents, O Jacob, your encampments, O Israel!" (24:5). While the immediate vision is yet of this nomadic people living in tents and camping in other nations' valleys, now Balaam's vision begins to spill over into the future, like the waters of the rivers he now begins to describe. Balaam envisions a day when Israel will stretch out not only like palm groves (which one can encounter in the desert), but like cedar trees beside the waters (a scene from a far more settled life; vv. 6–7a). Although Israel now has only one King, Balaam now foresees a day when Israel will have a human king and a kingdom of another kind, higher and more exalted that Agag's, or Moab's (v. 7b). Last, while Israel again appears now as just a sleeping giant, there will come a day when it is aroused to devour the nations that are its foes and break the bones of those who would oppose it (vv. 8–9). Balak, Balak, are you listening?

This oracle closes where the whole story began, with a quote right out of Genesis 12: "Blessed is everyone who blesses you, and cursed is everyone who curses you" (v. 9). Again, this battle was over before it even started. Indeed, it was over before any of its participants had even been born. It's a war of words, a battle over promises. And now it is hastening toward its end.

ANOTHER FOR THE ROAD
Numbers 24:15–24

24:15 So he uttered his oracle, saying:
    "The oracle of Balaam son of Beor,
        the oracle of the man whose eye is clear,
  16 the oracle of one who hears the words of God,
        and knows the knowledge of the Most High,
    who sees the vision of the Almighty,
        who falls down, but with his eyes uncovered:

¹⁷ **I see him, but not now;**
    I behold him, but not near—
a star shall come out of Jacob,
    and a scepter shall rise out of Israel;
it shall crush the borderlands of Moab,
    and the territory of all the Shethites.
¹⁸ **Edom will become a possession,**
    Seir a possession of its enemies,
    while Israel does valiantly.
¹⁹ **One out of Jacob shall rule,**
    and destroy the survivors of Ir."
24:25 **Then Balaam got up and went back to his place, and Balak also went his way.**

Though Balaam has now been dismissed and is ready to go home (24:14), the vision has so possessed him that he continues well past the desires of his employer and the dreams of any kings of that time.

Here Balaam sees someone, but not now. Here Balaam beholds someone, but not near (v. 17). For the first time, Balaam is straining to see something and someone beyond even Israel's imagining. For some, this "scepter" is just another king like that in the last oracle, well grounded in the historical listings of the other kings and nations he will vanquish, including the kingdom of Moab and our good king Balak, who has brought all this on (even though this listing continues to present problems and puzzles for the scholars). But for others, this "star" coming out of Jacob and arising out of Israel is even more than the kingdom of David and all the victories and territories he will gain. This is the true Lion of Judah, who will defeat God's enemies more soundly and spread God's blessings further and secure God's promises more reliably than even Balaam, the seer, can imagine. This is the king whose star some later seers will follow from the east to worship him. This is the king who will also rouse up lesser kings to oppose and deny him. This is the king who inspired the composer Felix Mendelssohn to lift up this verse from Numbers and use it for one of his choruses in *Christus*:

> Behold a star from Jacob shining
> And a scepter from Israel rising . . .

And all this was revealed through the eyes and mouth of Balaam, a seer from the east, while Israel was camping down in the valley, unaware! Again: "O the depth of the riches and wisdom and knowledge of God! How unsearchable are his judgments and how inscrutable his ways! 'For who has known the mind of the Lord? Or who has been his counselor?

[Other than Balaam!]' 'Or who has given a gift to him, to receive a gift in return? [Like Balak tried!]' For from him and through him and to him are all things. To him be the glory forever. Amen" (Rom. 11:33–36).

SOME CONCLUSIONS

Worship as a war of words, words as comfort, and words as terror. From the beginning of this narrative, we have been arguing that this confrontation in the valley of Moab is the most critical attack on God's people Israel since they emerged dry-footed from the Red Sea. This is more than a matter of life or death; this is a matter of curse or blessing; it thus goes to the heart of the central purpose for which this people was called, delivered, and equipped as a community. The stakes could not be higher, for Israel or for the world Israel is called to bless.

And yet it is all a matter of words. Yes, preceded by sacrifices and listening. Yes, accompanied by threats of violence and promises of payoffs. But at its heart, three songs, followed by a fourth for good measure: words, just words.

Read correctly, then, this story has the potential to put an entirely different spin on recent talk of "worship wars" in the church. The battle in this story is not between various factions who would restrict the proper words of worship to one style of voice or another. Rather, the struggle here is between those who trust in the power of God-given words to bring blessing (Balaam) versus those who would fashion their own words or buy them from the professionals to function as curse (Balak). It is a desert war of the principalities and the powers, and like Jesus' battle with Satan in the wilderness, it all takes place with words.

In a society that trivializes words outside the liturgy and bemoans the apparent impotence of words within the liturgy, this story should provide both comfort and terror to all who would bring words to worship, whether in the sanctuary or out.

Though all we may have to offer is words, the right words are often enough. Words of proclamation rather than propaganda. Words of witness rather than willfulness. Words of the sermon and words of the benediction. Words in the anthem and words in the aisle. Words offered in the hospital and the classroom and the office, by those who are ordained, nonordained, or not even in the family. When words are preceded by earnest listening to the Lord and followed by faithful proclamation, they do not return void but accomplish the things for which they are purposed (Isa. 55:11). Words can still storms (Mark 4:39). Words can cause the lame to walk (Acts 3:6). Words got the whole story started (Gen. 1:3), and words are the note on which the whole story ends (Rev. 22:20–21). There is no more powerful force on earth or in heaven, much less in the valley of Moab.

Words can be dangerous and destructive and defeating as well, especially when they are used to build up one's own power and prestige versus witnessing to the power and prestige of Another. If bearing false witness against one's neighbor makes it into the Ten Commandments, how much more serious is bearing false witness against God? Balak was indeed messing with fire when he tried to put words into Balaam's mouth. And so also are any who would utter their own words rather than a witness to the Lord's words in the context of worship. First and foremost, it's "just" a matter of words.

Insiders and outsiders. It is indeed deeply surprising, given the restriction of benedictory words to the mouths of the priests (Num. 6:24–26), that here toward the end of Numbers, the most extensive and profound benediction pronounced over Israel before the nation crosses over the Jordan comes from the mouth of a pagan seer from the east. Not from Moses and not from Aaron, but from Balaam, son of Beor, who will soon be identified with the wayward Midianites, drawn aside from the story, and killed (31:8, 16).

This story thus forces us to acknowledge both the radical *particularity* of this story, in Israel's election as God's peculiar people set apart; and the radical *inclusivity* of this story, in the kinds of people who find themselves part of Israel's saving history. There is no way around the fact that this is a story of a particular God, Yahweh, and this God's particular people, Israel, who alone have been chosen to serve as a blessing to the nations of this world. But there also is no way around the fact that Israel's arrival causes a division among the nations, which ends up with surprising coalitions on the sides "for" and "against."

Many we would assume to be allies (Balak, the Moabite, our cousin) end up as enemies; many we would assume to be enemies (Balaam, the seer from the east) end up as allies. No one who has met Balak will be surprised when he meets Herod (Matt. 2); no one who has learned from Balaam will fail to learn from an unnamed Samaritan (Luke 10). This is a story of surprises and surprising people overseen by a surprising God, and we get into the most trouble when we would decide the lines. In two books so full of boundaries and categories, this is no small observation at all.

The strife is o'er, the battle done. To get back to where we started, the most amazing aspect of this story is the scope it gives to God's providence, over God's people and beyond. After anyone has witnessed even tangentially how difficult it is to organize and implement human encounters in desert terrain, only then can one only begin to fathom the work it required of the Lord to bring Balaam, Balak, and Israel together on the plains and in the mountains of Moab. How long had God been at work in Balaam in order for his fame to spread all the way southwest to Moab? What hand did God have in matching Balak's fear with Balaam's invitation? How many meetings had God had with Balaam before the point where Balaam is able to receive the spirit of God upon him and thus to speak? From the birth and training of Balaam, to the fear and maneuvering of Balak, to the arrival of Israel on the scene with its fair tents and glorious encampments—the Lord is at work in it all. And all the while, Israel goes about its business.

Surely this story has the power to evoke similar questions with regard to our lives in and out of the church. How many bacteria and viruses has my immune system had to battle in order for me to crawl out of bed this day? What hidden victories has the Lord God won in order to preserve God's people the church down through the centuries and including this day? Where today in some corner of the world far away from our expectations (Iraq, Pakistan, Papua New Guinea?) is God raising up a seer who will help us see ourselves and God's purposes for our lives even clearer than we can on our own?

"Deep in unfathomable mines of neverfailing skill," goes the hymn, "He treasures up His bright designs, and works His sovereign will" (Wm. Cowper). Or in the words of *The Study Catechism*:

> Question 23. What comfort do you receive by trusting in God's providence? Answer. The eternal Father of our Lord Jesus Christ watches over me each day of my life, blessing and guiding me wherever I may be. God strengthens me when I am faithful, comforts me when discouraged or sorrowful, raises me up if I fall, and brings me at last to eternal life. Entrusting myself wholly to God's care, I receive the grace to be patient in adversity, thankful in the midst of blessing, courageous against injustice, and confident that no evil afflicts me that God will not turn to my good.

Or in the slightly more succinct words of Balaam: "Now it shall be said of Jacob and Israel, 'See what God has done!'" (Num. 23:23).

Yahweh, 6 (or 7, counting the ass!); Balak, 0.

This play, this game, this battle is now complete.

19. The People Rebel, Threat of Assimilation
Numbers 25:1–18

25:1 While Israel was staying at Shittim, the people began to have sexual relations with the women of Moab. 2 These invited the people to the sacrifices of their gods, and the people ate and bowed down to their gods. 3 Thus Israel yoked itself to the Baal of Peor, and the LORD's anger was kindled against Israel. 4 The LORD said to Moses, "Take all the chiefs of the people, and impale them in the sun before the LORD, in order that the fierce anger of the LORD may turn away from Israel." 5 And Moses said to the judges of Israel, "Each of you shall kill any of your people who have yoked themselves to the Baal of Peor." 6 Just then one of the Israelites came and brought a Midianite woman into his family, in the sight of Moses and in the sight of the whole congregation of the Israelites, while they were weeping at the entrance of the tent of meeting. 7 When Phinehas son of Eleazar, son of Aaron the priest, saw it, he got up and left the congregation. Taking a spear in his hand, 8 he went after the Israelite man into the tent, and pierced the two of them, the Israelite and the woman, through the belly. So the plague was stopped among the people of Israel. 9 Nevertheless those that died by the plague were twenty-four thousand. 10 The LORD spoke to Moses, saying: 11 "Phinehas son of Eleazar, son of Aaron the priest, has turned back my wrath from the Israelites by manifesting such zeal among them on my behalf that in my jealousy I did not consume the Israelites. 12 Therefore say, 'I hereby grant him my covenant of peace. 13 It shall be for him and for his descendants after him a covenant of perpetual priesthood, because he was zealous for his God, and made atonement for the Israelites.'" 14 The name of the slain Israelite man, who was killed with the Midianite woman, was Zimri son of Salu, head of an ancestral house belonging to the Simeonites. 15 The name of the Midianite woman who was killed was Cozbi daughter of Zur, who was the head of a clan, an ancestral house in Midian. 16 The LORD said to Moses, 17 "Harass the Midianites, and defeat them; 18 for they have harassed you by the trickery with which they deceived you in the affair of Peor, and in the affair of Cozbi, the daughter of a leader of Midian, their sister; she was killed on the day of the plague that resulted from Peor."

As God's people have just been saved from destruction, now would be a good time for a major service of thanksgiving. Call in the guards, lay aside your walking sticks, and bring out the fatted calf, for that which was almost lost (Israel's blessing) has been found and secured again, both now and out into the future. The scene (or scenes) in Numbers 25 could not be farther from the mark.

The first cue that must be noted is the very first word in this chapter in Hebrew, which is a form of the verb "to dwell." Up to this point in the story, Israel has been wandering and walking. The only references to "dwelling" (save some brief transitional points in Kadesh and the city and land of the Amorites; Num. 20:1; 21:25, 31) have been in the past tense (their living in Egypt; Lev. 18:3) or the future tense (their upcoming dwelling in the land; Lev. 25:18), or to describe the manner of existence of the peoples round about (e.g., the king of Arad who "lived" in the Negeb; Num. 21:1). This is a people made for sojourning. Even short stays in camp lead to problems. So what happens when this people drive their tent pegs in a little deeper and begin to "dwell," even temporarily, in a given spot? Well, to be blunt and to speak theologically, all "hell" (as in separation from God) breaks loose.

This story thus serves as a prologue and a warning for all that is to follow. As great as the trials and temptations of the wilderness may be, they are always and ever minor in comparison to the major temptations of "settled" life. At the beginning of this story, Israel got into major trouble when they became a little too "settled" while waiting for Moses to come down from Mount Sinai (read the story of the golden calf in Exod. 32). For the rest of Israel's story (beginning in Joshua), sins of the "settled" will be the focus of the tirades of Israel's prophets and the tears of Israel's God. This is what all the testing and preparation of Leviticus and Numbers is getting Israel ready for, and here at almost the end (as at the beginning and the rest of the way through), Israel fails. This too then becomes a sharp word and a critical story for any people or congregation whose leading verb becomes "to dwell."

Second, then, it is not surprising that Numbers 25 reads like a mixture of two stories: one about sexual relations with the women of Moab, which calls for the execution of all participants, be they leaders or followers (vv. 1–5); and the other, which involves intermarriage with the Midianites and the cessation of an already-burgeoning plague (vv. 6–18). Surely the writer could have added a long list of other stories specifying the many and various ways by which "settlement" works to lead God's people astray. The key word here is the second Hebrew verb in this chapter, *ḥālāl*, which means to profane or violate or pollute. God's people are to be a nation set apart, a distinctive people among the nations of this world. Yet when they settle down and begin to act like everybody else (sexually, materially, or religiously), things start to fall apart.

Therefore, while both of the stories merged together here have to do with sexual behavior ("fornication" in one case, "intermarriage" in the other), the overarching concept is one of "accommodation." A people that has no human king, no temple, and no land is, by default, "different" from all the other nations on this earth. But when they start to settle down and look around, they risk losing their ability to "transform" others and threaten to become "conformed" themselves. Yes, this is a story about sexual behavior. But it is also a story about church property and polity and methods to recruit and maintain members.

Last, by way of introduction, observe where all this leads: "These invited the people to the sacrifices of their gods, and the people ate and bowed down to their gods. Thus Israel yoked itself to the Baal of Peor" (vv. 2–3).

It would be encouraging for the forward progress of this story if here, toward the end, the failures of Israel amounted to minor transgressions, slight slipups in etiquette or camp arrangements. After all, they have been in training for a long, long time. But instead, their rebellion goes to the heart of the Ten Commandments, indeed the very first: "You shall have no other gods before me" (Exod. 20:3). Not only has Israel failed to throw a thanksgiving meal for the Lord, but they also have sat down to a festal celebration with other gods. Thus the language of "yoking" moves past matters of service and partnership toward the intimacies of husband and wife. The "yoking" of individual Israelites with women from Moab and Midian is just the surface symptom of a deeper disease. Here, on the east bank of the Jordan, after the Lord God has faithfully carried this people all the way through the wilderness, once they have even a slight taste of settlement, they forget their covenantal partner. In fact, they publicly replace him with another god with whom they are suddenly on a first-name basis. "The LORD's [not God's or a god's] anger" is now "kindled" (Num. 25:3). What is to be done?

With the guidance of the story here in Numbers 25, and ranging much farther abroad, at least three answers might be given:

Atonement must be made. Breaches in relationships are not easily healed. They require costly interventions and extravagant gestures. The penetrations of wayward alliances must be offset by penetrations of stake and spear, leading to the impaling of all those who had yoked themselves to the Baal of Peor, and the more explicitly described yoking of Zimri and

Cozbi on the tip of Phinehas's spear. The consuming jealousy of the Lord must in some way be slowed and redirected, like a fire break, by the "zeal" of the Lord's people—personified this time, not by Moses, but by Eleazar's son Phinehas, who will one day give the Zadokites their claim to the priesthood. The broken covenant made manifest both by Israel's meal with Baal Peor, and Zimri and Cozbi's all too obvious and intentional union must somehow be covered over by a new covenant of peace that is established between the Lord and Phinehas, thus making atonement for all the Israelites. Quick, immediate, and costly actions have to be made right here in the camp in Moab, or the rebellion and its requisite plague would continue, and the whole story come to an end. But the effects of this story rumble out farther.

Another generation must be raised. It surely is no accident that this is the last story of the first generation before the census of the second generation in the chapter to follow. Not only does this fulfill the promised discipline of this generation following their rebellion over the spies; it also demonstrates a deep need on the part of the narrative as a whole in some sense to begin again. The forward progress in this story has been limited to geography. Some new start is required.

Some space must be cleared. Two possible solutions to the sins of settlement may well have their genesis in this story of Israel's brief dwelling in Moab. One is the theme of "separation," made most tangible in the rejection of intermarriage, but also reflected in the general theme of necessary boundaries between Israel and all the other nations of the world. If Israel cannot be trusted to remain faithful to the Lord when settling down with other nations, then the Israelites must live separate from all such nations. Some space must be made. The other possible solution is that, if some of those nations become immediate neighbors of Israel, or if they occupy land necessary to give Israel some space within which to be set apart, well, then they must be eliminated, entirely, men, women, children, and cattle. This final solution is foreshadowed by the command of the Lord to "harass" the Midianites (a command that will bear fruit in Num. 31). But here it is already anticipated by the way the rebels within the camp are "cut off" before they can shatter the covenant cut between the Lord and this people. If this is a story not so much about travel (from Egypt to the Promised Land) as it is about relationship, then maintaining this relationship becomes the goal under which all other goals must be subsumed. Though violence and death may be undesirable, allowing Israel to partner with some other god is even less so. Some counteraction, some cutting-off, some making of space is necessary due to the hardness *not* of the Lord's heart but of *our own*.

Yes, the threats of settlement can begin with things as basic as sexual relations, but all too quickly they rumble out toward the objects of our sacrifices and the purposes of our meals and prostrations. Before we know it, we are yoked and reenslaved, and it is no longer a yoking to the Lord who brought us out of bondage (much of the training Israel has received thus far might be subsumed under the rubrics of "sexual relations," "sacrifices," "eating," and "bowing down"; 25:1–2).

Surely the church of Jesus Christ hears in this story the rumblings of another solution to such rebellion much later in the same story. Here, another Chief will be impaled and speared in order to create a safe space and a covenant of peace between God and God's people. The difference this time is that this violence and cutting-off will reveal not a breach in a relationship, but rather how deeply yoked this "Chief" of the people is with the Lord. And through this covenant, we, a new generation, will be invited to sit down and eat with the God now dwelling in our midst.

20. Taking a New Census
Numbers 26:1–65

26:1 **After the plague the L**ORD **said to Moses and to Eleazar son of Aaron the priest,** [2] **"Take a census of the whole congregation of the Israelites, from twenty years old and upward, by their ancestral houses, everyone in Israel able to go to war."** [3] **Moses and Eleazar the priest spoke with them in the plains of Moab by the Jordan opposite Jericho, saying,** [4] **"Take a census of the people, from twenty years old and upward,"** **as the L**ORD **commanded Moses.**

26:63 **These were those enrolled by Moses and Eleazar the priest, who enrolled the Israelites in the plains of Moab by the Jordan opposite Jericho.** [64] **Among these there was not one of those enrolled by Moses and Aaron the priest, who had enrolled the Israelites in the wilderness of Sinai.** [65] **For the L**ORD **had said of them, "They shall die in the wilderness." Not one of them was left, except Caleb son of Jephunneh and Joshua son of Nun.**

Read at a simple level, the Bible is a book of second chances. Abram becomes Abraham, Sarai becomes Sarah, Saul becomes Paul. Even Moses is a second-career person of sorts, as is Peter after the resurrection. Such a pattern should be no surprise in a story where conversion, redemption, and being born a second time serve as central themes.

Approached collectively, then, Numbers 26 serves as the second-chance chapter for a people called Israel. All of the previous generation, save Joshua and Caleb, have passed on. The tribes now renumbered are a second generation of redeemed folk who, while indebted to those who have gone before, are now free to live out a new and different chapter of relationship and service to the Lord. Some commentators have gone so far as to make this "new generation" the major division in their ordering of the whole book of Numbers, identifying various distinctions of faith and faithlessness between the narratives and laws before Numbers 26 and those afterward (see Olson, *Numbers*). Regardless of how hard and fast one makes this boundary, surely it represents a transition of sorts. As the assurance of pardon reconstitutes a congregation following the confession of sin, so this second census reconstitutes God's people and moves them one step closer to being a people fit for life on the other side. To paraphrase a Sunday Assurance of Pardon, The past is over and forgotten; a new future is waiting to be born. Though the long lists of names that constitute this chapter show up on no lectionary or Sunday school listings of favorite verses, they have a crucial role to play in the story as a whole.

The Lord is a God who knows people by name. The recitation of names is boring only when one expects to know no one on the list. Contrast this with the breathless excitement of reading lists for good or ill where one might expect to see a familiar name, such as a roster for teams, a blotter for criminals, or a roll call of faithful donors. What is most remarkable about this list is that everyone on it is known by God and is being used by God to move this story forward. For a people of faith, we should read this listing as we would read the faint script of a long-lost family genealogy, for it is through this generation that we gain a link with all the promises that have gone before. Not only will a single person not disappear from the Lord's roster without some accounting, but everyone on the list also will be known by name by God and be properly sorted into clans and tribes. The Lord does not work through humanity in general, but through tribes and disciples with names and particular stories.

The Lord is a God who keeps promises, both good and bad. Sometimes we might wish that God would simply erase the slate and start over. But God is faithful and will not go back on words that have been spoken, whether they be words of judgment or mercy. God has promised that no one in the first generation (except Joshua and Caleb) will cross over into the Promised Land, and with Numbers 26 this promise is accomplished. There is a cost for rebellion and unfaithfulness, and you can count it up face-to-face by placing this second census side by side with the first. But God has also promised God's people a land and a future, and with this listing that promise now takes on flesh in a particular way. Even within families, we can see how the Lord's judgment and mercy is working itself out, taking fathers but sparing sons (such as Korah in vv. 10–11) and producing generations with no male heirs, for which new arrangements will have to be made (such as the daughters of Zelophehad in v. 33). It might seem simpler for the Lord to simply wipe the slate and start over, but that is not in God's character, as Numbers 26 particularly makes clear.

New life and new hope is God's creation, not ours. As far as human beings are concerned, the whole notion of progress is problematic in the Bible. Although there may be an initial flare-up in human obedience after this new census in comparison to before, like the similar flare-up following

Pentecost, it does not last long. Thus the story of God's grace moves forward not so much in a steady and gradual way, as by repeated outbreaks of God's inspiration and re-creation. Just as no human being can become alive unless the Lord breathes the breath of life into her, so no group of people can continue on unless the Lord raises up a new generation out of the old, to start the story over. Whether in the New Testament or the Old, "the focus is not on a gradual spiritual improvement on the part of the people. Rather, the focus is on the activity of God, who, though intolerant of rebellion, remains faithful to his promise" (Olson, *Numbers*, 180).

What therefore takes place in Numbers 26 on a generational basis is what we testify takes place on an individual basis in baptism. A break and yet continuity occurs in baptism; something new is created out of the old. It can be described as burial and resurrection, death and life, or one generation and another. As Israel began its journey as one generation with a particular set of names, so Israel ends this journey (or this stage of the journey!) with another generation and another set of names. There is continuity on a human level, and yet discontinuity on the divine level. Ever since Numbers 13–14, the former generation has lived their lives under a sentence. With their deaths, this sentence has now been paid, and a new generation is named, claimed, and counted. "Do not remember the former things, or consider the things of old. I am about to do a new thing; now it springs forth, do you not perceive it?" (Isa. 43:18–19).

21. Last-Minute Instructions
Numbers 27:1–30:16; 36:1–13

Before an individual embarks on a fateful journey, before an army undertakes a dangerous crossing, and before a congregation launches out into some new form of mission, some tying up of loose ends is required. Are there gaps in the previous instructions? Have new developments in Israel's life as a community led to the need for new or revised legislation from the Lord? More important, as the Israelites begin to anticipate their future in the Land of Promise, can they imagine coming situations that might prove easier to handle if the people are prepared for them through instruction that treats this future as if it has already arrived?

A good coach anticipates shifts in game plans and plans alternative strategies to deal with them. A good pastor tries to envision changes in mission and lays the groundwork to prepare for them. A good general reviews the troops before the battle in order to spot holes in the ranks and discrepancies in the orders. So God's people pause on the far side of the Jordan to tidy up.

DAUGHTERS OF ZELOPHEHAD
Numbers 27:1–11; 36:1–13

27:1 **Then the daughters of Zelophehad came forward. Zelophehad was son of Hepher son of Gilead son of Machir son of Manasseh son of Joseph, a member of the Manassite clans. The names of his daughters were: Mahlah, Noah, Hoglah, Milcah, and Tirzah.** [2] **They stood before Moses, Eleazar the priest, the leaders, and all the congregation, at the entrance of the tent of meeting, and they said,** [3] **"Our father died in the wilderness; he was not among the company of those who gathered themselves together against the LORD in the company of Korah, but died for his own sin; and he had no sons.** [4] **Why should the name of our father be taken away from his clan because he**

had no son? Give to us a possession among our father's brothers." ⁵ Moses
brought their case before the Lᴏʀᴅ. ⁶ And the Lᴏʀᴅ spoke to Moses, saying:
⁷ The daughters of Zelophehad are right in what they are saying; you shall
indeed let them possess an inheritance among their father's brothers
and pass the inheritance of their father on to them. ⁸ You shall also say to
the Israelites, "If a man dies, and has no son, then you shall pass his inheritance on to his daughter. ⁹ If he has no daughter, then you shall give his
inheritance to his brothers. ¹⁰ If he has no brothers, then you shall give his
inheritance to his father's brothers. ¹¹ And if his father has no brothers, then
you shall give his inheritance to the nearest kinsman of his clan, and he shall
possess it. It shall be for the Israelites a statute and ordinance, as the Lᴏʀᴅ
commanded Moses."

Once the shepherd has accounted for all his sheep, or the officer called the
roll for all her troops, what happens next? It's time to move; it's zero hour;
the reader expects the narrative to lean forward once again. But here
comes the first of several "interruptions" in the march of this story. This
one takes place without the initiative of Moses or Eleazar or any of the
leaders of the clans. Rather, five sisters (whose names are listed not once,
but twice in the biblical text, compare 36:11)—Mahlah, Noah, Hoglah,
Milcah, and Tirzah—draw near to the seat of power and the place of the
Lord's presence (the verb is *qārab*, used elsewhere in settings of adjudication and justice; cf. Josh. 7:14). They come not meekly, or apologetically,
but as a group that trusts its membership in the family. They do not bow,
they do not scrape; rather, they stand and begin their appeal with a word
no one in the gathering can dispute: "Our father."

The reader may be tempted to think that the only thing that marks this
passage as radical is the *gender* of the protagonists. This is a band of sisters,
a coalition of women, the likes of which we have encountered nowhere
else in this story. Just a couple of chapters before, a group of non-Israelite
women are credited with leading God's people astray. Elsewhere, groups
of women appear almost exclusively in a nameless collective (such as the
women and children) or a passive part of the plot (standing by the flaps of
their tents). Yet here a group of women with names draws near, stands for
a purpose, and demands a hearing. "Give to us a possession among our
father's brothers." This is radical and this is new. But the gender is just the
tip of the iceberg.

First, like the earlier ruling regarding an alternative Passover observance
(Num. 9), a situation has arisen that demands further revelation. There the
problem was the presence of some who were ritually unclean on the day
designated for Passover. Here the difficulty arises from a family that has

produced no male heirs to receive their share of the Promised Land. In both cases, those who are threatened with exclusion come forward to plead their cases, trusting that this is appropriate and expecting to be heard.

Moses listens to their plea, and then brings their case before the Lord. This is followed by a whole new paragraph of legislation, provoked by this five-sister appeal. *Coming from this particular people*, this is remarkable. How do they know that this will not be received as another in their long series of complaints? *Brought before this God*, this is remarkable. After a book and two-thirds of legislation, you might think that the Lord had reached a limit. *Coming at this particular point in the narrative*, this is remarkable. It's time, it's past time to get on with the marching. There's work ahead to do.

And yet, here is a God and a leader who makes time to listen, adjudicate, and grant new wisdom appropriate for the occasion. Like the good pastor or the good parent, here is a God who recognizes "interruptions" as opportunities for further instruction and preparation. If driven by questions of justice (who gets what?) or inclusion (who gets in?), no matter is too trivial for a hearing, and no business more pressing. Surely occasions such as this created the expectation so evident in the Psalms, that the Lord of the Scriptures is a God who stands ready to listen: "Hear a just cause, O LORD; attend to my cry. . . . From you let my vindication come" (Ps. 17:1–2).

Second, though God's response here adds a few verses, it later leads to an additional excursus at the very end of this book, Numbers 36. Indeed, this issue of what to do when a woman (or group of women) has no man (or men) to represent her in matters of justice and property and protection rumbles through all of Scripture and produces a variety of responses. In some places, the solution seems to be the practice of levirate marriage, where a childless and widowed woman is forced to marry her husband's brother or brothers, until a male heir is secured (this is the practice that drives the story of Ruth, and perhaps that of the Samaritan woman at the well, and obviously the Sadducees' question about marriage in the kingdom; Matt. 22). Here a new word is given, allowing these women on their own to inherit the property that is their due through their membership in the clan (Num. 27:7). Only nine chapters later, however, this ruling will be qualified, limiting any future marriages of such female inheritors to weddings within the tribe, in order to prevent the gradual dispersion of any tribes' lands due to the greater desirability of another tribes' males (36:6).

Adjudications, words, revelations from the Lord thus are seen to be an ongoing activity, even within the confines of canonical Scripture. Unforeseen events arise. Unanticipated injustices develop. Matters that seem to be temporarily resolved spawn other matters from their resolution, and on and on it goes. One danger is that the complexity and sinfulness of the human community requires such detailed legislation that the whole parade bogs down with one addendum after the next, until the whole story becomes a wrangling over words and subwords. But the other danger is that the Scriptures become so fossilized that they are unable to speak to new situations and unforeseen developments. Here, through the daughters of Zelophehad, begins the practice of Scripture provoking Scripture, and Scripture demanding new interpretation. Yes, this is about far more than gender.

Third, and by no means least, such shufflings and readjudications and fresh words are particularly incumbent upon the Lord and the Lord's people whenever some individual or group of individuals is threatened with loss of the promise due to no fault of their own. The Scriptures and God's promises seem especially apt to crack open in fresh ways whenever someone or somebodies stand up and ask, demand, and plead not to be left out. Here we have a band of five sisters. There we have a strange coalition of Hebrew mother-in-law and Moabite daughter-in-law. Here a band of lepers cry out to a passing Messiah. There in a whole new category, Gentile Christians make an appeal through the apostles at a council in Jerusalem. Though the boundary lines between those who stand to inherit and those who don't are still within the family here in Numbers 27, the possibility of fresh revelations hints at the continuing possibility of fresh revelations elsewhere. One more time, gender is just the tip of the iceberg.

It therefore is not surprising that the tag "Daughters of Zelophehad" has become an umbrella for various justice groups appealing to church and synagogue for a new or revised word from the Lord. It is extremely important at least to recognize the possibility that this is an appeal that arises not *over against* but *within* the Scriptures themselves. Such a discovery is certainly worth a slight delay in the march, for these five sisters and for many sisters and brothers to follow.

APPOINTMENT OF JOSHUA
Numbers 27:12–23

27:12 The LORD said to Moses, "Go up this mountain of the Abarim range, and see the land that I have given to the Israelites. 13 When you have seen it, you also shall be gathered to your people, as your brother Aaron was, 14 because you rebelled against my word in the wilderness of Zin when the congregation quarreled with me. You did not show my holiness before their eyes at the waters." (These are the waters of Meribath-kadesh in the wilderness of Zin.) [15] Moses spoke to the Lord, saying, [16] "Let the Lord, the God of the spirits of all flesh, appoint someone over the congregation [17] who shall go out before them and come in before them, who shall lead them out and bring them in, so that the congregation of the Lord may not be like sheep without a shepherd." [18] So the Lord said to Moses, "Take Joshua son of Nun, a man in whom is the spirit, and lay your hand upon him; [19] have him stand before Eleazar the priest and all the congregation, and commission him in their sight. [20] You shall give him some of your authority, so that all the congregation of the Israelites may obey. [21] But he shall stand before Eleazar the priest, who shall inquire for him by the decision of the Urim before the Lord; at his word they shall go out, and at his word they shall come in, both he and all the Israelites with him, the whole congregation." [22] So Moses did as the Lord commanded him. He took Joshua and had him stand before Eleazar the priest and the whole congregation; [23] he laid his hands on him and commissioned him—as the Lord had directed through Moses.

As a new generation has been introduced in the second census, so a new leader must be commissioned before Israel is ready to cross over to the other side. While this scene will be repeated once more before the crossing begins (Deut. 31), it continues the theme of last-minute instructions of the chapter before. Joshua and Caleb will be the only members of the former generation to make this transition, and Joshua the only one specifically set apart and commissioned by the Lord.

God's discipline completed. This positive development, a "new" leader, comes about only due to the negative antecedent: the reclamation of the "old" one. It is now time for Moses to be gathered to his people, *in death*, as he has spent all his energies gathering them, *in life*. In later tellings, the blow is softened by describing Moses' advanced age and failing powers (Deut. 31:2). But here the cause is rebellion and failure to show forth the Lord's holiness (Num. 27:14), describing the sins of commission and omission all too familiar from the narratives before. Moses, Aaron, and Miriam all bear witness to the priority of God's words over human words in the life of this people. No matter how high one's rank or important one's office, failure to properly hear and obey God's words leads to discipline. Moses is commanded to go up another mountain, this time not to see the Lord's glory, but the land the Lord has promised to the next generation. Whether this sneak peek is a sign of God's judgment or mercy probably depends as much on the situation of the reader as the words of this passage. To see what one cannot attain, for some, is torture. For others, it is pure graciousness, a visible sign that the Lord's spoken promises will come true.

Moses' maturation continues. It is therefore all the more surprising that the provision of a new leader begins not with words from the one who is disciplining (God), but words from the one who is disciplined (Moses). Moses, who now stares his own humanity in the face, turns in his thoughts to that other flesh so close to and often under his skin: the congregation. He reminds the Lord that as God exercises authority over Moses' life, so God continues to bear responsibility for those God has brought out into the wilderness (27:16–17). Perhaps this is another reminder that God might prefer to remain the sole leader who goes out before them and comes in before them, who leads them out and brings them in (27:21; 10:33–36). Surely this is partly because the Lord himself would have this congregation experience his presence and power like that of a shepherd and thus have no wants (Ps. 23). But though this very congregation has often broken Moses' heart and bruised his face (with falling down!), he knows better than anybody how, lacking a leader in the flesh, they will be like "sheep without a shepherd." Moses has come a long way on this journey, from hot-headed anger to warm-hearted advocate. Only those who continue to look with compassion upon those who have wounded them are qualified to serve as leaders in the Scriptures (cf. a similar surveillance of the crowd by the new Moses in the Gospels: "When he saw the crowds . . ."; Matt. 9:36).

God responds and equips once more. As the Lord began this encounter in judgment ("Go up"; 27:12), so the Lord concludes this encounter with mercy ("Take"; v. 18). The very person who is refused entrance to the Promised Land because of rebellion against God's word and failure to show forth God's glory is now invited to recognize and call forth leadership for the future.

"In whom is the spirit." It might make sense to talk here of Joshua's strength or faithfulness or abilities to lead. All of these have been demonstrated in the story. But the qualification here cited is "the spirit." Such gifts may reflect the spirit, but it is the spirit that equips and qualifies a person for service and office. Here we are given a model for the setting apart of any person for the Lord's service: not sinlessness, not giftedness, but spirit (from God).

"Lay your hand upon him." Though Joshua already possesses spirit, and though the true setting apart is surely done by God naming Joshua, nevertheless, Joshua gains authority before the people, both through the touch of the hands of Moses and the tumble of the Urim by Eleazar, the priest. Moses had been commissioned by the Lord much more directly (through burning bush and mountaintop fire), but now God's people are

invited into the ceremony in a highly tangible way. The forms and practices may vary (who may lay on hands; resumes and recommendations versus lots), but the order is the same. The Lord names those with the spirit; God's people tangibly participate in this recognition of authority.

"The whole congregation." With a new leader comes a new dream, or at least an old dream revitalized. Though Joshua is presented to "all the congregation" (v. 19) and "the whole congregation" (v. 22) so that no one can claim not to have seen ("in their sight," v. 19), the repetition of "all" and "whole," both in the present ceremony and thereby in future campaigns ("at his word they shall go out, and at his word they shall come in, both he and all the Israelites with him, the whole congregation"; v. 21), make clear that this time, with this leader, maybe the community may mature as well. Here Moses may get to see a promise even more incredibly tangible than the Promised Land: God's people responding in unity (cf. Ps. 133). How fitting then that this scene of new leadership and new possibilities ends with the name of him who held on to this dream up to this end: "he [Moses] laid his hands on him and commissioned him [Joshua]—as the LORD had directed through *Moses*" (Num. 27:23, emphasis added).

REGARDING OFFERINGS
Numbers 28:1–29:40

28:1 **The LORD spoke to Moses, saying:** [2] **Command the Israelites, and say to them: My offering, the food for my offerings by fire, my pleasing odor, you shall take care to offer to me at its appointed time.** [3] **And you shall say to them, This is the offering by fire that you shall offer to the LORD: two male lambs a year old without blemish, daily, as a regular offering.** [4] **One lamb you shall offer in the morning, and the other lamb you shall offer at twilight;** [5] **also one-tenth of an ephah of choice flour for a grain offering, mixed with one-fourth of a hin of beaten oil.** [6] **It is a regular burnt offering, ordained at Mount Sinai for a pleasing odor, an offering by fire to the LORD.** [7] **Its drink offering shall be one-fourth of a hin for each lamb; in the sanctuary you shall pour out a drink offering of strong drink to the LORD.** [8] **The other lamb you shall offer at twilight with a grain offering and a drink offering like the one in the morning; you shall offer it as an offering by fire, a pleasing odor to the LORD.**

29:39 **These you shall offer to the LORD at your appointed festivals, in addition to your votive offerings and your freewill offerings, as your burnt offerings, your grain offerings, your drink offerings, and your offerings of well-being.** [40] **So Moses told the Israelites everything just as the LORD had commanded Moses.**

While the various kinds of offerings have already been spelled out (the Manual of Sacrifice, Lev. 1–7), and the schedule of sacred days and festivals previously rehearsed (Lev. 23), the types of sacrifices required for each particular day and festival have not been cataloged in one place. Before crossing over the Jordan and beginning the life of a settled people, a grand inventory of offerings is taken, as if to make sure the daily bread required for the people (now that the manna is ending) is also matched by the daily bread appropriate for God (the One to be served first each day). A grand inventory it is indeed. (See Table 2.)

First, every day is marked by a morning and an evening sacrifice consisting of animal, grain, and drink offerings (all without blemish if animal; choice if grain; and strong if drink). That makes six preparations, every day, or 2,190 per year. Every Sabbath day, there is an additional offering, equivalent to the daily offering, adding 312 preparations, for a running total of 2,502. Now add every month a first-day-of-the-month offering, which includes two bulls, one ram, seven lambs, plus a goat for a sin offering, for the animal sacrifice, plus the requisite and proportional grain and drink offerings, times twelve, for a running total of 2,538 preparations. Throw in the even more extravagant sacrifices required for the yearly festivals: Passover and Unleavened Bread (total of eight preparations); Firstfruits (one preparation); and Festival of Trumpets through Festival of Booths, including the Day of Atonement (total of nine preparations, seven of which include so many animal sacrifices that they are listed separately, beginning with the fifteenth day and onward to the twenty-first day). They end up with a grand total of 2,556 preparations, one of which, Day One of the Festival of Booths, requires thirteen bulls, two rams, fourteen lambs, one goat, and all the requisite grain and drink offerings, in addition to the daily offerings, and all without blemish, choice, and strong. No wonder this little detail needed to be attended to before they crossed over. For a subsistence people, embarking on a campaign of conquest, this style of worship appears to be extravagant to the point of foolishness. Clearly, some comment is in order.

A matter of priorities. Any planner today, poised as Israel is at this point, would be much more concerned with provisions for people and foodstuffs for army. With the Lord's daily provision about to be cut off, you would think that the inventory would be for some more essential function than providing a regular and large dose of pleasing odor for God. And yet, here once more, we get a glimpse into the radical nature of Israel's dream. The question is not whether this sacrificial system was ever put into full practice, much less in the years immediately to follow. No,

Table 2. Calendar of Offerings/Festivals, Leviticus–Numbers

Occasional Offerings	One-Time Offerings	Scheduled Offerings
For all the people		
Voluntary (Lev. 1–3; 6–7)	Ordination of original	*Daily* (Num. 28:2–6)
Burnt (Lev. 1:3–17; 6:8–13)	priests (Lev. 8)	*Weekly* (Lev. 23:3;
Grain (Lev. 2:1–16; 6:14–18)	Inauguration of	Num. 28:9–10)
Well-Being	tabernacle service	*Monthly* (Num. 28:11–15)
(Lev. 3:1–16; 7:28–36)	(Lev. 9)	*Yearly* (Lev. 23:5–43;
Thanksgiving		Num. 28:16–29:39)
(Lev. 7:11–15)		**Spring**
Votive and Free-will		Passover and Unleavened
(Lev. 7:16–18; 22:17–25; 27)		Bread (Lev. 23:5–8;
Atoning (Lev. 4–7)		Num. 28:16–24)
Purification		Firstfruits and Weeks
(Lev. 4:1–5:13; 6:24–30)		(Lev. 23:9–22;
Reparation		Num. 28:26–31)
(Lev. 5:14–6:7; 7:1–6)		**Fall**
For the priests		Trumpets (Lev. 23:23–25;
Ordination		Num. 29:1–6)
(Lev. 6:19–23)		Atonement
		(Lev. 16; 23:26–32;
		Num. 29:7–11)
		Booths (Lev. 23:33–43;
		Num. 29:12–38)
		Seven Years (Lev. 25:1–7)
		Sabbath Year
		Fifty Years (Lev. 25:8–55)
		Jubilee Year

the point is that this inventory is placed here at this place in Israel's memory as a pattern for its life once in the land. More important than satisfying the Israelites' own hunger and security was their desire to fill their need for worship: costly worship, extravagant worship, and worship first thing in the morning and last thing at night. The picture here is that of a worship center where the smell of smoke and the sight of blood are always just about to occur or have just happened. Not just one hour of worship and then six days vacant here. This is a picture of a nation whose whole productive capacity is geared toward sacrifice, most of which benefits nobody but God and those who offer it, as animal, grain, and drink go up in smoke. Here is a mission team that packs their bags thinking mostly of worship supplies, not money and medicine and passports. Rather than skipping over this and getting on to the action, it might well be worth spending a Sunday morning reading all of Numbers 28 and 29, just to get the cumulative effect.

Gifts from the center of their life. While this point was made in the Manual of Sacrifice, it must be made here once again. Animals, grain, and drink were at the core of Israel's economy. Yes, they represented their food, but they also served as the repositories for their wealth, their security, and their hope. Again and again in Scripture, these are the sorts of things that are counted as tangible blessings by this people from their God. If they are not going to sacrifice themselves, or their firstborn, those are the only lines they will draw. All else God has given them is fair game. Surely we should begin to cite a similar inventory for us: money, property, insurance policies, retirement accounts, liquid and nonliquid assets. How do these daily, weekly, and monthly go up in smoke?

The dailiness of it all. Most congregations gear up for a big blast once a year. Stewardship Dedication Sunday, we may call it. Sure, we try to do our little devotions every day, when we have time, but we usually come forward and make a large pledge just on special occasions. Verse 2 of Numbers 28 introduces the notion of God's "appointed time." This is not the time we may choose, or the time that makes sense to us, but the various times in our day, our week, our month, our year that make sense to God and remind us of God's saving story with us. This last-minute detail of offerings for appointed times reveals a God who knows our hearts well. Unless sacrifice is built into our daily living, unless we are constantly doing an inventory of worship appointed for this day, we will forget the daily, weekly, monthly, and yearly sacrifices the Lord is making for us, and our worship and praise and productivity will go elsewhere. Placed at this point in the story, this dream is even more poignant and provocative. More than conquest or the end of the journey, this is a people who see their whole existence summed up in this desire: to present a pleasing odor to the Lord. Odors, by their very nature, are evanescent. They must be engendered repeatedly, persistently, and constantly. What a vision for worship this little detail contains!

REGARDING VOWS
Numbers 30:1–16

30:1 **Then Moses said to the heads of the tribes of the Israelites: This is what the LORD has commanded.** [2] **When a man makes a vow to the LORD, or swears an oath to bind himself by a pledge, he shall not break his word; he shall do according to all that proceeds out of his mouth.** [3] **When a woman makes a vow to the LORD, or binds herself by a pledge, while within her father's house, in her youth,** [4] **and her father hears of her vow or her pledge by which she has** bound herself, and says nothing to her; then all her vows shall stand, and any pledge by which she has bound herself shall stand. [5] But if her father expresses disapproval to her at the time that he hears of it, no vow of hers, and no pledge by which she has bound herself, shall stand; and the LORD will forgive her, because her father had expressed to her his disapproval.

30:16 These are the statutes that the LORD commanded Moses concerning a husband and his wife, and a father and his daughter while she is still young and in her father's house.

As previously noted (esp. Lev. 27; Num. 6), the keeping of vows was a fundamental value for the Israelites. As a people whose sole hope was grounded in the vows the Lord had made to them ("I will bless you to be a blessing," "I will meet you on the mountain," "I will accompany you through the wilderness"), vows made in response were not to be taken lightly. This probably had something to do with the commandment not to take the name of the Lord lightly. It undoubtedly was especially stringent for vows of offerings to the Lord (human, animal, and otherwise). It hovers over stories in the Scriptures that otherwise would be completely unintelligible (most infamously, the dangerous story of Jephthah and his daughter; Judg. 11).

But what happens when a vow is made by a woman? Here we peer into another area of Scripture that we might prefer to avoid. But unlike the provision made for the daughters of Zelophehad, the provisions that emerge here are far less satisfying.

The principle here is quite simple, if quite offensive. Any vow made by a male is unbreakable and must be kept. As the Lord keeps promises, so must his people keep promises—as long as they are male. But if they are female, there is a window of opportunity for the male who sits in authority over her, either as father or husband. If such a male authority overhears such a feminine vow, dedicating a person, an animal, or herself to the Lord (some think the most pressing concern was the possibility of such a woman vowing her virginity to the Lord, thus depriving future males of their conjugal privileges!), then this male could exercise a veto power over this vow before it went into effect. Otherwise, such female vows, like their male counterparts, were inviolable ("then her vows shall stand, and her pledges by which she has bound herself shall stand"; v. 7).

What do we do with such a problematic "detail"?

First, we must place it in the context of wider Scripture, where Deuteronomy makes clear that vows are not necessary (23:22), and Christ explicitly preaches against them (Matt. 5:33–37). Despite recent usage, the Lord is the true "Promise Keeper," not we human beings, and our urge to underscore our words with vows is not only unnecessary, but also distracting from the main vow upon which we trust. Beware of all human beings obsessed with vows, whether male or female.

But second, here is laid bare a bias that runs through all of Scripture. Women are not seen as reliable witnesses. Their word is not to be trusted. They are prone to "thoughtless utterances" and "idle tales" and must be properly supervised in order to be trusted. Here again, we must allow Scripture to interpret Scripture. Which two Hebrews were sworn to devote Hebrew males to destruction, but in faith refused to do so? The midwives Shiphrah and Puah in Exodus 1. Which Israelite kept her vow to dedicate her firstborn to the Lord's service if the Lord would open her womb? Hannah in 1 Samuel 1. Which group of witnesses ran from the tomb in fear, saying nothing to anyone, but obviously at some point told someone, else we have no Easter story? The women at the tomb in Mark 16. Numbers 30, a part of Scripture that differentiates vow-making and vow-keeping on the basis of gender, must be set alongside the wider witness of Scripture in order to be corrected. Moses followed this pattern of respecting women in Numbers 27. This approach awaits the new Moses with regard to Numbers 30.

Finally, however, this entire chapter drives us back to the first point we have made. The Lord is indeed the Promise Keeper, the only one who is finally reliable. But given the grounding of this community in such vows that are spoken, it is incumbent upon this community to take spoken vows seriously. That is the reason that the breaking of marital, ordination, or baptismal vows is so serious a threat to the Christian faith. How can a community grounded in the reliability of God's promises in Christ ("Lo, I am with you always") be so cavalier about its own vows? We must not, whether man, woman, or child. Thus comes the constant need for forgiveness and redemption at the most fundamental level. We must be a community that takes vows seriously.

22. Final Victory in the Wilderness
Numbers 31:1–54

31:1 The LORD spoke to Moses, saying, [2] "Avenge the Israelites on the Midianites; afterward you shall be gathered to your people." [3] So Moses said to the people, "Arm some of your number for the war, so that they may go against Midian, to execute the LORD's vengeance on Midian. [4] You shall send a thousand from each of the tribes of Israel to the war." [5] So out of the thousands of Israel, a thousand from each tribe were conscripted, twelve thousand armed for battle. [6] Moses sent them to the war, a thousand from each tribe, along with Phinehas son of Eleazar the priest, with the vessels of the sanctuary and the trumpets for sounding the alarm in his hand. [7] They did battle against Midian, as the LORD had commanded Moses, and killed every male. [8] They killed the kings of Midian: Evi, Rekem, Zur, Hur, and Reba, the five kings of Midian, in addition to others who were slain by them; and they also killed Balaam son of Beor with the sword. [9] The Israelites took the women of Midian and their little ones captive; and they took all their cattle, their flocks, and all their goods as booty. [10] All their towns where they had settled, and all their encampments, they burned, [11] but they took all the spoil and all the booty, both people and animals. [12] Then they brought the captives and the booty and the spoil to Moses, to Eleazar the priest, and to the congregation of the Israelites, at the camp on the plains of Moab by the Jordan at Jericho. [13] Moses, Eleazar the priest, and all the leaders of the congregation went to meet them outside the camp. [14] Moses became angry with the officers of the army, the commanders of thousands and the commanders of hundreds, who had come from service in the war. [15] Moses said to them, "Have you allowed all the women to live? [16] These women here, on Balaam's advice, made the Israelites act treacherously against the LORD in the affair of Peor, so that the plague came among the congregation of the LORD. [17] Now therefore, kill every male among the little ones, and kill every woman who has known a man by sleeping with him. [18] But all the young girls who have not known a man by sleeping with him, keep alive for yourselves. [19] Camp outside the camp seven days; whoever of you has killed any person or touched a corpse, purify yourselves and your captives on the third and on the seventh day. [20] You shall purify every garment, every article of skin, every-thing made of goats' hair, and every article of wood." [21] Eleazar the priest said to the troops who had gone to battle: "This is the statute of the law that the LORD has commanded Moses: [22] gold, silver, bronze, iron, tin, and lead— [23] everything that can withstand fire, shall be passed through fire, and it shall be clean. Nevertheless it shall also be purified with the water for purification; and whatever cannot withstand fire, shall be passed through the water. [24] You must wash your clothes on the seventh day, and you shall be clean; afterward you may come into the camp." [25] The LORD spoke to Moses, saying, [26] "You and Eleazar the priest and the heads of the ancestral houses of the congregation make an inventory of the booty captured, both human and animal. [27] Divide the booty into two parts, between the warriors who went out to battle and all the congregation. [28] From the share of the warriors who went out to battle, set aside as tribute for the LORD, one item out of every five hundred, whether persons, oxen, donkeys, sheep, or goats. [29] Take it from their half and give it to Eleazar the priest as an offering to the LORD. [30] But from the Israelites' half you shall take one out of every fifty, whether persons, oxen, donkeys, sheep, or goats—all the animals—and give them to the Levites who have charge of the tabernacle of the LORD." [31] Then Moses and Eleazar the priest did as the LORD had commanded Moses.

31:48 Then the officers who were over the thousands of the army, the commanders of thousands and the commanders of hundreds, approached Moses, [49] and said to Moses, "Your servants have counted the warriors who are under our command, and not one of us is missing. [50] And we have brought the LORD's offering, what each of us found, articles of gold, armlets and bracelets, signet rings, earrings, and pendants, to make atonement for ourselves before the LORD." [51] Moses and Eleazar the priest received the gold from them, all in the form of crafted articles. [52] And all the gold of the offering that they offered to the LORD, from the commanders of thousands and the commanders of hundreds, was sixteen thousand seven hundred fifty shekels. [53] (The troops had all taken plunder for themselves.) [54] So Moses and Eleazar the priest received the gold from the commanders of thousands and of hundreds, and brought it into the tent of meeting as a memorial for the Israelites before the LORD.

For the first time perhaps since the Israelites left Mount Sinai, a story from the journey begins with no internal or external threat to mention. No fight is brewing in the camp, and no threat looms from the hills. Final preparations and details are being rehearsed before the crossing and the battles ahead. Into the midst of these discussions of precise boundaries and unanticipated vows and inheritances comes a command to mount an offensive, violent action. Before the chapter is over, the valley will be full of Midianite corpses (every man, nonvirgin woman, and all the male "little" ones) and the camp overflowing with the booty (human, animal, and precious metal) that this sudden action has provoked. To make matters worse, the whole story begins not with murmuring or rebellion on the part of God's people, but with a straightforward command from God: "The LORD spoke to Moses, saying, 'Avenge the Israelites on the Midianites; afterward you shall be gathered to your people.'" As we began this traversal of Leviticus–Numbers with the slaughter of cows, sheep, and fowls, now we end it with thousands of Homo sapiens added to the list. "Take us back to Leviticus!" you may cry.

However, as should be painfully clear to the fellow traveler by now, violence and casualties have been part of this story from the beginning. At the Red Sea back in Exodus and on the west side of the Jordan in Joshua, most of these casualties will be from the nations outside Israel; the Egyptians before, and the Canaanites to follow. In between, almost all of the casualties have been internal, due either to direct intervention (of earthquakes and fire, or plagues and serpents) or a generation-long moratorium on crossing (which led to the deaths outside the Promised Land of all the first generation except Joshua and Caleb and the now-about-to-die Moses). This journey of God's people is a costly journey from beginning to end, and all points in between. The question in this story therefore is not why some are dying, but who? by whom? and for what purpose?

War as vengeance. Hanging heavy over the wars in Joshua is the fact that people are being cleared out for territorial purposes. Yes, these are peoples who do not recognize the Lord as sovereign (with some notable exceptions; cf. Rahab, in Josh. 2). And, yes, these peoples' practices are worrisome due to their potential to lead these fickle Israelites astray (as we shall see in Num. 33:50–56). Nevertheless, all these battles have as their product "conquest" of the land (a detail that continues to haunt these stories down to the politics of the present day), a salient detail that contrasts them with all the battles of transit and the safe camps thus far. Even though this land of Moab, once cleared, will prove attractive to some of the Israelite tribes (the next chapter), this story is told not as a war for conquest, but as a war of vengeance. Whether that makes it better or worse depends solely on one's interpretation.

As blood continues to flow, the main thrust of this overall story continues to be the creation of a holy people traveling with a holy God in their midst. As this Holy Lord's fire has burst out against unholy words and actions *on the part of God's people*, so this Holy Lord's fire bursts out here against all the unholy words and actions of *other peoples* that Israel has encountered on its trip (hapless Balaam appears on the Midianite *casualty* list, "They also killed Balaam son of Beor" (31:8), and the *suspect* list, "These women here, on Balaam's advice, made the Israelites act treacherously against the LORD" (v. 16), though Balaam appears nowhere in the story of Num. 25). This is a tidying-up action from the larger perspective of the story as a whole, though one that painfully includes the names and numbers of those thus consumed. "Harass the Midianites, and defeat them," the Lord had commanded the Israelites after the affair at Shittim, "for they have harassed you by the trickery with which they deceived you in the affair of Peor" (25:16–17). Quite consistently, God has dealt with the grumblings and rebellion of Israel with immediate and appropriate discipline. Now we see how such discipline is applied to the accomplices of such waywardness as well (even though this very people had been invited to travel along with Israel much earlier in the story; Num. 10:29–32).

At this point the key danger for interpretation and application is the invitation for Israel to participate in such divine vengeance. This is no small detail at a time when all sorts of violent actions, both individual and national, are being attributed to divine vengeance or "holy war" or "jihad." Though the major qualifications of this story come in the sections that follow, a few might be listed in this section as well.

First, to repeat, the purpose of this engagement is not *conquest*, but *vengeance*. Though this may indeed sound worse at first glance, if true, it places a severe test on most of the violent actions with which we are familiar. Precious few are the engagements of the powerful that truly have no conquest in mind. Indeed, the lack of direct benefit for the aggressor continues to be one of the main ways to evaluate the "justice" of any war, no matter how large or small (cf. the just-war criterion of actions either in self-defense or to protect the innocent).

Second, the lack of any description or gloating in connection with the battle must not be overlooked or discounted. The glory of this engagement belongs to the Lord (as shall become clearer). The lack of room for human boasting, clapping, and rejoicing provides another severe test of the true motivation for such engagements yesterday and today. "They did battle against Midian, as the LORD had commanded Moses, and killed every male" (31:7). That's not much of a story, and an extremely poor example of narrative technique if the battle is the center of focus. All one has to do is imagine how Hollywood would film this story today to know that we are dealing with a story whose purpose is different from either the bellicose or the pacifistic accounts we have come to expect.

Last, the whole categorization of this war as one of vengeance makes certain biblical moves inevitable. First, it places this story in continuity with all the similarly retributive actions that the Lord has exercised in the past. As the Israelites cry out for meat and are buried in quails (Num. 11); as those who would handle fire are consumed with fire (Num. 16); so those who harass the Israelites will be harassed as well (Num. 25; 31). Actions have consequences in this saving story where God is not just along for the ride. Second, however, the whole theme of Israel as "avenger" for the Lord makes one begin to think of the role of "avenger" in general, a role that is circumscribed with all sorts of legislative and territorial checks and balances to prevent its abuse. Surely if such caution is exercised on the individual level, it must be required on the communal, national, and international levels. Finally, this language of "vengeance" forces the reader to lay it alongside the wider biblical witness, where such vengeance is usually restricted to the Lord alone (cf. "Vengeance is mine," Deut. 32:35; and "O LORD, you God of vengeance, you God of vengeance, shine forth!" Ps. 94:1); where such retributive justice is later associated with the turning of the other cheek (raising the issue of applying Matt. 5:38–48 on intercommunal as well as interpersonal levels); and where, finally, such activity is eventually lifted from human shoulders entirely and placed exclusively in the hands of the Lord ("Beloved, never avenge yourselves, but leave room for the wrath of God; for it is written, 'Vengeance is mine, I will repay, says the Lord'"; Rom. 12:19). All of this drives us on to the sections to follow.

War as worship. If the reader pays attention, this story of the Midianites' defeat may put a whole new spin on the talk of "worship wars." Note some details.

1. The leader of this expedition is not Moses or Caleb or the newly commissioned Joshua. No, this military campaign is led by Phinehas, the priest, the son of Eleazar, the priest. Like the surgical strike of this same Phinehas back in Numbers 25, and the various maneuverings of the knife the priests oversee in the practice of sacrifice, this action is more clerical than military, more the province of those with robes and collars than those with rifles and Kevlar.

2. Though the 12,000 who participate in this action go out "armed for battle," and though lone Balaam is explicitly cited as being killed "with the sword," the only instruments actually cited are "the vessels of the sanctuary and the trumpets for sounding the alarm," and all the other victims are simply reported as "killed." Like the later battle of Jericho, whose initial assault consists once more in a blast from

the trumpet and a shout (of praise?), there is something strangely "worshipful" about this engagement, from which so much blood flows (cf. Josh. 6).

3. Although the numeric tally of casualties (thousands for the Midianites, zero for Israel) have caused many to debate the historical nature of this account, it may also point toward an implied shift in categories. If this story was told first as a narrative of the journey through the wilderness, and next as a journey toward a new temple, it finally becomes a model for how God's people confront threats to their forward journey after the temple is gone.

4. None of this is meant to deny the fact that this story is told as a retributive action against a particular people who harassed the Israelites on the way through the wilderness: they paid for these actions dearly. It simply underscores the fact that this narrative does not work well as a straightforward story of military conquest at the hand of God's people. Rather, it begins to remind us of a later people whose mouths will function as swords and whose first response to threat are the musical "blasts" of hymns (cf. Acts 16:25ff.).

War as threat. The final observation about Numbers 31 may be, in the end, most important yet most easily overlooked. One-quarter of the chapter describes the victory, and three-quarters of the chapter deals with the results. Something is decidedly out of whack here if this is mainly an account of vengeance accomplished and evil overcome. Why spend such time and space on cleanup after the game itself is over?

First, we must remember that from the beginning we have found ourselves in the midst of a story that seeks to reorient our most basic fears and joys. If the point of this story were simply preservation, the victory should have been followed by a celebration. If the point of this story is to demonstrate the prowess of the warriors, somebody else needs to take charge of the details. But if the point of this story is forming a holy people for a journey, then Israel's victory over the Midianites creates at least three fundamental problems: purity, potential divisions, and threat to mobility.

1. *Purity.* How strange that the victors of this battle are not immediately ushered into the middle of the camp and feasted and feted as heroes. Instead, they are forced to camp outside the camp for seven days, to purify themselves, their captives, and "every garment, every article of skin, everything made of goats' hair, and every article of wood" (v. 20). This is a peculiar people who worship a peculiar God.

How strange, amid a world that celebrates the human spoils of battle with parades of captives through the streets, that all the males and all the sexually experienced females are slaughtered, and the virgins allowed in only by Moses' own decree (v. 18). Though we may blanch at the horror of Midianite girls so conscripted, a comparison with cultural practices might well make the Israelites' squeamishness regarding such spoils a cause for derision. This is a peculiar people who worship a peculiar God. How bizarre it surely is to take all the precious jewelry and metal now requisitioned and pass it through fire, while everything else desirable is doused with water (v. 23). Wouldn't we be rushing such booty to the appraiser's or locking it in our vaults? Yes, this is a peculiar people who worship a peculiar God.

Once more we are reminded that the most precious asset this people has been given is the presence of the Lord at their center. All the spoils of victory are therefore immediately experienced by them as a threat to their most precious treasure: proximity to God. Alongside this all else is refuse and dross.

2. *Divisions among the people.* Following division from God, next in order of threat for this people must be division from one another, a problem that has haunted them throughout this journey. Only the fool thinks that a problem prevalent amid scarcity will disappear in circumstances of plenty. Watch what happens to a family that wins the lottery, or gathers for the disposition of an estate, or comes back from battle with their arms full.

So much of Numbers 31 must be read as a word for the future. When and whenever Israel finds itself no longer a subsistence community, getting by on subsistence fare, watch out. The same kind of rules for distribution among leaders and people, between congregation, priest/Levite, and God must be maintained. This happens only with great difficulty and strong leadership. While Moses and Eleazar sat out the battle, they take charge to head off the war that may follow. Every cow and sheep must be counted, every donkey and goat properly assigned. The battle only takes a single verse. The distribution of the booty goes on for paragraphs.

3. *The threat to mobility.* Israel, in Numbers 31, confronts a problem brand-new to the story, but one that will become fundamental in future stages of its journey. What happens to a traveling people when they become weighed down with stuff, so encumbered with booty that they can no longer move forward? There the Israelites sit, with the Promised Land just over the river, counting their booty and

making their piles and dividing their treasures as their leg muscles go slack. Sometimes a community can be so blessed with people to assimilate and possessions to process that the whole affair comes to a halt. This traveling people becomes immobile while their portable temple sinks in the sand.

Hanging over this whole story of victory, then, are the clouds of a more fundamental defeat. Could it be that this is a people under greater threat when they are winning than they were when they were losing? Will there come a day when the manna of the wilderness will be remembered as more filling fare than all else? For the modern church, does this story offer a parable of what may happen when prayers are answered, and God's people become blessed to such an extent that they lose their love of travel and trust and offering things up to God? Before this chapter is over one begins to wonder, Who really won this battle? Who or what may be truly transforming whom?

23. Instructions for the Conquest
Numbers 32:1–35:34

With the defeat of the Midianites, all the wilderness business of Israel is now complete. No further action takes place in Numbers, save for some mopping-up actions of the half-tribe of Manasseh appended to the division of the land on the east side of the Jordan, which is about to begin (Num. 32:39–42). The narrative now pauses with a tilt toward the battle ahead, as the upcoming conquest begins to set the context for last-minute discussions of the land, the journey, and the establishment of boundaries. Rumbling beneath all the talk with which this wandering concludes is the prospect of the upcoming crossing, and the war that shall greet God's people on the other side. Before the trumpets are sounded and the battle engaged, the teller of this story wants to make sure that everyone is together, that they are clear from whence they have come, toward what they are headed, and why and for whom. In a basic way, the real pep talk follows with the second version of the law in Deuteronomy. But some of the necessary work of pulling together begins here, on the east bank of the Jordan.

REGARDING TRANSJORDAN
Numbers 32:1–42

32:1 **Now the Reubenites and the Gadites owned a very great number of cattle. When they saw that the land of Jazer and the land of Gilead was a good place for cattle,** [2] **the Gadites and the Reubenites came and spoke to Moses, to Eleazar the priest, and to the leaders of the congregation, saying,** [3] **"Ataroth, Dibon, Jazer, Nimrah, Heshbon, Elealeh, Sebam, Nebo, and Beon—** [4] **the land that the Lord subdued before the congregation of Israel— is a land for cattle; and your servants have cattle."** [5] **They continued, "If we have found favor in your sight, let this land be given to your servants for a possession; do not make us cross the Jordan."** [6] **But Moses said to the Gadites and to the Reubenites, "Shall your brothers go to war while you sit**

here? [7] Why will you discourage the hearts of the Israelites from going over into the land that the LORD has given them? [8] Your fathers did this, when I sent them from Kadesh-barnea to see the land. [9] When they went up to the Wadi Eshcol and saw the land, they discouraged the hearts of the Israelites from going into the land that the LORD had given them. [10] The LORD's anger was kindled on that day and he swore, saying, [11] 'Surely none of the people who came up out of Egypt, from twenty years old and upward, shall see the land that I swore to give to Abraham, to Isaac, and to Jacob, because they have not unreservedly followed me— [12] none except Caleb son of Jephunneh the Kenizzite and Joshua son of Nun, for they have unreservedly followed the LORD.' [13] And the LORD's anger was kindled against Israel, and he made them wander in the wilderness for forty years, until all the generation that had done evil in the sight of the LORD had disappeared. [14] And now you, a brood of sinners, have risen in place of your fathers, to increase the LORD's fierce anger against Israel! [15] If you turn away from following him, he will again abandon them in the wilderness; and you will destroy all this people."
[16] Then they came up to him and said, "We will build sheepfolds here for our flocks, and towns for our little ones, [17] but we will take up arms as a vanguard before the Israelites, until we have brought them to their place. Meanwhile our little ones will stay in the fortified towns because of the inhabitants of the land. [18] We will not return to our homes until all the Israelites have obtained their inheritance. [19] We will not inherit with them on the other side of the Jordan and beyond, because our inheritance has come to us on this side of the Jordan to the east." [20] So Moses said to them, "If you do this—if you take up arms to go before the LORD for the war, [21] and all those of you who bear arms cross the Jordan before the LORD, until he has driven out his enemies from before him [22] and the land is subdued before the LORD—then after that you may return and be free of obligation to the LORD and to Israel, and this land shall be your possession before the LORD. [23] But if you do not do this, you have sinned against the LORD; and be sure your sin will find you out. [24] Build towns for your little ones, and folds for your flocks; but do what you have promised."

Up to this point, the only way the story can think about ongoing life to the east of the Jordan is as punishment and judgment. Those who settle their bones in the land short of Canaan are those who have rebelled and fallen short, and are thus only allowed to look upon and dream about the land the Lord has promised. But now, out of nowhere, comes a request to voluntarily get off the train one stop before the destination. "If we have found favor in your sight," the Reubenites and Gadites say to Moses, "let this land be given to your servants for a possession; do not make us cross the Jordan" (v. 5). It has been forty years! All things are now prepared! They can see the hills of the Promised Land just on the other side of the river! "Do not *make us* cross the Jordan"? Where did that come from, and what does it mean?

Now the Reubenites and the Gadites owned a very great number of cattle. We must recognize that this is a story told from the backside. The tribes of Reuben, Gad, and Manasseh ended up in Transjordan, settled in the towns and cities of this place, and possessed much cattle. This story thus becomes a way of explaining what is to be and, in telling the account forward, therefore presents some problems that are probably insoluble: How did they get so much cattle? Was it booty from the Midianites? But why then would they have acquired so much more than others? And why did just these two and one-half tribes make this request? Or were they the only ones brave or foolish enough to give voice to this request? Such questions the story does not try to answer because it is bent on explaining other things: How did these tribes happen to stop short of the Promised Land? What might such behavior have to teach us?

For the first time in this narrative, some tribes decide to define themselves not by what they lack (food, water, safety) and not by Whom they serve and how (the Reubenites camp here in relation to the tabernacle and march along when God's people are on the move), but by what they have; indeed, by what they "own." This east-of-Jordan land, which is not the land of promise, is a land of cattle, and these servants have cattle; thus the conclusion seems obvious: here is the place we should settle down. The first threat is thus one of self-definition, understanding who we are not by Who owns us, but by whom (captives, slaves, families) and by what cattle we own. Even though the booty of chapter 31 has been properly distributed according to the rules of war, the more pervasive threat of becoming overly encumbered as God's traveling people begins to hover over the forward progress of the story as a whole.

One might begin one's hearing of this story then by asking when we draw up short of the kingdom because we have become enamored with those things we already have in hand. "As God has blessed me with these things in this place, this must be the spot for me to settle." How many disciples' and congregations' journeys have fallen short of the mark because of blessings given for worship and for travel, which instead become excuses for settling down? In this sense, this story of a people with livestock points toward the parable of a later owner of cattle who, when invited to the master's banquet, begs off: "I have bought five yoke of oxen, and I am going to try them out; please accept my regrets" (Luke 14:19). Do we own our possessions, or do they begin to own and define us?

But Moses said to the Gadites and to the Reubenites, "Shall your brothers go to war while you sit here?" Although the initial problem may be more one of misunderstanding the gifts of God, as usual it manifests itself as well in a problem with the neighbors. For Moses, the most imminent threat has less to do with mislocation and self-definition than with another potential threat to the unity of God's people, and to the forward tilt of their shared purpose. Moses immediately has the sense that he has been here before and does not want to repeat the mistakes of the past (see Num. 13–14). If the rest of the camp sees these members settling down short of the destination, everybody else will start unloading their packs and possessions, and the parade will come to a halt. This is not just a matter of *herds*, but especially of the *heart*; and hearts that we now know can be all too easily discouraged (in contrast to Caleb, who back in the earlier narrative is commended for being willing to follow the Lord "wholeheartedly"; Num. 14:24; cf. Josh. 14:6–14). The Lord has given Israel this land. All they have to do is cross over and claim it. But if too many stop following him and take to sitting, the whole enterprise may be lost once more. What seems like a reasonable and even generous request (after all, there will be fewer tribes and more land for those who continue!) is interpreted by Moses as the plot of a "brood of sinners" who have "turned away" from following the Lord. They thus invite the anger and abandonment of the Lord, and thereby the destruction of all this people. What at first appears as a minor pause now takes on the dimensions of a full-scale threat to survival.

It is helpful and instructive to think once more of fundamental sin not so much as doing something wrong, but as failing to do something right. Here sin is the sin of sitting when the journey is not over. At its core it is a turning away from following that requires a turning back toward following, or else the whole purpose for our existence be lost. A sedentary church full of people with discouraged hearts will attract few followers, thanks be to God! But a people always ready to "cross over" (can one hear somewhere in this the "crossing over" of baptism, as well as the vows taken in that regard?) will attract other travelers as well.

Then they came up to him and said, "We will build sheepfolds here for our flocks, and towns for our little ones, but we will take up arms as a vanguard before the Israelites, until we have brought them to their place." Given the trajectory of this story, one would expect the next action to be fire from heaven, a fresh wave of serpents, or another forty years of wandering. Instead, incredibly, a compromise is proposed that is accepted. The Reubenites and the Gadites will settle in the land in a limited fashion (sheepfolds for flocks, towns for their little ones), but also commit themselves to travel (v. 18). They promise both to "settle" and "cross over" by dividing up their clan into two groups: those who will live in these towns and cities ("our little ones, our wives, our flocks, and all our livestock"; v. 26) and all those "armed for battle before the LORD" (v. 29). The Reubenites and the Gadites thereby become the first examples of followers who can also settle, putting down roots on the east bank of the Jordan even while they continue their journey to the land God has promised.

If we think of this story as a narrative that is over once the conquest is completed, then it is simply a story about how the Reubenites, the Gadites, and the half-tribe of Manasseh ended up in the "trans-Jordan" for a few hundred years. But if the inheritance of all the Israelites, and through them the inheritance of all the nations is yet unfinished, then one must come to think of these people as both still on maneuvers and still settled as well. Every day, the members of this modern-day tribe leave some in place in order for the rest to cross over in service. Every week, this people is sent forth with charge and benediction, both back to home and out for continued maneuvers until the inheritance of everybody is won. If we do not do this, according to Moses, we sin "against the LORD; and be sure your sin will find you out" (v. 23). With the compromise brokered by these exceptional tribes on the east bank of the Jordan, we catch some glimpse of the strange dual existence of God's people down to this day, a people called to seek the welfare of the cities where they find themselves as well as search for a city not made with human hands. What starts here as a simple territorial compromise provides a pattern for God's people down through the centuries. We are to be in this world, but not of this world (cf. John 17:11-17). Keep this promise, and the story will go on.

REVIEWING THE JOURNEY
Numbers 33:1–49

33:1 **These are the stages by which the Israelites went out of the land of Egypt in military formation under the leadership of Moses and Aaron.** [2] **Moses wrote down their starting points, stage by stage, by command of the LORD; and these are their stages according to their starting places.**

Before God's people are ready to "cross over" and confront the challenges of both conquest and settlement, a review of from whence they have come may be of assistance as they now think forward to whither they are headed. For those who just pick up Numbers 33 as a chapter to read or a lesson to lead, it seems overwhelming in its detail and length, and an unnecessary citing of names and places best forgotten. But for those who have endured this entire story beginning in Leviticus, such reactions drive us back to the fundamental purposes for this narrative as a whole, beside which Numbers 33 seems incredibly brief and orderly in comparison. It may prove helpful here to think first about how this summary *differs* from the account of Israel's journey in Leviticus–Numbers as a whole, then shift toward the fundamental themes upon which these two versions of the same story *agree*.

Differences. For the reader who arrives at this chapter after slogging through all the conflicts of places and trajectories and loyalties of this people to this point, one might well wonder whether the author of Numbers 33 has the same story in mind.

First, as many scholars have pointed out, there are discrepancies between this account of the stages of Israel's journey, and the "wanderings" that we have read about all along the way. Stated bluntly, the order and place names here listed are difficult to harmonize with the more chaotic accounts that have preceded it. Surely then, in some basic sense, Numbers 33 must be read as the summary of a final group of editors, whose goal is to impose some order on the multiple versions of this story as a whole and the individual chapters that comprise it. They made earlier attempts to draw together sometimes divergent strands and traditions regarding individual stories (e.g., the several stories of the conquest of the Midianites in Num. 31; or the revolts of the Reubenites, the Levites, and the people in Num. 16–17); now the editors try to do the same for the story as a whole. Like a harmonized version of Jesus' or Paul's journeys in the New Testament, there are some places where the two fit, and some where they do not (for a more extended discussion of these discrepancies, see Dozeman, *Numbers*).

Second, there is so much missing from this account that it seems, in a more basic sense, more than a little "misleading." In this version of the story, every stage begins with Israel "setting out" and ends with Israel "camping" at individual places that do not overlap or cut back on one another, but lead forward to the final destination in a beautiful succession of hikes and stops along the way. Where, we might ask, are the stories of rebellions and reversals? Where is the constant sense of "one step forward, two or three steps backward" that has haunted us throughout this narrative? If all we had to remember these stories of Israel's days in the wilderness was this summary chapter, the whole label of "wanderings" would never have been applied to this story. Numbers 33 remembers a story that is told as a military march or parade (v. 1), all under the rubric of the command of the Lord and the response of his people (v. 2). Thankfully, we all might say, there are other more complete and accurate summaries of the journey available elsewhere in Scripture, which have been far more influential on the synagogue's and the church's memory of these events than Numbers 33 (cf. Ps. 106, where Israel's rebellions gain equal space with its parade).

Maybe third, and most problematic, is the way Numbers 33 introduces the whole narrative as a "bold" going forth: "On the day after the passover the Israelites went out boldly in the sight of all the Egyptians" (33:3). The goings out of Israel described in Leviticus–Numbers might be characterized in many ways (fearful, hesitant, distrustful, divided, rebellious), but "boldly" is not the first adverb that would come to mind. The reason Joshua must repeatedly exhort these same people to "be strong and courageous" (three times in the course of four verses, Josh. 1:6–9) to get them moving out of the camp at Moab must be because they in some fundamental way have given in to the opposite ("Do not be frightened or dismayed"; Josh. 1:9). This portrait of an organized army marching out of Egypt and through the wilderness—in full sight of its enemies, and experiencing the Lord's judgments not only on all who would stop them, but also on these peoples' gods ("The Lord executed judgments even against their gods"; Num. 33:4)—seems as out of sync with the main narrative as can be imagined. It is almost as if one of the disciples, following the resurrection, had looked back and described their journey from Nazareth to Jerusalem as a unified and single-minded assault on the forces of evil, with none of them wavering or hesitating along the way (first we won over the north, then the south, then confronted head-on the powers of the palace and the Temple, and overcame!). Or are we reading and understanding this summary in a fundamentally misguided way?

Agreement. First, this parade did *begin* boldly. Way back in Exodus, the Israelites responded with no hesitation to Pharoah's command to rise up and go away (12:31), the Egyptians' plea to do so hastily (12:33), and Moses' and Aaron's passing on of the Lord's marching plans: "All the Israelites did just as the Lord had commanded Moses and Aaron" (12:50). Even later, as we have seen, the Israelites have no trouble in getting started (see Num. 10; cf. the disciples: "Immediately they left their nets and followed"; Mark 1:18). It is the "keeping going" that presents the problem. That this parade began boldly and with a sense of purpose and direction is true to both the story as a whole and this summary.

Second, the place names do demonstrate a kind of order and symmetry (reflecting the kind of symmetry typical of other "remembered" military campaigns in the ancient Near East; see Dozeman; as well as the numerical symmetry so prized in Jewish accounts of ordering, as in Leviticus–Numbers). Yet the names themselves call to mind many individual stories along the way, where disorder was more the order of the day: Marah, "bitterness" (Exod. 15:23); in the wilderness of Sin, "the whole congregation of the Israelites complained against Moses and Aaron in the wilderness" (Exod. 16:2); Kibroth-hattaavah, "graves of craving" (Num. 11:34); in the wilderness of Zin (around Kadesh), the spies bring back an "unfavorable report" (14:37); on the plains of Moab, "the people began to have sexual relations with the women of Moab" (25:1). Numbers 33 thus identifies this journey not only as a real-world journey to places that really existed and could still be visited today, but also by a group of people yet recognizable to those who continue to follow in their footsteps even now, for good and ill.

Last, then, the grand sweep of this summary proves most helpful, both for looking backward and for looking forward. Though this story has indeed seemed chaotic when viewed closely and on a day-by-day basis, now, as they stand on the banks of the Jordan, looking backward, the patterns of forward movement reemerge. As is often the case, both individually and collectively, in the midst of the journey each step is uncertain and each action ambiguous. But looked back on from a distant-enough vantage point, most of our stories do take on the shape of a journey someone other than we ourselves have planned. Before Israel can once more be courageous and bold on the next stage of the journey, the storyteller pauses to remind the Israelites of the distance already traveled, and now, quite miraculously, the path appears almost straight. Whether the reader experiences this summary as more or less truthful than the narrative as a whole may have less to do with who compiled the final summary than with the reader's own experience of providence. It truly is a theological reality, whose truth is more evident in the "looking back" than the "looking ahead."

REGARDING CONQUEST
Numbers 33:50–56

> 33:50 In the plains of Moab by the Jordan at Jericho, the LORD spoke to Moses, saying: 51 Speak to the Israelites, and say to them: When you cross over the Jordan into the land of Canaan, 52 you shall drive out all the inhabitants of the land from before you, destroy all their figured stones, destroy all their cast images, and demolish all their high places. 53 You shall take posses-

sion of the land and settle in it, for I have given you the land to possess. [54] You shall apportion the land by lot according to your clans; to a large one you shall give a large inheritance, and to a small one you shall give a small inheritance; the inheritance shall belong to the person on whom the lot falls; according to your ancestral tribes you shall inherit. [55] But if you do not drive out the inhabitants of the land from before you, then those whom you let remain shall be as barbs in your eyes and thorns in your sides; they shall trouble you in the land where you are settling. [56] And I will do to you as I thought to do to them.

God's people have now reviewed their journey all the way up to this point, "in the plains of Moab by the Jordan at Jericho" (33:48, 50). Now, the last-minute details shift from the conquest and division of the Transjordan (Num. 32), to the conquest and divisions of Canaan itself (once more we encounter the key phrase that sets this material off from all the experiences thus far: "when you *cross over* into the land of Canaan"; 33:51, emphasis added). Although we have encountered a similar review of final plans as far back as Leviticus 26 (in the form of rewards for obedience and punishments for disobedience), here the emphasis is on the action of conquest itself (versus the rules for living once there). As we have just experienced a "dry run" at such a conquest in Israel's defeat of the Midianites (Num. 31), it might prove helpful to examine the similarities and differences in this campaign already completed and the campaigns of conquest now dead ahead. These six verses are heavily loaded: they are the last instructions in this material before the "crossing over," and thus they are placed in creative tension with Moses' "second" run-through of the rules for warfare in Deuteronomy 20.

Similarities with Numbers 31. The first similarity is the emphasis on total destruction, made obvious by the repetition of the word "all," occurring four times in one verse (33:52), three times in conjunction with the verb "to destroy." This is no war simply for the sake of winning. It whispers once more of a sacrifice where everything is consumed on the altar ("the priest shall turn the whole into smoke on the altar as a burnt offering"; Lev. 1:9), both as a sign of extravagant worship and to prevent any improper use of the offering by the worshiper. From the beginning it is clear that this manual for conquest reflects both the peculiar demands of a God whose claims on his followers are all-inclusive, and the necessary clearing of a space for a people whose allegiance is far more compromised. As with the Midianites, the reason for such wholesale destruction has as much to do with the Israelites' fickleness as with the Canaanites' wickedness. "But if you do not drive out the inhabitants of the land from before you [all of them!], then those whom you let remain shall be as barbs in your eyes and thorns in your sides; they shall trouble you in the land where you are settling" (Num. 33:55). If anyone needs any depiction of what such barbs and thorns look like, just go back a few chapters to Numbers 25, where one of the Israelites became yoked side by side "in the sight of Moses and in the sight of the whole congregation of the Israelites" (v. 6). Similar drastic actions were required then, and similar drastic actions are anticipated here. Perhaps a more steadfast people would require less lethal orders. But for a people of wandering eyes ("no idols") and wavering commitments ("no gods before me"), such total destruction seems almost inevitable.

Second, these orders point toward the time for settlement (33:53). Though certain rules of engagement may apply when God's people are traveling and "passing through" (We will stay on the path, drink our own water, or pay for any that is yours; 20:17–19), when these people begin to "stay" or "settle" anywhere, different rules of engagement are required. Again, the story of Israel in camp at Shittim becomes the narrative that drives the plans for settlement in these verses ("while Israel was staying at Shittim"; 25:1). While Israel may or may not be showing much progress in its attempts to stay faithful "on the road," this passage reminds us that such tests always pale in comparison to the trials that loom ahead once "in the land."

Third, as the earlier story of conquest (Num. 31) is followed by rules for dividing or apportioning the spoil, so these instructions anticipate the means by which the land will be divided once the battles are over (33:54). Curiously, for a matter of such supreme importance, the mechanism for division seems a strange hybrid: apportionment "by lot" on one hand, and proportional apportionment on the other (v. 54). Once more we see an unexpected flexibility in a matter of no small import (cf. 26:52–56), making us wonder once more regarding the ultimate purpose of these instructions and this story, which now drives us forward toward some key differences.

Differences with Numbers 31. We began our listing with the emphasis on "all," linked with destruction. Yet at this very point, a key difference arises. While the story of the conquest of the Midianites was awash in blood, and full of the verb "to kill," it must be noted in this key summary that all the things destroyed are objects of worship, while all the human beings must be "driven out" (33:52). This is no small detail. Surely there will be many casualties in such a "herding" maneuver, but it still sounds quite different from the discussions regarding human booty in Numbers 31 (and Deut. 20). As we flagged the "priestly" aspects of the campaign against the Midianites, now the liturgical aspects of this conquest become even more unavoidable. Could it be that these instructions are as much about preparing a place for worship as they are about gaining property for settlement?

Second, and hidden from view in this passage alone, is the recognition that this conquest, unlike the story of the Midianites, is never accomplished, not even in the Scriptures. Almost from the beginning of the conquest, certain inhabitants of the land are not "driven out," beginning with shrewd Rahab and her family in Joshua 2 and continuing with the wily Gibeonites in Joshua 9 (cf. Judg. 1). As with Hobab back at the beginning of this parade (Num. 10:29–32), this is a people who follow a God who loves to accumulate surprising fellow travelers along the way (cf. Exod. 12:38). It therefore is a strange mixture of God's graciousness and the peoples' faithlessness that leads Israel to the point of a mixed conquest ("Now these are the nations that the LORD left to test all those in Israel who had no experience of any war in Canaan"; Judg. 3:1), from which the Israelites never recover, either in the first conquest of the land, or in their later return.

It is this later "driving out" of Israel itself to which this passage alludes in its final, oddly dangling sentence: "And I will do to you as I thought to do to them" (Num. 33:56). That this people ended up living as a people more "driven" than "driving" finally puts an odd spin on these instructions in particular, and on our story as a whole. We must come back to this theme in our conclusion; for now, in this portion on instructions regarding conquest, some summary comments must be made.

For a passage that purports to be the final instructions for a war of conquest, this passage thus reveals itself to be strangely "pacifistic" at its core. Like Jesus in the Temple (who overturned or destroyed the tables for money changing, but drove the money changers out), and like most of the words of the prophets (who focused more on the smashing of idols than the enemies of Israel round about), this passage on the banks of the Jordan near Jericho seems to talk more about destruction of things and driving out of people than we would or should expect. This then points out the difficulty of establishing any unified biblical guidelines on the topic of "holy war," much less issues of settlement and possession. Again, one wonders if this summary has more to do with worship than real estate, a question this entire journey keeps pushing to the fore.

For some reason, the image that keeps coming to my mind is the gift of communal Bible study. It can take place anywhere and at any time on the journey. All that is required is for any competing, ultimate authorities to be demolished or demoted (like "figured stones" and "cast images"; v. 52), and any who would finally disrupt the study to be driven out (like all the inhabitants of the land; v. 52). Then God's people will be given a place to settle in a transient world, to discuss and apportion their inheritance in a kingdom that has room for all. For a people of the Book, and for followers of the Word, this may well be all the conquest that God and we require.

REGARDING BOUNDARIES
Numbers 34:1–35:34

34:1 The LORD spoke to Moses, saying: [2] Command the Israelites, and say to them: When you enter the land of Canaan (this is the land that shall fall to you for an inheritance, the land of Canaan, defined by its boundaries), [3] your south sector shall extend from the wilderness of Zin along the side of Edom. Your southern boundary shall begin from the end of the Dead Sea on the east; [4] your boundary shall turn south of the ascent of Akrabbim, and cross to Zin, and its outer limit shall be south of Kadesh-barnea; then it shall go on to Hazar-addar, and cross to Azmon; [5] the boundary shall turn from Azmon to the Wadi of Egypt, and its termination shall be at the Sea. [6] For the western boundary, you shall have the Great Sea and its coast; this shall be your western boundary. [7] This shall be your northern boundary: from the Great Sea you shall mark out your line to Mount Hor; [8] from Mount Hor you shall mark it out to Lebo-hamath, and the outer limit of the boundary shall be at Zedad; [9] then the boundary shall extend to Ziphron, and its end shall be at Hazar-enan; this shall be your northern boundary. [10] You shall mark out your eastern boundary from Hazar-enan to Shepham; [11] and the boundary shall continue down from Shepham to Riblah on the east side of Ain; and the boundary shall go down, and reach the eastern slope of the sea of Chinnereth; [12] and the boundary shall go down to the Jordan, and its end shall be at the Dead Sea. This shall be your land with its boundaries all around. [13] Moses commanded the Israelites, saying: This is the land that you shall inherit by lot, which the LORD has commanded to give to the nine tribes and to the half-tribe; [14] for the tribe of the Reubenites by their ancestral houses and the tribe of the Gadites by their ancestral houses have taken their inheritance, and also the half-tribe of Manasseh; [15] the two tribes and the half-tribe have taken their inheritance beyond the Jordan at Jericho eastward, toward the sunrise.

35:1 In the plains of Moab by the Jordan at Jericho, the LORD spoke to Moses, saying: [2] Command the Israelites to give, from the inheritance that they possess, towns for the Levites to live in; you shall also give to the Levites pasture lands surrounding the towns. [3] The towns shall be theirs to live in, and their pasture lands shall be for their cattle, for their livestock, and for all their animals. [4] The pasture lands of the towns, which you shall give to the Levites, shall reach from the wall of the town outward a thousand cubits all around. [5] You shall measure, outside the town, for the east side two thousand cubits, for the south side two thousand cubits, for the west side two thousand cubits, and for the north side two thousand cubits, with the town in the middle; this shall belong to them as pasture land for their towns. [6] The towns that you give to the Levites shall include the six cities of refuge, where you shall permit a slayer to flee, and in addition to them you shall give forty-two towns. [7] The towns that you give to the Levites shall total forty-eight, with their pasture lands. [8] And as for the towns that you shall give from the possession of the Israelites, from the larger tribes you shall take many, and from the smaller tribes you shall take few; each, in proportion to the inheritance that it obtains, shall give of its towns to the Levites. [9] The LORD spoke to Moses, saying: [10] Speak to the Israelites, and say to them: When you cross the Jordan into the land of Canaan, [11] then you shall select cities to be cities of refuge for you, so that a slayer who kills a person without intent may flee there. [12] The cities shall be for you a refuge from the avenger, so that the slayer may not die until there is a trial before the congregation. [13] The cities that you designate shall be six cities of refuge for you: [14] you shall designate three cities beyond the Jordan, and three cities in the land of Canaan, to be cities of refuge. [15] These six cities shall serve as refuge for the Israelites, for the resident or transient alien among them, so that anyone who kills a person without intent may flee there.

Finally, before the crossing over begins, a plan for the drawing of boundaries is placed on the table. Heretofore most of the crucial boundaries for this people have been the ones within the camp (particularly necessary boundaries between the people and the Lord) and without the camp (with specific regard to the various nations and lands they desired to pass through). But now, as settlement stares them in the face on both sides of the Jordan River, it is time to break out the transepts and the stakes and establish tangible boundaries that will not shift and move. If God's promises for the people had always been merely spiritual in nature (gifts such as patience, trust, and perseverance), there would be no need for two whole chapters drawing lines in Palestinian dirt. But just as promises of descendants have produced clans with flesh-and-blood cohorts; and just as promises of cattle, goats, and sheep have produced creatures with blood, organs, and entrails; so the promise of land now gets down to wadis, wildernesses, and coastlines that can be measured, plotted, and mapped out, for past, present, and future generations. Make no mistake. Wars are still being fought over the sites and cities that appear in these two chapters. But just as surely, let us continue to listen for something more.

Boundaries in the dirt. All through this story we have followed a tendency to draw boundaries that create a threefold division: between human beings (Gentile, Jew, and priest) and between animals (unclean, edible, and sacrificial). Here, in our last two chapters, such a threefold division continues.

First, there is the boundary between Israel and its neighbors, transcribed by the southern, western, northern, and eastern boundaries described in 34:1–15. Some of these boundaries are simple, such as the Great Sea on the west, and the Jordan River on the east. Some are more difficult, such as the "wilderness of Zin." But however simple or complicated, all these boundaries are meant to be measured, with real sightings and footsteps, and real stakes and pegs driven into the ground. How do we know? Because many of these places are real-life landmarks, still visible and measurable down to today. But also because this is a real-life people who have revealed their deep need for real-life space, so they can settle down and flourish versus being led astray. Without real lines in real dirt, this is a people who will forget who they are as they continue to try to live out their peculiar witness to their peculiar God, as settled members of the worldwide human community.

Second, there is the boundary between Israel and Israel's God, still necessarily maintained by a group of people set apart for that purpose, the Levites. Now, even after the camp is dispersed, the person traveling through this land will know that this people's God is nearby. How? By the forty-eight cities set aside for those who will tend God's service. This is a substantial sacrifice of real estate, especially with the 1,000-cubit buffer zones, and thus must be implemented proportionally (35:8). But this is a necessary investment for a people for whom the boundary between them and their God is at least as important as the boundary between them and their neighbors. All visitors have to do is walk this land, and they will be able to see that this people is different: What is that city over there? It's a city for the Levites. And why do you need a city for the Levites? Because we worship a God who is very near.

Third, there is a boundary between those in Israel with blood on their hands and those called to slay the murderers: the cities of refuge, counted among the forty-eight cities for the Levites, but set up with three to the west of the Jordan and three to the east. These cities establish a boundary within the community itself, which recognizes that sometimes the worst things that can happen ("the shedding of human blood") may take place "unintentionally" (35:11, 15, 23). Therefore, this is a society that would forswear any boundary between the slayer and the avenger of blood for intentional killings (whether the person is as vulnerable as a "transient alien," in v. 15; or as invulnerable as someone able to pay a large ransom, in v. 31); yet this is also a society that recognizes the messiness of life in this world, where ax heads may fly off inadvertently and stones be dropped without first looking below (v. 23). This then is a society determined to strike the right balance between the sanctity of life on the one hand ("The murderer shall be put to death"; 35:16), and the insanity of life on the other (where someone may push someone without enmity or hurl an object without lying in wait, only to cause the death of someone he holds dear). This is a people who are commanded to draw boundaries between themselves and their neighbors, between themselves and their God, and between themselves as a community (rich and poor, strong and vulnerable), not because they are perfect people living in a perfect world, but because they and their world are not perfect. These are imperfect people living in an imperfect world, yet in proximity to the Lord, their God. Boundaries must be drawn, and yet—

Boundaries not in dirt. As we have recognized since the beginning of this journey, this story (Leviticus–Numbers) stops short of settlement, for reasons that are historical, literary, and theological. It is therefore highly significant that on drawing lines in the dirt, a countertext is yet evident for those who would look more closely.

First, the divine apportionment of the land is immediately followed by the appointment of flesh-and-blood leaders to carry this division out. Surely part of this provision arises from the fact that it will take human conversation, cooperation, and compromise to figure out just where to draw the line through "the wilderness of Zin." Nevertheless, it is quite clear that the major apportionment in this story is "handed down" to this people by God rather than "handed over" to them by God. This is not a committee founded to figure out where the proper boundaries are, but a task force charged with putting into action a divine decree. It is therefore somewhat strange that the story would need to name the leaders from each clan one by one, and preserve this record, unless . . .

Could it be that one day the boundaries between the tribes in the family and those outside the family will be more important than any particular geographical divisions? We have already seen how these boundaries can flex, as is made evident even in these verses with reference to the clans of Reuben, Gad, and Manasseh (34:14–15). So what happens when these boundaries become flexed even more, and the tribes are scattered to the four ends of the earth in the Diaspora? Well, then the boundaries between God's people and the nations are drawn more in genealogy than geology, as a comparison of this list of tribal leaders and the genealogies of the New Testament attest. Yes, God's people need some real-life space, but it gradually becomes more familial than physical.

Second, as we read the accounts of Levitical cities, we must go back and remember an earlier solution for the feeding and provision of the Levites and the priests. From the beginning of the sacrificial system, we have seen a twofold process at work. While the whole burnt offering offered everything to the Lord, most of the other offerings accrued some benefit to the priests. The farther we journeyed in Leviticus–Numbers, the more explicit such priestly "set asides" became, until it began to be clear that these portions were being given to the priests and the Levites in order to free them up for worship by setting them free from production. Just as the apostle deserves his bread in the New Testament, so the priests and Levites are reserved a portion in the Old.

Why then would cities be set aside within which the Levites become their own producers? Could the ideal numbers and measurements, and the proportional nature of this division, point back to this sacrificial system, serving more as a sign here on the east bank of the Jordan, than an actual rezoning to come? Again, once this people becomes a group of wanderers and travelers, the prospect of providing for priests with real estate becomes problematic. Shared ownership by the people and special provisions for the apostles now become the order of the day.

Finally, the driving motivation for the cities of refuge must now be brought to the fore. Today we might assume that the primary rationale for such set-aside city is one of justice and mercy in this broken world. This is undoubtedly true, as made clear in the painstaking if difficult distinctions between intentional and unintentional deaths that claim the bulk of this material. But at the end of this chapter—and given our framing, at the end of this story as a whole—comes a quite different rationale, which is fraught with difficulties in interpretation for traveling tribes today: "You shall not pollute the land in which you live; for blood pollutes the land, and no expiation can be made for the land, for the blood that is shed in it, except by the blood of the one who shed it. You shall not defile the land in which you live, in which I also dwell; for I the LORD dwell among the Israelites" (35:33–34).

Here at the very end are several shifts that we must observe. Though we began this section with explicit language regarding the land of Canaan (34:2), we end here with "the land in which you live." Could it be that boundaries originally meant for a particular piece of land are now applied to any lands within which Israel may live, even temporarily?

Recognize also the shift in language regarding pollution and expiation at the end of this section, so different in tone and origin from the warnings about "driving out" and being "troubled" by the inhabitants in the sections just before. One cannot help but look back once more to where we began this journey (in Lev. 1–7), with talk of sacrifices and blood, all for the purpose of atoning for sins that are classified as "unintentional," though that interpretation remains as difficult there as here in Numbers 35. Is it really true that no expiation can be made except by the blood of the one who shed it—for the Israelite back then, or for the Christian today? Having reached the end of this story, are we being asked to go back and begin again where we began?

Last, observe the shift in the language of the Lord's dwelling. From the beginning of this story, much of the motivation for the rules and the stories has been grounded in the way in which God's presence is located. At the start of Leviticus, I argued that the preceding descent of the Lord upon the tent of meeting was the precipitating cause of the sacrificial rites that spun out one after another. The Lord had requested a sanctuary consisting of a tent so that he might dwell in their midst (Exod. 25:8; 29:45–46). This dwelling then comes to fruition fully when the worship of the people begins in Leviticus 9 ("The glory of the LORD appeared to all the people"; v. 23). After that, as the march through the wilderness begins, the Lord keeps his promise to be a God who goes with this people (Exod. 33:14), by the cloud over the tabernacle regularly lifting off when it was time to journey, and then settling down over the tabernacle when it was time to camp (Num. 9:15–23). And so, there is nothing new to the language in Numbers 35:34 about the Lord dwelling among the Israelites.

But 35:34 includes not only language about God's dwelling among the Israelites. It now also implies that God dwells *in the land*: "You shall not defile the land in which you live, in which I also dwell." We have already encountered the problems that confront God's people when they transition from traveling to dwelling (Num. 25). Now we are confronted with similar concerns with respect to God. *On the one hand*, we might follow this theme out into the wider world of the rest of Scripture, where the dwelling place of God shifts from tents ("I have been moving about in a tent and a tabernacle"; 2 Sam. 7:6) to Temples ("I have built you an exalted house, a place for you to dwell in forever"; 1 Kgs. 8:13); and from a tabernacling rabbi (in whom "the whole fullness of deity dwells bodily"; Col. 2:9) to those to whom his Spirit is given ("Do you not know that you are God's temple and that God's Spirit dwells in you?" 1 Cor. 3:16). *On the other hand*, within our smaller story of Leviticus–Numbers, a drama about traveling ends with a passage about dwelling, but then stops before that dwelling can occur. Surely it is no accident that while there is a story about God's glory coming to dwell *in the tabernacle* (the scene in Exod. 40, with which this study began), there is no parallel scene about God's glory coming to dwell *in the land* versus the Temple (either here in Leviticus–Numbers or later in the Scriptures).

At the conclusion of this section on boundaries, it remains somewhat unclear how these boundaries are to be interpreted. Read in one way, they become a pattern for how God's people should set up camp in whatever land they find themselves, so that the proper divisions between the nations, Israel, and the priests within Israel are maintained. These may well be boundaries drawn in dirt, even if only the dirt of a temporary camp or sanctuary. Discussions regarding the setting apart of sacred space for worship might find guidance in the patterns of Numbers 34–35.

But as these books draw to a close on the far side of the Jordan, before any crossing over and much less any dwelling can occur, it is proper to ask whether this entire discussion of boundaries in dirt is the primary focus. How does a people who are yet on the journey go about establishing boundaries, planning for conquest, and plotting their trajectory? We will try to answer some of those questions in the epilogue that follows.

Epilogue

Having traversed this long and strange stretch of territory (and Scripture), we may well benefit from spending just a little time looking back. As we began this journey together, we argued that such "blue highways" might provide us a clearer portrait of the character of God and God's people than some other more "well-traveled" roads. Not only has this journey convinced this reader of the soundness of this argument; it has also raised the suspicion that perhaps our preference for other pathways in Scripture is less than accidental. Surely it is always a good exercise to ask ourselves what portions of Scripture we skip over, and then have the courage to examine why.

We began our discussion by reminding ourselves of the threefold nature of the composition of Leviticus–Numbers. In succession, these were a journey from one land to the next, a journey from one temple to the next, and a journey from one kingdom to the next. This was a useful construct for reading this story *forward*, since it helped resolve some of the apparent contradictions of this story as a story. Why is the route of this march so difficult to discern? Why have all these regulations for worship for an army on the move? Why don't the travelers ever get to their destination, or is their destination all that clear after all?

After walking this journey forward, we may now find it helpful to *look back on the story* from its end: camped out with the Israelites on the plains of Moab, with the crossing over of the Jordan dead ahead. What, we might ask, are the primary stages of this journey? What have we learned about the relationship between God, God's people, and the rest of God's world at each of these stages along the way?

In the camp. First, let's think about God's people in the camp. Most of the material from Leviticus 1 to Numbers 10 has to do with organizing Israel's life in the camp. With hindsight it is now clear that the greatest threat for Israel in this location comes not from within the family and not from the world outside, but from the proximity of that person or force or

Other at the heart of the camp: the Lord God. It was one thing for God to set this people free from Egypt. That requires a response of extravagant praise: "I will sing to the LORD, for he has triumphed gloriously; horse and rider he has thrown into the sea" (Exod. 15:1). It is another thing for God to promise to go with this people on the way. That, as we shall see, requires a response of trust rather than fear as we face the future as God's people together. But what do we do if God chooses to come and dwell in our midst? Something extravagant. Something peculiar. Something costly each and every day. "You shall be holy as the LORD God is holy!" (cf. Lev. 19:2; etc.) becomes the central theme song for God's people "in camp."

The church has often responded to this dilemma by shouting, "We can't do this! And, thank the Lord, we don't have to, because God has done it for us in Christ Jesus!" There is indeed some truth in this. We believe that Jesus is the perfect and once-for-all sacrifice. There is nothing we can do to surpass this or to gain what he alone has accomplished. But what rereading Leviticus–Numbers makes clear is that neither could Israel. That's not what this is about. God has chosen to draw near, a decision that is costly to God, in both the Old Testament and the New. There is nothing the people can do to earn this. There is nothing the people can do to deserve it. But once the Lord has not only made this decision, but also carried it out, whether in Exodus 40:34 ("Then the cloud covered the tent of meeting, and the glory of the LORD filled the tabernacle") or John 1:14 ("And the Word became flesh and lived among us, and we have seen his glory, the glory as of a father's only son, full of grace and truth"), then something must be done. "You shall be different, set apart, holy, as God has chosen to be different, set apart, and holy in your midst."

The deep wisdom and the great challenge of Leviticus–Numbers are its recognition that such a response cannot be made in one fell swoop. Some individuals may do so, by sacrificing themselves as witnesses or martyrs (and we catch some glimpses of this in Moses as he lays down his life for the very people who, at times, would take his life). But for God's people, as a community "in the camp," this is only accomplished concretely, day by day, in small actions as well as large. It is this daily practice of holiness, inspired by a situation of too much God in our midst, that is the primary gift from this stage of Israel's journey, a gift to the synagogue and the church today.

For too long we have thought that we could maintain our awareness of God's immediate proximity through polishing our *faith* rather than rehearsing our *practice*. We have too quickly dismissed Israel's worries over food and clothes and camp arrangements as "lack of faith" and "subservience to the law," rather than a day-to-day "incorporation" of our gratitude for God's election of us as the Lord's own peculiar people in this world. Anyone who reads the New Testament in conjunction with Leviticus–Numbers will know that both Moses and Paul were calling God's people to an embodied versus a disembodied faith. One could not be around this people Israel, and one should not be able to be around God's people the Jews or the Christians—watching them eat and dress and mark time—without beginning to wonder what guest they must have hidden somewhere in their midst. Ordinary people don't act or live this way. Something or Someone must be "in their midst," indeed at the very center of their lives. "Christian practice is always a response, always inadequate, to merciful divine presence" (Amy Plantinga Pauw, in Volf and Bass, *Practicing Theology*, 36).

Maybe it is providential that at the very same time that the prooftexting of this material has become most absurd and outlandish, other works have appeared, both in biblical studies of this material (see Balentine; Gerstenberger) and in the necessary practices of the Christian community (see Bass; Dawn). The most exciting next step might be a coming together of these two streams in a concrete, specific, and radical discussion of what "life in camp" should look like with God in our midst today. What foods should we eat in a starving *and* oversated world? What clothes should God's people wear when some go naked *and* elsewhere almost everybody but the priests are decked out in the latest fashions? What impact might the Sabbath have in a society obsessed with time management, or the Jubilee in a world both driven and riven by land and property and possessions? Why now, looking back, do *you* think this material is so little read?

On the road. Next, let us look back and think together about life on the road, God's people on the march, especially the passages we have encountered in Numbers 10–21. If the primary threat to Israel in camp came from God, it is equally clear that the primary threat to Israel on the road comes from God's people themselves. Although the presenting problem might be threats in the present (food and water) or potential threats up ahead (their enemies), whenever they found themselves in camp while on the way, the greatest threat was what we today call "friendly fire," casualties brought on by divisions among themselves. Any church or synagogue terribly concerned about enemies without might benefit from rereading these stories regarding enemies within.

In an era of constant schism in the church (has there ever been a time when it was otherwise?), the narrative sections of Leviticus–Numbers have some pointed lessons to teach us. First, most fundamental divisions within

God's people arise out of fear, especially fear of the future, which causes God's people to turn on one another ("All the Israelites complained against Moses and Aaron; the whole congregation said to them, 'Would that we had died in the land of Egypt'"; Num. 14:2). Second, such turning on one another is ultimately a turning on God, who is traveling with this people and calls us to trust ("How long will this people despise me? And how long will they refuse to believe [or trust] in me, in spite of all the signs that I have done among them?" 14:11). Third, the best solution for such divisions is to break camp and keep moving (unless the Lord has just disciplined you for not moving; 14:39–45); most fights break out when God's people are standing still or sitting, versus marching (cf. the names of most of Israel's camp-sites, e.g., Kibroth-hattaavah, "Graves of craving," in 11:34).

Such observations may sound obvious and unavoidable when stated bluntly and without elaboration, but when discovered in the process of walking through this stage of Israel's journey together, they take on an immediacy and urgency that has caused them to remain central for the synagogue if not the church. Again we must ask ourselves pointedly, Why is this material so little read? As we move into a new millennium as God's yet-traveling people, stories about spies and imaginary enemies and a people with a forward-moving tilt may be the very texts for what ails *us*—church and synagogue—and, in many ways *because of us*, what ails the *world*. How responsible is the divided witness of church and synagogue for the ongoing divisions among all the world's peoples? In contrast, how alluring is the unity of God's people when their forward motion gains them some rest on the way: "How fair are your tents, O Jacob," declares the foreign seer, Balaam, "your encampments, O Israel! . . . Blessed is everyone who blesses you, and cursed is everyone who curses you" (Num. 24:5, 9).

In the land. Last and in many ways most difficult, we come to the stage that the latter chapters only anticipate: God's people in the land. Clearly the primary anticipated problem here has to do with those *not* in the family: the Canaanites and their kin, who threaten to lead God's people astray. At first glance there is much truth in this. God's people are sent to be witnesses to a peculiar God in the midst of peoples chasing after gods of other sorts. When Israel shifts from *camping* on the way to *settling* in one place, even temporarily, all hell does break loose, and it is grounded in accommodation to the world (Num. 25). Israel and the church are called to be in the world but not of the world, so some setting of ourselves over against the rest of the world's people is in order.

However, all along this journey there has been some ambivalence on this matter. All one has to do is think about the Midianites and those with whom they are associated to see how mixed the picture can become. At one point in Israel's journey, a Midianite, Hobab, Moses' father-in-law, is asked to come with God's people so that "whatever good the LORD does for us, the same we will do for you" (10:32). At another point, Balaam, who is later associated with the Midianites, shows himself to be obedient to the Lord, even when threatened by a wealthy king (Num. 22–24). But then the Midianites, along with Balaam, are all destroyed, save for the booty (material, animal, and human) that is painstakingly distributed among God's people while in camp (Num. 31). How do we explain the discrepancies in these stories with regard to the Israelites' attitudes toward those *outside* the family, and what the appropriate barriers and/or boundaries might or might not be?

We then return to the "land," that obvious and not-so-obvious destination toward which this whole story points ("You shall take possession of the land and settle it, for I have given you the land to possess"; 33:53). If what makes the non-Israelite so threatening to God's people is their threat to Israel's settled life, what happens if Israel forgoes a settled life altogether? Then no space has to be permanently cleared. Then no concessions other than "transit" are required ("It is only a small matter; just let us pass through on foot"; 20:19). Then the threat of "assimilation" and the burden of booty are both reduced and transformed into an invitation to come and travel with us "on the way." Boundaries drawn in the dirt, and even boundaries drawn between peoples, become less important than establishing the boundaries of the path which leads forward, a task for which God's people need all the help they can get ("Do not leave us, for you know where we should camp in the wilderness, and you will serve as eyes for us"; 10:31).

We arrive back then where we first started, wondering why two books about a journey from one land to the next end short of the land and in a camp with a people gathered around a portable shrine. Does God truly want to dwell *in this land*, or *in this people* on the way? And does God want to dwell in this people alone, or to invite all the world's people to join them on a journey where God will dwell in their midst? Then boundaries will remain important, but only the boundaries that radiate out from the Lord at the center of camp, and those boundaries that point out the way of the path moving forward—for all fellow travelers.

Maybe at its best, Leviticus–Numbers calls us toward the kind of settled and unsettled life worked out for the two and one-half tribes on the far side of the Jordan. They are allowed to set up cities and corrals for their little ones and livestock so that they might have some security in this threatening world. But they must also pledge to send people forward on a march. This march will prove costly and require courage. Yet this march will not only unite all these disparate tribes as one people, but also join them around the one Lord who both travels with them and dwells in their midst. They are then not so much a people limping between two opinions as living between two worlds. In some sense, they have already arrived in the land, and they are given guidelines for how to live in this land without losing focus on the Lord, who dwells at their center. In another sense, they are yet on the journey toward this land, and God is always out front and moving, calling them to get up and follow, to adapt and to trust.

It is finally this call to adapt and trust that may prove to be the greatest challenge of Leviticus–Numbers for God's people today. True, the forward march seems to come to an end. But what of the forward momentum? A new generation and new leadership emerge from the old. Dreamed-of victories bring with them challenges of their own (e.g., the disposition of booty) that call into question the precise shape by which God's promises might be fulfilled. Unanticipated situations (tribes with lots of cattle; families with no male heirs; murders that occur unintentionally) require new consultations with God and revisions to already-received rules and regulations, making clear that God's people will need guides through the Scriptures just as they have needed guides through the wilderness. Such a conclusion leads not so much to a blurring of the boundaries, but more to a bold attempt to redraw such boundaries at each stage along the way. No wonder then that we would prefer to avoid such stretches of Scripture and of faith. This is not and shall not be an easy journey for God's people to make. It will require courage and trust every step of the way.

Thus, as we get to the end, we have a strange sense that we are back at the beginning. One camp is at Moab and the other at Sinai, but they are both camps "on the way" just the same. Once again it is time for sacrifice and worship. Once again it is time to prepare for the march. Soon it will be time for a new census to be taken, new leaders to be set apart, and new challenges and tests to be faced. Just as these passages roll back round in the lectionary, so these "traveling stories" and "practices for living" roll round in our lives. Slowly but surely, we begin to realize that *all* of our days are but preparation for and witness to a "crossing over" always, in its fullest sense, out ahead of us all.

And so the final shape of Leviticus–Numbers helps us see once again how both the peoples of the Jewish Scriptures and of the Christian Scriptures understand themselves to be peoples "of the way." Whether the way be the right path through the wilderness or the words of Scripture, it is not surprising that even later Jewish disciples found themselves uncertain of direction: "Lord, we do not know where you are going. How can we know the way?" (John 14:5). The answer in both testaments remains the same: *The Lord* is the way, and the truth, and the life. When the cloud arises from the tent in the morning, follow the Lord. When the cloud settles down over the tent at night, make camp. Then, even as you continue your journey toward an uncertain destination, your hearts will not be troubled, neither will you be afraid (John 14:27). Why? Because the same Lord who dwells with you also goes before you to prepare a place for you. *This* Lord will surely watch over your "going out" and "your coming in," from this time forth and forevermore (Ps. 121:8).

Bibliography

Commentaries

Bailey, Lloyd R. *Leviticus–Numbers.* Macon: Smyth & Helwys, 2005. An aesthetically pleasing combined commentary that is rich in archaeological detail and Jewish/Christian interpretive issues.

Balentine, Samuel. *Leviticus.* Interpretation. Louisville: John Knox Press, 2002. A theologically challenging commentary that stresses the formative nature of ritual worship practices.

Calvin, John. *Commentaries on the Four Last Books of Moses.* Grand Rapids: Eerdmans, 1948. Reprint of 1852 translation. A necessary supplemental commentary for readers of the Reformed tradition.

Dozeman, Thomas B. *Numbers.* In *The New Interpreter's Bible.* Vol. 2, *Numbers–Samuel.* Nashville: Abingdon Press, 1998. A clearly written and thorough exposition of Numbers, with helpful applications for theology and practice today.

Gerstenberger, Erhard S. *Leviticus.* The Old Testament Library. Louisville: Westminster John Knox Press, 1996. An English translation of a German work that details the intimate connection between faith and practice in the social life of postexilic Israel.

Mays, James L. *Leviticus–Numbers.* The Layman's Bible Commentary. Richmond: John Knox Press, 1963. A brief but theologically rich commentary on both books as revelatory of the character of God.

Olson, Dennis T. *Numbers.* Interpretation. Louisville: Westminster John Knox Press, 1996. An accessible commentary theologically structured on the distinction between the first and second generation.

Other

The American Heritage Dictionary. 3rd ed. New York: Houghton Mifflin Company, 1992.

Bass, Dorothy, ed. *Practicing Our Faith: A Way of Life for a Searching People*. San Francisco: Jossey-Bass, 1997.

Bass, Dorothy, and Richter, Don C., eds. *Way to Live: Christian Practices for Teens*. Nashville: Upper Room Books, 2002.

Book of Common Worship. Louisville: Westminster/John Knox Press, 1993.

The Book of Confessions. Louisville: The Office of the General Assembly, Presbyterian Church (U.S.A.), 2002.

Dawn, Marva J. *Reaching Out without Dumbing Down: A Theology of Worship for This Urgent Time*. Grand Rapids: Eerdmans, 1995.

Lischer, Richard. *The End of Words: The Language of Reconciliation in a Culture of Violence*. Grand Rapids: Eerdmans, 2005.

McWhorter, John. *Doing Our Own Thing: The Degradation of Language and Music and Why We Should, Like, Care*. New York: Gotham Books, 2003.

Marty, Martin, ed. *Context: Martin Marty on Religion and Culture*. Chicago: Claretian Publications, 1995.

Miller, Vincent J. *Consuming Religion: Christian Faith and Practice in a Consumer Culture*. New York: Continuum, 2005.

Moon, William Least Heat. *Blue Highways: A Journey into America*. Boston: Little, Brown & Company, 1983.

The Presbyterian Hymnal. Louisville: Westminster/John Knox Press, 1990.

The Study Catechism, Full Version. Louisville: Geneva Press, 1998.

Tyler, Anne. *Saint Maybe*. New York: Ivy Books, 1991.

Volf, Miroslav, and Bass, Dorothy, eds. *Practicing Theology: Beliefs and Practices in Christian Life*. Grand Rapids: Eerdmans, 2002.